How to
Write, Publish,
and *Promote*
a Novel

Steps to Making
Your Writing

✓ Credible,
✓ Engaging, and
✓ Marketable

Florence Osmund

How to Write, Publish, and Promote a Novel
Steps to Making Your Writing Credible, Engaging, and Marketable

Cover by Tugboat Design
Edited by Carrie Cantor

ISBN: 978-0-9998074-1-5

Library of Congress Control Number: 2020903982

Contents

Part 3: **The Final Stretch**

Part 4: **Marketing and Promotion**

Part 5: **Conclusion**

Preface

I am a novelist in the literary fiction genre who got a rather late start as a writer. After a long career working in corporate environments, I published my first book at the age of sixty-two. I am now eight times self-published (as of 2020). I have made my share of mistakes along the way, but because of this I have a good store of knowledge about the industry.

My goal with this, my first nonfiction book, is to share with you what I've learned during the past ten years so you can avoid making the same mistakes I did, as the opportunities for making mistakes were (and remain) numerous. There are still times I refer back to pages in this book and others to remind myself of things I need to do to improve my writing—to make it more credible, engaging, and marketable.

My wanting to share what I know about the business started with a website. When that became too large and cumbersome to manage, I revamped it into this how-to book. Then I turned my website into an interactive blog www.florenceosmund.com where I post excerpts from the book and related articles about the more dynamic side of the writing business—current events, industry changes, recent laws, and new marketing and promotion strategies.

It is important for you to know that the contents of this book are just the tip of the iceberg for each topic. You can find elsewhere more in-depth discussions on every subject I touch upon. Think of me as your general practitioner—I am aware of and can help you with most things, but you may have to consult with a specialist from time to time.

I suggest that you start your writing journey by reading this book in its entirety before you begin. That way you will be familiar with all the potential pitfalls. Then, as you write and are faced with specific issues, you can go back to review the relevant chapter or delve deeper into the subject by referencing more in-depth works on the subject, such as the ones listed at the end of each chapter under "Suggested Reading."

I would like to acknowledge a few wonderful people for their assistance in helping me make this a better book. I thank my sister (and avid reader), Marge Bousson, for being my beta reader and catching problematic areas that I had overlooked. I owe thanks to Deborah Bradseth of Tugboat Design for her valuable insight into the industry and talent in creating a great book cover. Thank you, Stephanie Anderson at Alt 19 Creative for your adept attention to detail in the formatting process. And, finally, I thank my editor, Carrie Cantor, for sharing her wisdom in relevant subject matters, her skillful editing of this book, and the valuable things she has taught me over the years about the craft of writing.

Florence Osmund

Introduction

I f you are a new or aspiring writer with a story inside of you aching to get out but don't know where to start, you've picked up (or downloaded) the right book. Even if you're an experienced writer, you may find the contents of this book useful. After having written several novels myself, I can tell you that I too am still learning.

I cover the following subjects in this book: how to get started; establishing goals and timetables; self-publishing versus traditional publishing; building an author platform; approaches to crafting a story; writing tips; how to self-edit; how to spot a scam; working with editors; marketing and promotion; setting up an effective book launch; and securing valuable reviews. (See Appendix A for a comprehensive summary list of things to do before, during, and after the writing of your book.)

No two writers will take the exact same approach to writing—it's not cookie-cutter work. But even though what works for one author may not work for another, some things apply to most writers across the board, and that's where I have tried to focus the contents of this book.

You can publish your book in one of two ways—through a traditional publisher or by self-publishing. Most of what is included in this book pertains to both, but you'll notice I don't talk as much about going through a traditional publisher as I do self-publishing—I'll leave that to others who have done that. My experience comes from self-publishing fiction, but much of what is included here applies to other genres as well.

If you choose to disregard my advice to read this book *before* you begin writing, I strongly advise that you at least read "Part I—Before You Start Writing." Here I talk about a variety of things to do that may take time up-front but that I assure you will save time and frustrating rewrites in the long run. If you read the entire book before you begin to write, you'll save even more time.

I can't guaranty that by reading this book and following the advice herein you will become a successful, award-winning author, but I *can* promise you that by reading it and applying what you've learned, you will have a better chance at it.

Unfortunately, the publishing industry has become a haven for scam artists who are adept at targeting new and aspiring authors—those who are anxious to get published and naïve about the seamier side of the industry. To alert you to these, I have included a "Scam Alert" in applicable chapters. One site that does a decent job at vetting self-publishing services is ALLi, The Alliance of Independent Authors, a global nonprofit association for self-published authors. This page on its website, selfpublishingadvice.org/self-publishing-service-reviews/, provides ratings for publishing services, contests, and awards. You might want to visit this site before engaging service providers.

To furnish additional insight into the topics covered in this book, I have included links to articles at the end of each chapter to supplement and expand upon my thoughts. You will find links that are of a more general nature in the "Additional Resources" section at the end of the book.

If you have a question about the writing process, self-publishing, or promoting your work, please feel free to shoot me an e-mail at info@florenceosmund.com. I would love to hear from you.

I wish you the best of luck in your writing projects and hope that publishing a best-selling book becomes your reality!

PART 1

Before You Start Writing

*There is no greater agony than
bearing an untold story inside you.*
—MAYA ANGELOU

CHAPTER 1

So, You're Thinking about Writing a Book...

Y ou've thought about writing a novel, perhaps many times throughout your life. You've imagined how the characters will look and
how certain scenes will play out. You fall asleep with a smile on
your face as you picture your story being acted out on the big screen.
Friends and family are encouraging, and now you have finally committed
yourself to doing it. You carve out a writing sanctuary in your house,
buy a new computer and ergonomic chair, dust off the thesaurus, and
are ready to start.

Not so fast—I know you're eager to begin writing, but there are a few
important things to consider first, and I can assure you that taking the
time to do them will pay off tremendously. Furthermore, you are more
likely to actually finish your novel if you have done the preliminary work.
So, bear with me while I outline a plan to put you on the right path. Be
patient—you'll get to the writing part soon enough. Think of it as the
blueprint for building a house—without one, it could be done, but the
end product wouldn't likely be well constructed and there wouldn't be
much in the way of sales value.

I can't tell you how many times I have heard an aspiring writer say, "I have lots of ideas, but I don't know where to start." And the response most often heard is, "Just begin to write." The "just do it" approach may work for some, but there are methods you can use that will make the process more efficient before you invest hundreds of hours in writing a first draft. The idea you have, while a great accomplishment in itself, is just the first step in writing your book. And, by the way, if you don't have an idea yet, there are many story-idea and plot-generator guidelines available online (see the "Suggested Reading" section at the end of this chapter).

Not every writer will take the same approach—what works well for some may be cumbersome for others. For example, the right place for me to start writing is at the beginning, but that's not true for all writers. Some writers will craft the ending first and work backward. Some in the middle. You'll know early on whether the method you have chosen is working for you. If you choose one that's holding you back, try something else. There is no one right way.

And remember what Somerset Maugham said.

> *There are three rules for writing the novel. Unfortunately, no one knows what they are.*

Your book is an extension of you, and the same amount of care should be given to publishing it as is given to any other major aspect of your life. With that said, and at the risk of imposing a sense of doom and gloom on your writing dream, I would be remiss if I didn't point out these five reasons for *not* writing a novel.

Do *not* write a novel if:

1. You need to support yourself on the royalties. Without proper education and training, the vast majority of first-time authors sell fewer than 100 books—total. That's under $400 in royalties for most printed books. Not $400 a month or a year. $400 total.
2. You cannot afford to hire a professional editor ($0.01–$0.10/word depending on the condition of your manuscript, level of editing

you choose, and editor experience). A good editor will ensure your writing is clear, credible, and marketable.

3. You are not ready to spend as much time promoting and marketing your book as you did to write it.
4. You don't have a thick skin.
5. Your main goal is to become an overnight sensation and appear on *Good Morning America* as this year's newest best-selling author.

Educate Yourself

Now that that's out of the way, before you start putting one word after another to make those intriguing thoughts of yours turn into chapters of a book, I suggest you read, read, and then read some more. Read books in your genre and make notes on what you liked about them, what you didn't like about them, and then emulate what you think the authors did well. Maybe your favorite author created a compelling character, one you will remember for a long time. Analyze and understand how he or she did that. Or maybe another author made you feel like you were on the journey right along with the protagonist. How was that accomplished? If you can figure these things out, you will be on your way to writing a successful book yourself.

You may also want to consider taking some writing classes. There are scads of opportunities out there to learn the craft of writing—trade associations, conferences, webinars, Internet articles, websites, online discussion groups, colleges, and universities. (See the "Additional Resources" section at the end of this book.)

There are numerous reference books available that will help you produce a well-written, compelling novel, but these two are on my list of must-have books (besides this one, of course).

> *The Chicago Manual of Style*—most U.S. editors, proofreaders, copywriters, and publishers use this reference guide for rules on grammar, spelling, punctuation, and so much more. It is

available in hardcover, or you can subscribe to the electronic version by visiting chicagomanualofstyle.org.

The Elements of Style by William Strunk and E. B. White—the best little reference book you'll ever find on word and punctuation usage; sentence and paragraph structure; misused words and expressions; and more.

Your Writing Routine

Writing requires discipline, and whether you are going to make writing a full-time project or something to do in your spare time, establishing a writing routine will help you keep moving forward. If you say, "I'll fit it in when I can," chances are you won't finish the project. My writing is a full-time job, and what works for me, what I find to be most productive, is to leave mornings open for responding to e-mails, checking in on social media, participating in online discussions, and promoting my books—all things related to writing books other than the actual writing. This leaves the afternoons open for writing.

Most writers will tell you that in order to keep their perspective fresh, they need a break every three to four hours. That goes for me too, as I have found that taking breaks that involve something unrelated to what I'm writing helps to clear my head and keep the creative juices fresh and flowing.

Distractions are counterproductive for most writers, so it's important to keep them to a minimum. Choose a quiet area of your home to write—away from family members, pets, and other diversions. Unless it's beneficial to you, turn off the TV, stereo, and phone while you're writing so you can focus all your attention on your craft.

Writing and editing require different skill sets. To achieve optimal productivity, I recommend keeping them separate. I find it best to write a complete first draft of the book before doing any self-editing—it keeps my creativity flowing freely for an extended period of time before I start the arduous task of making improvements. If you're like me—and like most writers—you'll spend more time self-editing than you did writing the initial manuscript.

I also find it useful to take a break between finishing the first draft and starting the self-editing process. Too many times upon rereading some sections with the benefit of a fresh perspective, I find myself saying, "I can't believe I actually wrote that!"

I learned the hard way that if you intend to write full-time, it is imperative to take frequent exercise breaks. If you don't, you could end up with serious back, neck, and shoulder problems. In addition, according to the Mayo Clinic website, sitting for long periods of time is linked with a number of other health concerns, including obesity and metabolic syndrome—a cluster of conditions that includes increased blood pressure, high blood sugar, excess body fat around the waist, and abnormal cholesterol levels. It has also been reported that too much sitting increases the risk of death from cardiovascular disease and cancer. One study compared adults who spent less than two hours a day in front of the TV or other screen-based entertainment with those who logged more than four hours a day of recreational screen time. Those with greater screen time had a nearly 50 percent increased risk of death from any cause and about a 125 percent increased risk of events associated with cardiovascular disease, such as chest pain (angina) or heart attack.

You may want to try a height-adjustable desk. Switching between sitting and standing throughout the day while I write has reduced back and neck pain and enabled me to work more hours per day.

Know Your Audience

Forget the notion that you can write a book everyone will love. That has never happened and never will. Another myth is that the larger the target market, the more books you'll sell. In fact, the opposite is often true. The larger the target market, the more competition you are likely to face, and the more money and time you'll spend trying to get noticed. Furthermore, striving to appeal to a wide market can result in your writing being too general, and then it becomes very appealing to no one. It is advantageous to identify your target audience before you start writing because having a picture in your mind of who you are writing for will help you focus on creating the right content and then later make your marketing efforts more productive.

To appeal to a specific group of readers you must understand their needs, wants, and desires. Finding and narrowing your niche will help you reach and appeal to more of the people who will ultimately buy your book.

Sometimes understanding the demographics of your target audience will help you to find your niche. When determining reader demographics, you may want to consider the following:

- **GENDER** – Are males or females more likely to read your book? Interesting fact—according to Amazon and Goodreads, the vast majority of all fiction is purchased by females.

- **AGE** – Which age group(s) will be most interested in your book? Consider this breakdown by generation (from the Center for Genetic Kinetics):
  - Mature – older than 65
  - Boomers – born 1946–1964
  - Generation X – born 1965–1976
  - Generation Y – born 1977–1995 (also called Millennials)
  - Young adult – Ages 12–18
  - Children – younger than 12

- **EDUCATION LEVEL** – What level of education do you expect most of your readers will have? Some novels will appeal to readers regardless of their level of education, while others will appeal to a smaller group of people at a particular intellectual level. Be sensitive to the intellect of your target readers and write accordingly.

Think about your genre and your story line. Based on demographics, who will be the people most likely to buy your book? Then, keep them in mind as you write. If you market your book to one audience, but the content of your book appeals to a different audience, your book will be in trouble.

SUGGESTED READING:

Crawford, Sara. Live Write Thrive (blog): *What Does It Take to Be a Real Writer?* https://www.livewritethrive.com/2019/09/16/what-does-it-take-to-be-a-real-writer/#more-10793.

Jenkins, Jerry. Reedsy (blog): *How to Become an Author: The Ultimate Guide.* https://blog.reedsy.com/how-to-become-an-author/.

Sansevieri, Penny. Author Marketing Experts (blog): *10 Myths and Facts About Publishing a Book.* https://www.amarketingexpert. com/10-myths-and-facts-about-publishing-a-book/.

CHAPTER 2

Story Structure

S tory structure is the framework for how the story is told—what holds the plot together, how the story and plot are logically arranged and presented to the reader so that the action unfolds in an optimum fashion, how the various story components meld together to make the story easy to read. Structure doesn't just happen—it needs to be carefully considered by the author for the story to be supported by a solid foundation. If you disregard establishing the structure for your story and dive right into writing, you risk losing coherence and perhaps your readers if you don't eventually fix it.

Here are things to consider when structuring your narrative.

Basic Story Components

If you Google "components of writing fiction," you'll discover numerous trains of thought from a variety of writers and educators. Listed below are those common to most of their theories—the ones that I and most experts agree every story must have to be complete.

Character

One could argue that characters are the foundation for the whole story. They are the vehicle that drives the story and through whom your reader experiences the story, so making them feel real to the reader is extremely important. Without believable characters, readers won't have someone in the story to like, dislike, or care about in any way, making the other elements of the story rather irrelevant. (See Chapter 3 for more on character development.)

Setting

Setting includes the physical location, social/cultural environment, time period, climate, and surroundings. Setting not only provides your readers with a visualization of where the story is taking place, but components of it can also affect the plot and the characters. (See Chapter 13 for more on setting.)

Conflict and Roadblocks

Conflict and roadblocks are usually what enables the protagonist to grow. They give purpose to the story. They are what makes a story worth reading. Whether external and internal, conflict and roadblocks are what keep your readers engaged. (See Chapter 9 for more on conflict.)

Plot

The plot of the story determines the way you shape the narrative—the organized structure of the action your characters take when they face things, the important points and/or events that have significant consequences within the story. But plot is broader than that—without a plot, a story is nothing but a series of events. Plot motivates the characters to do what they do, which garners interest and emotional connection for the reader. (See Chapter 5 for more on plot.)

Theme

Theme is what your story is *really* about—that often-subtle message that readers figure out on their own while or after reading the story. Common themes are love, war, reunion, death/tragedy, good versus evil, coming of age, family, innocence, heroism, power, survival. The list goes on and on. (See more on theme in Chapter 19.)

Point of View

Point of view (POV) specifies through whose eyes the story is being told. (See Chapter 4 for more on point of view.)

Pulling It Together

While each story component is individually essential to the story, how they interconnect with one another is even more important—it's their interaction that drives the events and outcomes of the story, keeping it running smoothly and easy for readers to follow. Appropriate interconnection of story components is fundamental for making a story interesting, cohesive, and complete.

Following is a simplified explanation of how these six story components are pulled together to form an integrated story line.

> Most fiction includes the same six basic components. A (1) main character in a contributive (2) setting is faced with (3) conflict and roadblocks that prevent him or her from reaching a (4) goal. The narrative incorporates a (5) common theme that is laced throughout the story as told from one or more (6) points of view.

If you're writing fiction, this guideline is a good place to start. Let's dissect it a bit. The *main character* (or protagonist) is obviously the most prominent character in the story and needs to be present and accounted for in all the important scenes. *Setting* plays a significant role throughout the story by anchoring where the story takes place, establishing mood, and supplementing characters' motivations and feelings in specific scenes. The story's plot revolves around how the protagonist overcomes *conflict and roadblocks* that keep him or her from reaching a *goal(s)*. A story's *theme,* the underlying concept that flows through the narrative, is the common thread that helps to connect all the other components of the story. The essence of the story can change depending on who is narrating it and his or her *point of view,* so keeping this consistent is extremely important in tying it all together.

Organization

Most novels will be born from some inkling of an idea that the author thinks will make a good story.

> **INKLING EXAMPLE #1.** Mary Lou's next-door neighbor disappears. The missing woman's husband claims she ran away with someone she met on the Internet. But when the missing woman's husband seeks out Mary Lou for comfort in a clandestine way, she suspects he may have had something to do with his wife's disappearance.

> **INKLING EXAMPLE #2.** The local hospital begins to be the site of unexplained deaths. When a man dies from a relatively minor ailment, his family members devote all their energy to getting to the bottom of it.

> **INKLING EXAMPLE #3.** Jennifer learns she has a twin sister who is alive and well and living two towns away. But Jennifer isn't sure how much her sister knows about their biological family, making a possible reunion problematic and potentially dangerous.

Once you have a solid idea in your head, you will likely have thoughts as to how to begin fleshing it out to make the story full and compelling. I find it useful to jot down these wonderful thoughts. (If you have a better memory than I do, you may be able to skip this step.) To get things organized in my head, I start with an outline, and the way I do it is by creating a spreadsheet with the following column headings:

> Chapter Number
> Time Period
> Plot Points
> Number of Words

Before I start writing, under the Chapter Number column, I create twenty-five rows by entering 1 through 25 down the page (this assumes I'll end up with twenty-five chapters—just a guess, a place to start). Then, in the Plot Points column, I write a few brief sentences for chapters 1, 3, 12, and 25 based on the narrative arc (See Chapter 6 for more on story structure) that many authors use to structure their work.

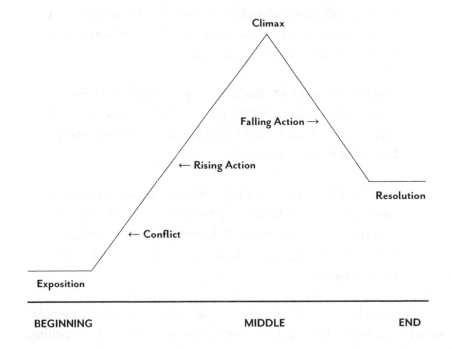

CHAPTER 1: This is where I establish the setting and at least the main character.

CHAPTER 3: Novels need conflict, drama, tension, and/or crisis to grab reader attention and keep them turning the pages. I include at least a hint of the problem early on, and it is very evident by this chapter.

CHAPTER 12: By now, approximately halfway into the novel, I have included the most impactful conflict, drama, tension, or crisis.

CHAPTER 25: This is where I predict how the story ends. (Very important because if you establish the ending before you start writing, you will have a goal in front of you while you write.)

I choose these plot points because they are typically the ones I know in my head before I start writing. That's not to say they don't change during the course of my writing, but I find they provide a good starting place.

Then, as I write, I note the time period for each chapter, expand on the plot points, and when I'm finished with a chapter, I record the word count.

For me, this evolving outline proves to be invaluable throughout the entire writing process. It keeps me on track with the story line, saves time from going back into the text looking for specific scenes, and monitors the number of words I've written. (I like to keep chapters more or less the same length, and the total number of words between 75,000 and 90,000.)

If you decide to use an outline, keep in mind that you don't have to follow it exactly. Sometimes when you're writing, the story will (seemingly) take off in a direction on its own. If it feels right when that happens, go with it. It's relatively easy to revise an outline.

Whether you are a "planner" (you prepare an outline and develop the characters and major plot points before you start writing) or a "pantser" (you do no up-front planning but write by the seat of your pants), whether you write love stories or dark fantasy sagas, every story needs structure to make the narrative components meld together and make sense for the readers.

SUGGESTED READING:

Card, Orson Scott. "4 Story Structures That Dominate Novels." Writer's Digest. August 24, 2010. https://www.writersdigest.com/ writing-articles/by-writing-goal/write-first-chapter-get-started/ 4-story-structures-that-dominate-novels.

Lyons, Jeff. "How to Structure a Premise for Stronger Stories." The Writer. October 26, 2018. https://www.writermag.com/improve-your-writing/fiction/how-to-structure-a-premise-for-stronger-stories/.

Ogorek, Keith (owner). "How to Structure a Story: The Fundamentals of Narrative." Author Learning Center. (No date.) https://www. authorlearningcenter.com/writing/fiction/w/plot-planning/6366/ how-to-structure-a-story-the-fundamentals-of-narrative---article.

CHAPTER 3

Character Development

Creating believable, memorable characters that come to life on the page and engage the reader is key in writing fiction. A physical description of them is never enough, and in fact, the current trend is to minimize the physical descriptions of characters. Instead, layers of personality and history should be embedded in characters, especially the main characters, to properly develop them. Your job as a writer is to make the reader relate to them in some way, feel empathy for them, want to know more about them, and care about what happens to them.

This is not to say that believable characters need to be "realistic" ones—we all have superheroes we adore, admire, fear, or envy. But even if your story takes place in a magic kingdom (for example), your characters need to be believable given the setting, time period, and other aspects of the story. The most brilliant plot is doomed if the characters are implausible or fall flat.

Don't be afraid to draw from your own relationships to inspire your fictional characters. If your character needs to be shy, think of someone you know who is shy and create a scene from what you've observed in real life. Similarly, if your character is in a situation that requires mustering up an incredible amount of courage, think about someone you know who has been in that situation. Just be careful not to infuse too much of the real person into your fictional character, as that can lead to sensitive familial/friendship issues if the real person doesn't take to the likeness. And speaking of that, do add this important disclaimer at the front of your book:

> This is a work of fiction. Names, characters, places, and incidents are either the product of the author's imagination or are used fictitiously. Any resemblance to actual persons, living or dead, business establishments, events, or locales is entirely coincidental.

I have found it helpful to have the major characters in the story fully imagined before I start writing, as their actions and dialogue will depend on their many individual characteristics, such as physical condition, likes and dislikes, values, obsessions, fears, lifestyle, needs, habits, desires, and flaws. I also find it useful to keep a picture of each main character nearby. For example, the female protagonist in my first two books is in her thirties and of mixed race but can easily pass for white. So I Googled "images of mixed-race women," found one I could relate to for my character, printed it, and taped it to my computer screen. The photo provided inspiration when I was trying to get inside the character's head.

Browse the Internet or magazines and catalogs for pictures of your characters. For example, does your protagonist like to ski? Pick up an issue of *Freeskier.* I bet you'll find a picture of him in there.

Protagonist versus Antagonist

The *protagonist,* the main character in your book, is at the story's heart—it is the protagonist's story. The key to creating a compelling story is having the protagonist chase after a goal—the story being the journey taken to achieve this goal.

The protagonist is typically identified by the character in your story who:

- Has the greatest passion to reach a specific goal.
- Faces the greatest challenges that keep him or her from reaching this goal.
- Makes the hardest choices and decisions within the story.
- Undergoes the most significant transformation.

Protagonists need roadblocks, and the most common ones are created by an *antagonist*—some person or thing that stands in the way of the protagonist reaching his or her goals. The antagonist may be in the form of the traditional villain working alone, a group of people, a force of nature, or even an intrinsic conflict that the protagonist has to overcome. Here are some things to consider when developing your antagonist:

- Give the antagonist powerful, realistic goals of his or her own.
- Make the antagonist's backstory believable.
- Create antagonist misdeeds that require decisive action for the protagonist.
- Make the antagonist smarter, more powerful than the protagonist.

Antagonists don't necessarily need to be evil characters. In order for characters to be antagonists, they need only to meet one criterion—their goals must conflict with those of the protagonist. As with protagonists, antagonists need a reason to do what they do in the scope of the story— they need a motivation that often is created from their backstory.

Physical Characteristics

Stating physical characteristics—gender, weight, height, age, body build, hair, eyes, posture, voice, and clothing—is the easiest way to portray a character, but be careful to not overuse it.

TOO MUCH DESCRIPTION: She was slim and tall, close to six feet, with broad bony shoulders and long legs. Her brightly colored blazer over a sheer, white blouse contrasted nicely with her long blond hair, tanned skin, and blue eyes.

BETTER: She stood out—close to six feet tall and dressed in a stunning, brightly-colored blazer over a sheer, white blouse.

BEST: Based on her physical attributes and attire, she appeared to belong on the cover of *Vogue.*

Once you have provided enough description for the reader to have a good picture of your character, it is not necessary to repeat any of it unless, of course, one of these features is germane to the plot.

Avoid providing the entire description of a character in one place—break it up by scattering snippets of it throughout multiple scenes. A few well-placed descriptive words throughout the story will usually be enough to help readers form a mental image.

Given his scruffy appearance, she had half a mind to ask him for some identification.

A graceful and subtle way to show physical characteristics is to include them within action.

She'd pulled her thinning, ash-blond hair into a loose ponytail, her bony fingers revealing a telltale symptom of her eating disorder.

Other physical traits may be revealed in any number of ways through dialogue, actions, internal thoughts, likes and dislikes, background, mannerisms, speech patterns, lifestyle, and habits.

Character Flaws

In real life, no one is perfect. Your fictional characters shouldn't be either. If you don't give your characters a flaw or two—a bad habit, an insecurity, or a weakness—readers may not accept them or feel empathy for them. Flaws add depth and make characters more memorable. In the end, a character isn't defined by his flaws but by what he or she does in spite of them, and this deepens their characterization.

Character flaws fall into one of three categories:

1. **MINOR IMPERFECTIONS**—ones that serve to distinguish a character from the others.
2. **PROMINENT FLAWS**—flaws that impede the character from reaching his or her goals.
3. **FATAL FLAWS** (also called hamartia)—ones that cause an otherwise noble character to bring about their own downfall and, often, their eventual death.

Character flaws don't necessarily make your character a bad person. Readers will still like a character who is flawed. Of course, you don't want to go overboard—most story lines call for a main character with more strengths than flaws for readers to like them enough to root for them when their flaws get in the way. The right flaw doesn't detract from a character's appeal. Instead, it makes their strengths shine in comparison, their mistakes make sense, and their conflict more gripping.

For the purpose of this discussion, I am going to focus on prominent flaws—ones that impede the character from reaching his or her goals.

Here are a few examples of character flaws that have potential for getting in the way of a character reaching his or her goal.

- Gullibility
- Hypocrisy
- Idealism
- Impatience
- Impulsiveness
- Indecisiveness
- Nosiness
- Paranoia
- Skepticism
- Stubbornness
- Vanity

Let's say your protagonist is idealistic, and her main goal is to find the love of her life. She's smart, fun to be with, attractive, and likable in every way. With each new relationship, there is the possibility that this might be the one…until reality sets in and she realizes he's not perfect. Her character flaw—her idealism when it comes to relationships—will resonate with many readers.

Or think of a character whose goal it is to earn a living as a musician. He's good at it but unknown, and his indecisiveness keeps getting in his way—indecisiveness about getting a degree in music, accepting wedding and bar mitzvah gigs, playing in a house band, and teaching music on the side. Readers won't be turned off by this—they'll root for him.

And then there could be the character who is determined to find his sister's murderer but has little patience when it comes to getting to the truth. That character flaw could be a problem on many levels—frustration while waiting on information that only others can give him, tracking down tedious leads, and taking time to ensure he's not doing anything illegal—all things that get in the way of reaching his goal.

Flaws can be uncovered through backstory, the character's internal thoughts, other characters pointing them out, or by the character's own actions. When you choose a flaw, keep in mind that there has to be a reason behind it—don't include it unless it has meaning. That's not to say you have to provide a detailed explanation of the flaw, as sometimes hints are more effective. Provide enough explanation to justify it to the readers and help them understand why the character is the way he is.

Get the most out of the flaws. Put your character in different situations where the flaws become apparent and have consequences for the character. Make the flaws part of the story.

Keep in mind that perfect characters are boring. Giving them flaws will not take anything away from their persona—it will only make them appear more human.

Character Evolution

Whether your character is a fairy princess, a ten-year-old boy coming of age, a hopeless romantic, or an ex-con just released from prison, your characters need to evolve throughout the story. If the main character hasn't changed in some meaningful way by the end, their story won't be very interesting or compelling. This is especially true in literary fiction where the story line is character driven compared to genre fiction (mystery, suspense, science fiction, romance, or horror), where plot drives the story and is more important and prominent than character change. But in either case, the main character must change in some way in the course of reaching his or her goals. Whether your protagonist is someone who was weak and became strong, was miserable and became happy, was bad and became good, or some other transformation, the difference between the character at the beginning of the story and who the character became at the end is essential to the story.

In order for your characters to evolve, you have to allow them to make mistakes, like putting them in uncomfortable situations that force them to make difficult choices. The crises they face need to change their life or their outlook on life, and the change needs to come from choices they've made.

Character change can be prompted by a number of different circumstances. Here are three common ones:

1. The character discovers something about himself or herself that was always there.
2. An outside force changes the character.
3. The character goes through an inner transformation.

One of the best examples of character evolution is the change that occurs in Ebenezer Scrooge in *A Christmas Carol* by Charles Dickens. Scrooge is described early in the story as a "cold-hearted, tight-fisted, selfish, money-grabbing" man who refuses to help needy people and has difficulties with relationships in general. As the story evolves, Scrooge is haunted by three spirits who remind him of his troublesome childhood, the bad choices he's made, and how that led to his current state of mind and loneliness. Through the spirits, he sees how other people live and what he's been missing. And then finally, when he sees his own grave, he recognizes his need to change and wants another chance at life. In the end, Scrooge becomes a completely different man.

The bigger the transformation, the more you must justify it in the story—the character must change for a reason, or it won't make sense to the reader. You want your readers to say "Ah" at the end of the story, not "Huh?"

Change can't just happen—it's not enough to make the character different from one scene to the next. Characters need to evolve—it's a gradual process.

Internal Dialogue

What a character is thinking—called internal or interior dialogue—is often important in allowing the reader to better know the character. In fact, the ability to experience what life is like inside someone else's head—even though the someone is merely a fictional character—may be one of the main reasons people read novels.

Internal dialogue can be effective before a scene, after a scene, or even in the middle if it's kept short. The trick is to find the right balance between writing the character's internal dialogue and writing the action that will enable readers to deduce on their own what the character is thinking.

Two different technical styles may be considered when writing internal dialogue. You should choose the style that is least distracting from the flow of the story and then keep it consistent throughout.

1. **MULTIPLE POVS, TAGS**—Margaret felt uneasy and inched closer to Kevin as the disheveled man approached their table. He's not someone we want to talk to, she thought.
2. **SINGLE POV, NO TAG**—I kept my eye on the disheveled man approaching my table. *He's not someone I want to talk to.*

In the first example, assuming the story has been written in both Margaret and Kevin's POV, there could be some question as to whose thought it is, and the dialogue tag will help to clarify this. In the second example, there is no reason to add a dialogue tag—it's written in first person, and the dialogue is in italics, so readers automatically know whose thought it is.

Some points to keep in mind when writing internal dialogue are:

START WITH ACTION—and then follow it with the character's reflection on it rather than opening a scene with internal dialogue followed by the action.

> **Example**—He's not someone I want to talk to, Margaret thought as she kept her eye on the disheveled man approaching her table.

> **Better**—She kept her eye on the disheveled man approaching her table. *He's not someone I want to talk to.*

BREAK UP ACTION—use internal dialogue to give readers a break from long periods of action and to let them know what is going through the character's mind.

DON'T OVERDO IT—a little bit of internal dialogue can be effective, especially if you are able to create intrigue for the reader. Resist the urge to tell everything—allow readers to figure some things out for themselves.

Uniqueness

In order to create reader interest, each character needs to be distinct from the others —if too many characters have similar characteristics, the reader may become bored or confused. Here are some tips for keeping your characters unique.

- Use physical "tags" to help to initially set characters apart from each other and provide a visual image of them—wide-set eyes, a crooked smile, messy hair, ruddy complexion, petite body structure, buxom, beefy fingers, missing digits, tattoos, no neck, facial hair, to name a few. Unless the story line calls for it, be careful not to describe them in a distasteful way or create characters that are stereotypical.

- Make a character exceptionally good at something.
- Create unique voices and mannerisms for your characters. If five different characters try to make the same point, the reader should know which character it is without a dialogue tag.
- Give a character an obsession.
- Use your character's past to establish something unique about them.
- Consider dressing a character in unique outfits—ones that depict his or her personality.
- Intrigue readers with strange, unpredictable, irrational, peculiar, or curious behavior—make them stand out from the crowd.
- Give your characters conflicting traits—ones that pit them against each other.
- Avoid characters having closely similar names.

Characters shouldn't be created merely to fulfill some aspect of the plot. Make them unique and real by weaving in their history, family background, ethics, strengths, flaws, and goals. Dig deep into their psyche. Make them fully rounded, complex, and lifelike.

Emotions

In order for readers to become completely engrossed in your story, to be moved by it, they need to know what emotions are being triggered as characters go through major events. Even a story with a brilliant plot won't work if readers can't connect on an emotional level with the characters, the protagonist in particular. Their emotions are what make characters believable and compelling.

Emotions may be shown in many different ways. Here are the main ones.

- Describe a character's physical reactions to an event—crying, yelling, becoming withdrawn, trembling, etc.
- Use dialogue (including internal dialogue) to let the reader know what emotions the character is experiencing.
- Force your character to make difficult decisions that bring about strong emotions.
- Use setting to influence readers and deepen their emotional responses—sounds, smells, location, time of day, atmosphere, geography.

When you induce emotion in your characters, you will make readers feel it as well. Keep the readers engaged by making them feel the fear, enjoy the love, and be excited along with the characters.

Character Motivation

If you want to make your story believable, it is crucial that readers fully understand a character's motivation for his or her actions. Knowing this makes it easier for readers to put themselves into the head of a character, making the character more compelling. If they don't understand the motivations, readers will find the actions by the characters less meaningful. For example, let's say your protagonist volunteers at a local soup kitchen every Wednesday afternoon. Does he or she do it out of guilt because other family members do it? Are they "paying it forward" because of something someone did for them in the past? Or do they want to spend time with someone they want to get to know better?

Your character's reasons for doing what they do says a lot about who they are. They give insight into your character's values, morals, beliefs, hopes, dreams, fears, strengths, and weaknesses. Whether the character is the hero or the villain, they need to have motivation for their actions. Readers don't have to like, approve of, or share a character's motivation— they just have to believe it.

Here are some common motivations that drive characters to do what they do:

- Achievement
- Companionship
- Competition
- Conflict avoidance
- Curiosity
- Escape from something or someone
- Fear

- Fulfillment
- Guilt
- Pleasure
- Power
- Purpose in life
- Revenge
- Survival
- Threats

Take time to craft riveting motivations in your characters. Make use of the strength and power a strong character motivation can add to your story.

Backstory

Incorporating backstory—the aspects of the character's history that underlie the story's plot—is almost always needed in character development, as a character's past usually influences his or her current behavior and motivation. A complex and engrossing backstory can make a character more interesting, engaging, and believable.

Sometimes the backstory becomes the premise of the story, in *Citizen Kane* for example when the "present" is used to frame the real story, which is told in flashbacks where the majority of the action has taken place.

When backstory isn't the main story, sufficient background information on the characters will need to be included while not impeding the story to move forward. Then the question becomes how much to include. Mixing in the right amount of backstory is tricky—you want to include only what has a bearing on the present story or just a pinch of detail to add flavor. Balancing backstory with the other narrative elements is often a trial-and-error exercise as you add certain details and then remove them to see what works best. Here are some questions to ask yourself when deciding whether to include backstory.

- Do readers have to know something the character has done or experienced in the past to understand the current action?
- If readers do need to know something about a character's past, will one episode from the past or one piece of information be sufficient, or is more needed?
- Can you adequately show a character's personality without having to refer to his or her past?
- How much of a character's past is necessary as a setup to a future book in the series?

Relevant backstory may be created from the character's family background, nationality, schooling, or past experiences. When done properly, adding backstory will add layers to the character's personality.

A hint at the character's backstory in the beginning can go a long way—you may want the reader dying to know what in the character's past is now causing this behavior.

Backstory may be revealed through the character's dialogue with another character, others talking about the character, the character's internal thoughts, or flashbacks.

> "When I was growing up, it was acceptable to beat up on one another to show who was boss," he said to his son. "My father beat the crap out of me on a daily basis."

> "Richard's brother took his own life when he was Richard's age," Merlyn said. "That explains a lot."

> As I headed to the hospital room, I couldn't shake the image— one that had been buried in my memory for over twenty years—of my father lying in a similar bed, in a similar room, dying from a similar disease.

Here are some reasons for *not* including backstory.

- If there is too much backstory, readers might skip over it. You don't want them thinking *Get on with the story already.*
- The backstory slows the story's momentum.
- More than one instance of backstory butts up against another.

Incorporating backstory is a balancing act—too much will bog down the narrative flow, and too little may leave readers confused.

Relationships

Relationships are an excellent way to develop characters, whether it's one-on-one or in a group scenario. As characters develop, character relationships change, and that's one of the things that can make your plot engaging.

The relationships that exist between your characters are just as important as the characters themselves. Well-developed character relationships can reveal all sorts of things about your characters and their stories and can be a catalyst for action and story events.

Creating meaningful, believable character relationships may seem like a simple thing to do. It *is* simple in that you, the writer, know the characters well—what they want, their fears, their strengths, and all the rest—so all you have to do is put them in a situation and let them respond accordingly. But effective relationships are not easy to depict because (as in real life) they are complex and often difficult. Readers need to feel the authenticity of each relationship for them to be believable.

Some questions to consider as you're developing character relationships are:

- What type of relationship do you want to develop? Romantic? Familial? Business? Friendly? Adversarial?
- Is the relationship positive or negative? Supportive or neglectful? Comforting or abusive? Healthy or unhealthy? Or more likely, somewhere in between?
- How did they meet?

- What do they like and dislike about each other?
- Is one dominant over the other?
- What do they have in common? What are their differences?
- How do their feelings toward each other change over time? And what caused them to change?
- How do they treat each other as they work out their differences?
- How does each character think they are perceived by the other character?

When you're creating a scene that involves two or more characters, think about how it affects or contributes to their relationship(s) and how that fits into the story line. If it doesn't contribute to the relationship, it's best to leave the scene out.

Character Development Tools

Of the tools available for developing characters, I find the Myers-Briggs Personality Type Indicators most helpful. Developed back in the 1950s, when they still called them personality tests, it was used mostly in business for classifying temperament and behavior patterns in employees. Myers and Briggs identified four continuums of temperament, which resulted in sixteen unique combinations, each describing a person's typical behavior.

The four continuums are:

Introverted-Extraverted
Intuition-Sensation
Thinking-Feeling
Judging-Perceiving

The way I use this tool is by creating a spreadsheet that lists all of the personality traits for each of the sixteen types (listed on myersbriggs.org). Then I pigeon-hole each of my characters into one of the types. As I am developing a character, I refer to the typical traits of their personality type and weave these traits into the character's personality.

For example, a character in one of my books is an ESTP (extrovert, sensing, thinking, perceiving). Myers-Briggs describes this type of person as (among other things) someone who loves people, gossip, social activities, and entertainment. My character was all that, but what I didn't know was that this type of person is often impulsive and a thought jumper, so I weaved that into the story line as well to develop a more fleshed out and believable character.

Other tools include Character Builder (onestopforwriters.com), Persona Character Development Software (writersstore.com), and Character Writer (characterpro.com).

SUGGESTED READING:

Brown, David Griffin. "How to Create Memorable Characters." The Creative Penn. August 2, 2019. https://www.thecreativepenn.com/2019/08/02/writing-tips-creating-memorable-characters/?utm_source=feedburner&utm_medium=email&utm_campaign=Feed%3A+TheCreativePenn+%28The+Creative+Penn%29.

Chapman, Harvey. "Creating Characters in Novels." Novel Writing Help. (No date.) https://www.novel-writing-help.com/creating-characters.html.

Letourneau, Sara. "What Is Character Evolution, and Why Is It Important?" Sara Letourneau Writing. July 15, 2015. https://saraletourneauwriter.com/2015/07/15/what-is-character-evolution-and-why-is-it-important/.

Marks, C. S. "Five Traps and Tips for Character Development." LifeRich Publishing. (No date.) https://www.liferichpublishing.com/AuthorResources/Fiction/Five-Traps-and-Tips-for-Character-Development.aspx.

CHAPTER 4

Point of View and Narrative Tense

Two important elements of writing—point of view and narrative tense—need to be decided before you start writing. If you fail to do this, when you're finished with the book, you may end up having to go back to make things consistent and up to professional standards.

Point of View

Point of view (POV) specifies through whose eyes the story is being told. Just like in life, a story can change completely depending on the POV. The inability to grasp this concept is a common problem with new writers, so if this is your first exposure to it, please read on carefully.

There are three basic POVs from which to choose, and the time to establish it is with the first sentence of your book.

FIRST PERSON – In first-person narrative, the story is narrated using the pronouns *I, we, me, mine* and *my.*

> Call me Ishmael. Some years ago—never mind how long precisely—having little or no money in my purse, and nothing particular to interest me on shore, I thought I would sail about a little and see the watery part of the world.—Opening line of *Moby Dick* by Herman Melville

SECOND PERSON – Probably the rarest writing mode is second-person narrative, in which the narrator tells the story using the pronoun *you,* often transforming the reader into a character.

> You have brains in your head. You have feet in your shoes. You can steer yourself any direction you choose. You're on your own. And you know what you know. And YOU are the guy who'll decide where to go.—From *Oh, the Places You'll Go!* by Dr. Seuss

THIRD PERSON – Most novels are written in third-person narrative—using *he, she, it,* and *they*—from a narrator's perspective of the story.

> The Dursleys hadn't even remembered that today happened to be Harry's twelfth birthday. Of course, his hopes hadn't been high; they'd never given him a real present, let alone a cake—but to ignore it completely…—From *Harry Potter and the Chamber of Secrets* by J. K. Rowling

There are several reasons most novels are written using third-person narration: 1) it is arguably the easiest style in which to write, 2) it tends to be more objective, 3) it gives the writer more freedom to introduce information, and 4) it can allow the narrator to know everything there is to know about some or all of the characters.

But there's more to know about third person. You also need to choose between third-person limited and third-person omniscient. In third-person limited, the narrator knows only the thoughts and feelings of a single character—the protagonist—and not what's going on in the heads of other characters. If not done properly, what results is narration that hops into the heads of characters who are not the POV character—a sin known as head-hopping.

In the following example of third-person limited, Jillian is the POV character, and we the reader know only what she sees and hears and what is going on inside her head and nobody else's.

> Jillian stood behind her podium contemplating how she would answer the moderator's question. She had less experience than the rest of her running mates and no experience managing a multi-million-dollar budget. She looked over at Darin on her left. He glanced back at her and smirked.

But in this next example of third-person omniscient, while Jillian is still the main character for this particular scene, the narrator knows what is going on inside everyone's head.

> Jillian stood behind her podium contemplating how she would answer the moderator's question. She had less experience than the rest of her running mates and no experience managing a multi-million-dollar budget. On her left, Darin chuckled to himself, knowing he was the one on the dais with the best experience for the position.

Writing in third-person omniscient—with multiple POVs—is acceptable if done properly and if it is indeed most fitting for the story. If your story calls for multiple POVs, and you decide to write in third-person omniscient, it is best to make the POV character change obvious to the reader, placing it between chapters or major breaks in the narrative. To avoid confusion, some authors name the chapters after the person whose POV it is, eliminating any guesswork for the reader.

While writing in multiple POVs is permissible as well as fun and challenging, my advice for first-time writers is to stick to a single POV. Then, once you have more writing experience, you might want to try multiple POVs, but only if the story calls for it and you fully understand how to do it gracefully.

The most important POV rule is to be consistent. Once you pick a POV, stick with it throughout the entire manuscript.

Narrative Tense

Another decision to make before you begin writing is whether to use past- or present-tense verbs for the main action in the story.

> **PAST TENSE:** Grace raced to the finish line. Her ponytail whipped about as she took each stride.

> **PRESENT TENSE:** Grace races to the finish line, her ponytail whipping about as she takes each stride.

Past Tense
Past tense is most widely used in fiction for these reasons:

- Since past tense is familiar to readers, many have come to expect it and may actually be annoyed by present tense—they don't have to adjust to something different from what they're used to when they begin reading the story.
- It's arguably easier to write in past tense because it allows you to more freely jump around the timeline of your story, resulting in the story being told in a more fluid/natural manner than it can be in present tense.

- This may be a stretch, but some readers are more likely to believe a story where the events seem to have already taken place, as opposed to events that are happening as they are reading it. After all, the events must have taken place in order for the author to have written about them.

Present Tense

You might want to consider using present tense in the following situations:

- When the story is told within a short time frame, and especially when there is constant action. Think of *The Hunger Games,* which follows the harrowing experience of the heroine over a twenty-nine-day period.
- When the action unfolds with a sense of urgency and immediacy, and you want the reader to experience it while the action is happening. Like if the protagonist is one who lives in the moment or is impulsive or foolhardy, and you want the reader to experience the character's dilemmas and then growth as they happen.
- When it is important for the reader to feel particularly close to the protagonist as in "We are all in this together," making it easier for the reader to connect or empathize with the character. Veronica Roth does this well, especially in *Divergent*, where assigned personality factions within the social structure—the brave, the kind, the intelligent, the selfless, and the honest—are meant to complement each other but instead cause them to compete. The author's use of present tense brings the reader in close to the tumultuous relationships between the factions.

There is no right or wrong narrative tense choice, as long as you stick to one or the other. Most editors and readers do not care which tense is used, as long as it is used properly and consistently—failure to do so can be incredibly distracting. For example, you don't want readers to wonder if a particular event is happening now or if it was a flashback.

Refresher Course in Tenses

Even after you choose the narrative tense, you will find it necessary at times to use tenses other than simple present or past to show the reader the sequence of events throughout the story. For those who may need a refresher lesson, here are examples of other verb tenses you may need to use from time to time.

> **SIMPLE FUTURE TENSE**—used to indicate an action or feeling that will occur in the future.
>
> > Grace will run this marathon.
> > The baby will be hungry in about an hour.
>
> **FUTURE PERFECT**—used for actions or feelings that will be completed before some other point in the future.
>
> > The marathon will have ended by the time Grace leaves her home.
> > The baby will have calmed down by the time we get to the day care center.
>
> **PRESENT PERFECT**—used for an action that started in the past and the event still has some influence in the present.
>
> > Grace has run this marathon in previous years.
>
> **PAST PERFECT**—used when talking about an action that happened further back in the past than some other event that also happened in the past.
>
> > Grace had run marathons before she became ill.

As with POV, narrative tense is not an arbitrary decision. You will want to choose the one that works best for the story, the genre, and your readers.

SUGGESTED READING:

Bunting, Joe. The Write Practice (blog): *How to Choose the Right Tense for Your Novel*. https://thewritepractice.com/past-tense-vs-present-tense/.

Chapman, Harvey. "Point of View: The Complete Guide." Novel Writing Help. (No date.) https://www.novel-writing-help.com/point-of-view-in-literature.html.

Jauss, David. "The Pros and Cons of Writing a Novel in Present Tense." Writer's Digest. March 25, 2014. https://www.writersdigest.com/online-editor/the-pros-and-cons-of-writing-a-novel in present-tense.

Smith, Jack. "Tips on Handling the Omniscient Point of View in Fiction." The Writer. October 21, 2018. https://www.writermag.com/improve-your-writing/fiction/omniscient-pov/.

PART 2

Writing Tips

"There are three rules for writing a novel.
Unfortunately, no one knows what they are."

—W. SOMERSET MAUGHAM

CHAPTER 5

Story, Plot, and Hook

STORY: A narrative—either true or fictitious, in prose or verse—designed to interest, amuse, or instruct the reader; a tale.

PLOT: The important points and/or events that have significant consequences within the story.

HOOK: A technique used typically in the opening of a story but often throughout the story that captures the reader's attention so that he or she will continue reading.

In this chapter, I talk about the difference between story and plot and the hooks that are needed to grab readers' attention to keep them reading the whole story.

Story

A story is merely an account of events—typically with a beginning, middle, and end—targeted at readers for their enjoyment. What makes up a story is simply the main characters and what happens to them. Think of a story as a journey for one or more characters that starts in one place and time and ends up somewhere else.

For example, the story line in J. K. Rowling's *Harry Potter: The Sorcerer's Stone* is:

> Orphaned Harry Potter discovers he's a wizard and embarks upon an adventuresome journey after enrolling in Hogwarts School of Witchcraft and Wizardry.

The above statement explains who the main character is and what he does—the essence of the story.

The ability to write a great story is an awesome skill that involves a deep understanding of basic human emotions (anger, disgust, fear, happiness, sadness, and surprise) and what motivates people to do what they do. If you couple this with a unique situation and a main character battling against all odds to achieve his or her goal, you have the makings of a great story.

So how does one go about doing this when crafting a story line? I write literary fiction, so my stories are more character oriented than plot oriented, and my protagonists' conflicts are usually a combination of internal and external forces. I have my characters seeking something that is universally understood—acceptance, purpose, the truth. I think that pushes readers to appreciate and be sensitive to the feelings, thoughts, and experiences of the characters, perhaps even living vicariously through them. When people you care about are treated unjustly, you tend to care about them even more—it's human nature—so I sometimes weave that into the story. When the character faces danger, grief, or some other adversity, readers tend to feel their pain—another good strategy to get readers interested in the story because wounded, vulnerable characters tend to reveal what is at their core, which tugs at the reader's heartstrings.

If you're reading this book, you probably already have a story line in your head—one that will intrigue readers, entertain them, draw an emotional response from them, take them on a journey they have never experienced before. But if you don't already have a story concept, there are ways to arouse ideas in your head.

- Check out one of the many online story-idea generators. You'll find a list of them at writerswrite.com/fiction/plot-generators/.
- Let someone else's story idea influence you. It's not okay to steal it outright, but you can use certain aspects of other stories to shape yours into something unique.
- Create a unique story from a real life situation.
- Play the "what if" game. What if an up-and-coming politician fell in love with a covert operative from another party? What if a small country was secretly planning something that would affect the rest of the world? What if someone discovered a drug that would make people more intelligent?

For inspiration, here are some great story lines that are unique and have sold well, some of which have held the interest of an untold number of readers for many years:

Alice in Wonderland by Charles Lutwidge Dodgson is the story of a girl who falls down a rabbit hole into a fantasy world populated by an assortment of peculiar creatures.

Where the Crawdads Sing by Delia Owens is the heartbreaking coming-of-age story of a reclusive young woman locals refer to as "the marsh girl," and who is suspected of murder.

The Lord of the Rings by J.R.R. Tolkien is the story of men, elves, dwarves, and hobbits who attempt to overcome the dark forces of villains out to destroy a magical ring.

Into the Water by Paula Hawkins is the tale of a struggling young novelist with a severe case of writer's block who learns more than she bargained for after having accepted a dubious yet generous offer from a woman working for an obscure company.

Girl on the Train by Paula Hawkins is the story of a woman on a commuter train who witnesses something shocking in one of the backyards along the route. She reports it to authorities but gets into trouble when she decides to conduct her own amateur investigation.

Anyone can write down an account of events that add up to a story, but it takes great skill to write a compelling story line—one that makes the reader think and feel, one that captivates their attention.

Plot

The plot—the main events that make up the story—is important to the story in that it highlights the primary characters and their roles and connects the events in an orderly manner. "Plot is structure" seems to be a standard belief in literary circles. I've also heard, "Plot is the skeleton or the framework that holds the story together," and also "Plot is the series of events that make up a story." A compelling plot gets readers emotionally embroiled and keeps them entertained.

Using the Harry Potter story line as our example, we can appreciate J. K. Rowling's skill as a master plotter.

Orphaned baby Harry Potter lives with his aunt and uncle Mr. and Mrs. Dursley and their son Dudley. When they go to the zoo one day, Harry communicates with a snake, steals it from its cage, and brings it home. Soon afterward, mysterious letters start arriving for Harry, and his uncle, who is furious about the letters, takes the whole family to a deserted island to escape all of the mail. But the letters eventually catch up with

Harry, informing him that he's a wizard and that he's been admitted to the Hogwarts School of Witchcraft and Wizardry.

At Hogwarts, Harry makes many friends, and they begin taking classes in magic. During his first broom-flying lesson, Harry realizes he's a natural at flying, and although he often breaks the rules by flying unsupervised, he is rewarded by being put on a very important position on the team.

One day, while Harry and friends are hurrying to get back to the dorm, they discover a hidden part of Hogwarts where they bump into a three-headed dog that is guarding what they learn to be a magical stone that can guarantee immortality. After revealing too much about the stone to other people, Harry and his friends suspect that others are after it and try to retrieve it. In their attempt, they face horrific roadblocks including running into nemesis Voldemort. In the end, Harry defeats Voldemort and saves the stone.

This plot summary reveals and connects the events within the story. While researching the basic categories of plots, I ran into quite a difference of opinion—everything from there being one basic category (the main character wants something that he or she has to work for) to 1,462 (too many to list here) categories. Then I discovered author Christopher Booker's theory of seven basic plot types—a conclusion he arrived at after spending thirty-four years working on his book *The Seven Basic Plots: Why We Tell Stories*. Anyone who spends thirty-four years on this topic deserves some recognition, so it's his list I'll use to break down the various plot choices you can make.

OVERCOMING THE MONSTER: The protagonist must defeat an antagonistic force (most often a person but can be the protagonist himself via internal conflict, a social/cultural issue, or even the weather) that keeps goals out of reach. Historical examples: *Dracula, The War of the Worlds, The Guns of Navarone, Star Wars*. Contemporary examples: *Attack on Titan, The Hunger Games, Harry Potter*.

47

RAGS TO RICHES: The main character begins in poverty and/or hardship and makes something of himself or herself after overcoming great odds. Historical examples: *Cinderella, Jane Eyre, A Little Princess, Great Expectations, David Copperfield, The Prince and the Pauper.* Contemporary examples: *The Servant Boy, Fortune Is a Woman, The Windfall.*

THE QUEST: The main character(s) sets out to acquire something important and along the way faces substantial obstacles and temptations. Historical examples: *King Solomon's Mines, Jane Eyre, Brave New World.* Contemporary examples: *At the Water's Edge, The Pilgrim's Progress, Harry Potter and the Deathly Hallows.*

VOYAGE AND RETURN: The main character travels to or somehow ends up in a strange land where he or she faces and overcomes daunting threats. Historical examples: *Alice in Wonderland, Gone with the Wind, The Third Man, Apollo 13, Gulliver's Travels.* Contemporary examples: *Maiden Voyage, Finding Nemo, Endurance: Shackleton's Incredible Voyage.*

COMEDY: The main character(s) triumphs over adversity in a humorous way that results in a happy ending. Historical examples: *A Midsummer Night's Dream, Bridget Jones's Diary, Four Weddings and a Funeral.* Contemporary examples: *Eleanor Oliphant, Never Have I Ever, Where'd You Go, Bernadette.*

TRAGEDY: The main character is brought to ruin or death by a sorrowful or terrible event that results in a fall from prosperity to disaster, often through no fault of his or her own. Historical examples: *Macbeth, The Picture of Dorian Gray, Bonnie and Clyde.* Contemporary examples: *Beneath a Scarlet Sky, Ordinary Grace.*

REBIRTH: Important events force the main character to amend his or her ways, which results in the character becoming a better person. Historical examples: *The Frog Prince, Beauty and the Beast, The Snow Queen, A Christmas Carol.* Contemporary examples: *A Separate Peace, The Kite Runner, Because of Winn-Dixie.*

Some would argue that you can't start writing a story without a plot in mind. Others say it's possible to plan the ending first, and then later create the plot that leads to that ending. Still others say it's possible to just start writing and let the plot evolve on its own. There are planners (those who prepare an outline and develop major plot points before they start writing), and there are "pantsers" (those who do no planning but write by the seat of their pants). The truth is there is no right or wrong way to develop a plot. Just remember that regardless of the method you choose, plot development is a process that occurs throughout the story, so it is important to never lose sight of it.

Hook

Most people won't spend time reading the first fifty pages of your book to get into the story, so when readers pick up your book, it has literally only seconds to impress them. One good trick is to begin the story at an important moment that makes readers desperate to know what happens next. That's the hook. Hooks need to be crafted in a way that draws readers in, and the first one needs to appear earlier rather than later.

Here is the first sentence in *Lie Down with the Devil* by Linda Barnes:

> A man with plenty of secrets, Sam won't tell her anything, much less let her help—and she isn't having any more luck getting info from her old friends at the Boston PD. Sam's exile could have something to do with his mob connections, but it can't be that simple. Nothing involving Sam ever is.

That's a first sentence that will hook most readers to reading further.

Here are some ways to create "hooky" opening sentences for your book:

Curiosity

A screaming comes across the sky.

—*Gravity's Rainbow* by Thomas Pynchon

Contradictions

It was the best of times, it was the worst of times, it was the age of wisdom, it was the age of foolishness, it was the epoch of belief, it was the epoch of incredulity, it was the season of Light, it was the season of Darkness, it was the spring of hope, it was the winter of despair.

—*A Tale of Two Cities* by Charles Dickens

Ambiguity

I am an invisible man.

—*Invisible Man* by Ralph Ellison

Intrigue

"I was born twice: first, as a baby girl, on a remarkably smogless Detroit day in January of 1960; and then again, as a teenage boy, in an emergency room near Petoskey, Michigan, in August of 1974."

—*Middlesex* by Jeffrey Eugenides

Temperature

The heat was beginning to scorch my cheeks; beads of sweat were gathering in my eyebrows. It was just the same sort of heat as at my mother's funeral, and I had the same disagreeable sensations—especially in my forehead, where all the veins seemed to be bursting through the skin. I couldn't stand it any longer and took another step forward. I knew it was a fool thing to do; I wouldn't get out of the sun by moving on a yard or so. But I took that step, just one step, forward. And then the Arab drew his knife and held it up toward me, athwart the sunlight.

—*The Stranger* by Albert Camus

Sarcasm/Cynicism

If you really want to hear about it, the first thing you'll probably want to know is where I was born, and what my lousy childhood was like, and how my parents were occupied and all before they had me, and all that David Copperfield kind of crap, but I don't feel like going into it, if you want to know the truth.

—*The Catcher in the Rye* by J. D. Salinger

Emotions

"She left me the way people leave a hotel room. A hotel room is a place to be when you are doing something else. Of itself it is of no consequence to one's major scheme. A hotel room is convenient. But its convenience is limited to the time you need it while you are in that particular town on that particular business; you hope it is comfortable, but prefer, rather, that it be anonymous. It is not, after all, where you live."

—*The Bluest Eye by* Toni Morrison

Shock and Awe

They shoot the white girl first.

—*Paradise* by Toni Morrison

But hooks can't stop with the first sentence—you need to intertwine them throughout the story to hold the reader's attention. You can do this by keeping readers intrigued, guessing, shocked, bewildered, humored, scared, and/or saddened every so often. Here are some places to consider hooks.

- Begin and end chapters with a hook. Force readers to start reading the next chapter by ending the previous one right in the middle of high drama.
- Just when the narrative is rolling along at a gentle pace, give the reader a sense that something is "not quite right." Make it subtle yet deeply unsettling.
- Use foreshadowing (a subtle clue to the reader about what is going to happen in the future without completely revealing it) to give the reader a hint of what is to come later in the story.

Knowing how to craft a captivating story, properly structure the plot, and hook readers into it are key to writing successful novels.

SUGGESTED READING:

Kantey, Jordan. Now Novel (blog): *How to Plot a Novel: 7 Tips for Success.* https://www.nownovel.com/blog/how-to-plot-novel/.

Shepard, Sara. BookBub Partners Blog: *How to Start Your Novel to Hook Readers.* https://insights.bookbub.com/start-novel-bang-hook-readers/.

Sweetland, Robert. "Elements of Story or Fiction." Home of Bob. (No date.) http://www.homeofbob.com/literature/genre/fiction/ficElmnts.html.

Whitcomb, Laura. "Rescue Your Story from Plot Pitfalls." Writer's Digest. May 1, 2009. https://www.writersdigest.com/writing-articles/by-writing-goal/improve-my-writing/rescue-your-story-from-plot-pitfalls.

CHAPTER 6

Story Structure

When structuring a story, it's helpful to think in terms of a beginning, middle, and end, with each part fulfilling a distinct purpose. But the three elements don't necessarily have to occur in that order. For example, it can be quite effective to have the main character die at the beginning of the book and then devote the rest of the story to what led up to it. Consider the flashback method of storytelling, in which the narrator starts the story in the middle of things and then thinks back (or uses some other means) to reveal past events to fill the reader in on pertinent information before continuing with the story.

There are no hard-and-fast rules with regard to how much of the book each phase should occupy, and the sections are not clearly delineated. You won't go wrong if you devote roughly 20 percent of your novel to the beginning, 70 percent to the middle, and 10 percent to the end.

Sounds like a simple concept, right? Perhaps it *is* simple in some respects, but keep in mind that getting from beginning to end requires a certain structure in order to create an engaging and exciting experience for the reader. How the book is organized—how the plot is unveiled to the reader—makes a difference.

Let's dig a little deeper by starting with some definitions.

- **BEGINNING**—where the stage, mood, time period, and tone for the rest of the story are established; the main characters are introduced; and the protagonist's problem is defined.
- **MIDDLE**—where the story builds; everything comes apart; the tension is the greatest; and the conflict climaxes.
- **END**—where the major conflict in the story is resolved; (in most cases) all loose ends are tied up; and the reader learns how the story has changed the protagonist.

It is essential to include all the elements of each section—skimping on any of these will leave the reader confused, bored, or just plain uninterested.

Great novels grab readers' attention right away and keep it. This takes work—a lot of work. Not only does your novel need a good beginning, middle, and end, but so does each chapter, paragraph, and scene. While most of the following discussion applies to an entire novel, much of it applies to chapters, paragraphs, and scenes as well.

The pattern of the beginning, middle, and end of a story is called narrative arc, as is illustrated in the following graphic.

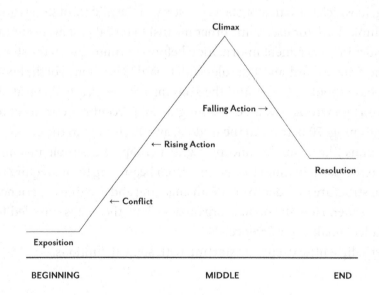

Narrative arc gives a story backbone and is the overall structure and shape of rising and falling action and/or emotion in a story. A good arc will help to engage readers from start to finish and deliver a satisfying conclusion.

Beginning

In addition to grabbing readers' attention with a great hook, the beginning of a novel needs to set the stage, the mood, the time period, and the tone for the rest of the story. It should introduce the main characters, the protagonist's goal(s), and his or her problem or challenge(s) in reaching this goal—the situation that drives them from their "normal" life toward something different, a conflicting situation that will give the story its reason for existing. Without the above elements introduced early on in the story, readers may become confused or frustrated and put the book down.

In plot-driven narratives, events tend to be more important than characters, and the writer must make sure all the plot points tie together smoothly and logically. As you focus on the events, tie in the characters' roles and their motivations for doing what they do. In plot-driven stories, it's about how your character reacts to and participates in the events.

Character-driven narratives tend to focus more on internal conflicts than external ones. Your focus should be on developing characters that readers can connect with by putting them in situations that showcase who they truly are.

By the end of the beginning of the story, readers should:

- Understand what type of story it is—romance, mystery, fantasy, etc.,
- Have a feel for the world in which the story takes place,
- Know the main character and his or her goals,
- Have formed a bond with the main character,
- Know what obstacles lie ahead for the main character in reaching his or her goals,

- Be familiar with the other significant characters in the story, and
- Feel compelled to continue reading.

By accomplishing these things, you will have built a strong foundation for the rest of the story.

Middle

The middle of the story is where tension, character conflict, the protagonist's journey, and narrative momentum build to a peak. Middles contain the meat of the story, and therefore something needs to be happening at all times for readers to maintain interest. The middle—typically much longer than either the beginning or the end—consists of three primary phases.

Rising Action

In the first phase of the middle, a series of events that raises the stakes for the main character begins to complicate matters, causing an upsurge in the story's suspense or tension. The rising action further develops the conflict between the main character and whatever obstacles he or she is facing, creating a series of predicaments that eventually rises to a climax.

A good example of rising action occurs in *Twilight by* Stephenie Meyer at the Cullen family (rescued vampires) baseball game where Bella is a spectator. When some outsider vampires fixate on her in the stands, and one of them smells Bella, the action rises. The miscreant vampire chases Bella while the Cullen family attempts to protect her. The chase rises toward a near-deadly climax.

Climax

This is the point of greatest tension in the story and is the turning point in the narrative arc from rising action to falling action. The point of climax is where everything goes wrong for the protagonist, where conflict is the greatest. No matter what form it takes, whether it's intense action or a quiet internal realization, the climax needs to be tied to the protagonist's conflict—which was conveyed in the beginning of the book. The climax should reflect the ultimate test of the protagonist's capabilities against the odds he or she is facing.

Here are three examples of story climaxes:

> *Gone Girl* by Gillian Flynn. Nick Dunne is a big-city magazine writer married to Amy, a woman with a substantial trust fund. After she goes missing on their fifth wedding anniversary, everyone (including the authorities) thinks he had something to do with her disappearance. The climax of the story occurs when Nick discovers and then plans to disclose the true story of what Amy did to create her disappearance.

> *Harry Potter and the Philosopher's Stone* by J. K. Rowling is about Harry, an orphaned boy raised by his aunt and uncle. When he is invited to join Hogwarts School of Witchcraft and Wizardry, he discovers he's a wizard, and his adventures begin when he and his new friends attempt to unravel the mystery of the Philosopher's Stone. The climax occurs when a professor puts a hex on Harry during one of their games, bringing to light tension between good and evil and shifting Harry's concern from winning the game to surviving.

> Set in the early 1930s in a racially divided Alabama town, *To Kill a Mockingbird* by Harper Lee is the story of lawyer Atticus Finch, who strives to prove the innocence of a young black man accused of raping a white woman. The story climaxes when the verdict is read, which leads to Finch's loss of faith in his fellow man.

The climax is where the protagonist will often have to make critical choices—where a change in their thought process, ideals, beliefs, physicality, or lifestyle occurs—one that will guide their actions through the rest of the story.

Falling Action

Immediately following the climax, when conflicts and problems in the story have come to a head and prior to the story ending, events will begin to unfold that cause a release of tension in the plot. This connective bridge between the climax and the resolution is called falling action. This is the time in the story when, given the circumstances of the climax, the protagonist deals with the consequences. The protagonist's world has changed since the beginning of the story, causing him or her to change and figure out how to reach his or her goal(s) in spite of the roadblocks.

This is not to say that during the falling action phase there has to be a lack of conflict, drama, or tension. These elements are merely aimed in a different direction—toward a conclusion—giving the reader satisfaction that rooting for the main character all this time has been worthwhile.

Ending

Three primary things need to happen at the end of the novel—loose ends are tied up, the major conflict in the story is resolved, and the reader knows how the story has changed the protagonist. It should be clear what truth protagonists have learned or not learned about themselves in the ending—their inner growth, how they've changed, how they've evolved. A good story ending must make the plot meaningful and the purpose of the story clear for the reader. An effective ending is often a new beginning for the protagonist.

Most readers want to feel some sense of satisfaction when they've completed reading a book. That's not to say every story has to end with the character(s) living "happily ever after." While most readers prefer a happy ending, they generally do not like overly predictable ones. My fourth novel, *Regarding Anna*, has an unpredictable ending, and in the more than 800 reviews it has gotten on Amazon, the most frequent comments are about how the reader loved the ending because they hadn't seen it coming. Even in romance novels and good-versus-evil stories, for example, where the general outcome is predictable, a slight twist to the ending will keep them from being boring.

A good ending won't be too abrupt, flat, or drawn out. But whether the ending is gradual or sudden, it should make the reader feel some strong emotion, such as happiness, sadness, surprise, pleasure, or shock.

As much thought should be given to the last sentence of the book as the first one. Whether it's a leisurely sentence or a sharp one, it should reinforce the book's central theme, portray a sense of completion, and leave the reader satisfied. A good ending will make the reader sorry to see the story come to an end.

Here are a few different types of endings to consider:

- **STRAIGHTFORWARD** The protagonist accomplishes his or her goal.
- **FULL CIRCLE**—The ending completes a loop, bringing the reader back to the prologue, opening line, scene, or chapter.
- **SURPRISE**—Something happens that is unexpected by the reader.
- **LESSON LEARNED**—The story ends with a lesson or moral you want the reader to get from the story.
- **CLIFF-HANGER**—You leave the reader in suspense, often setting the stage for a sequel.
- **HAPPILY EVER AFTER**—You close with a fairy-tale ending where everything turns out for the best for the protagonist and usually all the other characters.
- **SAD**—An ending that leaves readers feeling sad but intellectually satisfied.
- **SHOCK AND AWE**—Typically created by introducing a final twist to the plot, you leave readers horrified, appalled, astounded, outraged, angry, disgusted, or disturbed. (Most often used in horror, crime, and thriller novels.)

You do not want your ending to be any of the following:

- **VAGUE**—Especially in genre fiction, when important plot points are left up in the air, it leaves readers to speculate what happened, which will not be satisfying for them.

- **FLAT**—Regardless of genre, readers expect to feel some type of emotion at the end of the book. Bland endings are generally disappointing.
- **DRAWN OUT**—Once all the loose ends have been tied up, it's time to end the story.
- **UNSATISFYING**—If you promise readers something, and then you fail to deliver, they will feel cheated, dissatisfied.
- **CLICHÉD**—Overused endings generally aren't well received. Examples include: It was all just a dream. The character had been talking to a ghost all this time. The butler did it.
- **COINCIDENTAL**—Having lightning strike the bad guy just before he's going to do his dirtiest deed is not very insightful.

No hard and fast rules exist for structuring a story. But whatever path you choose, the story should flow in a logical, understandable order.

SUGGESTED READING:

McNulty, Bridget. Now Novel (blog): *Novel Structure: 7 Tips for Structuring Your Book.* https://www.nownovel.com/blog/novel-structure-writing-tips/.

Telfer, Jonathan (editor). "How to Structure a Novel." Writers Online. (No date.) https://www.writers-online.co.uk/how-to-write/how-to-write-fiction/how-to-structure-a-novel.

CHAPTER 7

Active Versus Passive Voice

There are many ways to structure a sentence to convey the same information and still be grammatically correct. In this chapter, I talk about where the subject and verb fall within the sentence, resulting in all sentences being essentially written in one of two voices: active or passive. Voice is the term used to describe whether a verb is active or passive. When a sentence is written in the active voice, the subject performs the action; in the passive voice, the subject receives the action.

ACTIVE VOICE—the subject performs the action.
Example: The teacher handed out the instructions.

PASSIVE VOICE—the subject is a recipient of the action.
Example: The instructions were handed out by the teacher.

While it is not wrong to use passive voice, active voice is generally preferred by editors. The point of the active voice is to highlight the logical flow of the action, from the subject (or *doer*) to the object (or *receiver*) of the action, making sentences more direct.

PASSIVE: Antonio's jugular was slit open by the intruder.
ACTIVE: The intruder (doer) slit open Antonio's (receiver) jugular.

PASSIVE: The tainted crackers that had fallen to the ground were eaten by the baby.
ACTIVE: The baby (doer) ate the tainted crackers (receiver) that had fallen to the ground.

Consider these two paragraphs describing Samantha's reaction to having been fired.

First example: A short, emotionless letter signed by Samantha's manager and obviously written by the company's legal department terminated her employment. Her attention was caught by the statement, "This decision is not reversible." Why there was no opportunity for discussion angered her. The bogus reason given for the termination made her cringe—she had never been told that her performance had been unsatisfactory. Her next month's rent would not even be covered by the meager severance check she would be getting. Desperation was etched on her face as tears made their way down her cheeks.

Second example: Samantha read the short, emotionless letter terminating her employment. Signed by her manager, but obviously written by the company's legal department, one particular statement caught her attention: "This decision is not reversible." She cringed at the bogus reason given for the termination—never having been told that her performance had been unsatisfactory—and was angered by the lack of opportunity for discussion. The meager severance check she would be getting, not even enough to cover her next month's rent, caused her to cry.

Not only is the second account of what happened—the one written in active voice—more direct than the first one that is written in passive voice, but it was written with fewer words, making it a more succinct paragraph.

When to Use Active Voice

Using active voice in your writing means that the subject of the sentence comes first and performs the action that the rest of the sentence describes.

Active voice...

- clearly identifies the action and who is performing that action.
- conveys energy and directness that passive voice isn't capable of conveying.
- helps readers to experience what the character is experiencing right along with them.
- usually results in sentences that are less wordy.
- is more apt to keep readers interested and engaged.

Using active voice can be a way for writing to flow seamlessly, be clear and concise, and be free from unnecessary words and confusingly long and awkward sentences. It is the most straightforward way to present your ideas, because it creates a clear image in the reader's mind of who is doing what. This makes your writing much easier to understand and is why good writers, editors, and readers prefer active voice.

How to Detect a Sentence in Passive Voice

To spot passive voice sentences, look at what happened and look at who was responsible for doing it. If the person or thing responsible for doing the action is either omitted or occurs in the sentence after the thing that happened, *and* you see a past participle following some form of "to be," it's passive voice, as in these examples.

1. The film is (form of "to be") viewed (past participle) by the students.
2. The old woman was (form of "to be") driven (past participle) to the store by her neighbor.

3. The grapes are (form of "to be") crushed (past participle) in a barrel by Gianna.
4. The biscuits were (form of "to be") eaten (past participle) by the street beggars.

Problems with Passive Voice

Sometimes passive voice can lead to awkward, lengthy, and/or convoluted sentences instead of straightforward ones.

> **PASSIVE:** Her body odor was found to be disgusting by Matt.
> **ACTIVE:** Matt found her body odor disgusting.

> **PASSIVE:** By then, the pancake batter will have been thoroughly mixed by the children.
> **ACTIVE:** By then, the children will have thoroughly mixed the pancake batter.

When to Use Passive Voice

Passive voice is not always the worse choice to make. It is perfectly acceptable and recommended to use passive voice when:

- You do not know who performed the action.
  Example: The NO DUMPING sign had obviously been ignored.

- The person who performed the action is not important to the meaning of the sentence.
  Example: Your performance was evaluated by three people.

- You want to emphasize the action rather than the one performing the action.
  Example: Each spring, the town was infiltrated by thousands of college students.

- You want to create an authoritative tone.

Example: After a long discussion, the amendment was ratified by the majority of members.

- When the person or thing receiving the action is more important than the subject performing it.
  Example: The president was sworn in on the steps of the White House.

Understanding the difference between active and passive voice is an important skill for writers. Both styles have a place in writing fiction when used appropriately—the choice between the two depending on the purpose, context, and content of the sentence.

SUGGESTED READING:

Shiau, Yvonne (content marketer, USA). Reedsy Blog: *Passive Voice Vs Active Voice: Finally Understand the Difference.* https://blog.reedsy.com/passive-voice-active/.

Strathy, Glen C. "Avoiding the Passive Voice." How to Write a Book Now. (No date.) https://www.how-to-write-a-book-now.com/the-passive-voice.html.

CHAPTER 8

Show, Don't Tell

"Show, don't tell" is often referred to as the golden rule of writing fiction and is arguably one of the most important rules for all new writers to learn and follow. Simply put, "show, don't tell" means to allow the reader to experience the story through the character's actions, dialogue, facial expressions, or through specific details rather than tell the reader what to believe.

> **TELLING**—He was really tired.
> **SHOWING**—He slouched in the recliner, eyes struggling to stay open, his hand gradually losing its grip on the can of Miller Light.

Showing will pull readers into the scene you've created so they can draw their own inferences, whereas *telling* imparts information and leaves no room for readers to deduce anything. A successful "show, don't tell" will make readers feel like they are inside the character's head and will know from that perspective what's going on.

Telling is usually boring and tends to slow the narrative down, causing readers to skip over parts or all of it. Extreme telling is a form of talking down to readers, not letting them think for themselves.

I love this advice from author/agent Evan Marshall.

Don't just write: The subway station was shabby. Write: Near the edge of the platform, a man with knotted hair held out a Dixie cup to no one in particular, calling, "Spare some change? Spare some change?" Swirls of iridescent orange graffiti covered the Canal Street sign. The whole place smelled of urine and potato chips.

And this by author/playwright Anton Chekhov.

Don't tell me the moon is shining; show me the glint of light on broken glass.

Here are some more examples of "telling" versus "showing."

TELLING—She was surprised at his remark.
SHOWING—She jumped up from the chair, shrieking, "You've got to be kidding me!"

TELLING—He was musically talented.
SHOWING—He played first violin for the Chicago Symphony and strummed a mean banjo as well.

TELLING—She felt as though she looked really nice in the outfit she had chosen.
SHOWING—Seeing her reflection in the mirror made her smile.

Surprisingly, a "showing" sentence isn't necessarily longer than a "telling" one.

FLAT: She moved to within a few inches of his face. When they kissed, she felt a tingle go down her spine.
BETTER: She leaned in for the kiss. His lips felt warm, soft, and pulsating.

To liven up a flat "telling" sentence, try incorporating one or more of the five senses into it—sight, sound, touch, smell, and taste.

> **FLAT:** He couldn't tolerate the smell in the bedroom.
> **BETTER:** The foul, dead odor coming from the bedroom caused him to gag.

> **FLAT:** He sweated.
> **BETTER:** Beads of sweat trickled down his face, onto his lips, and into his mouth with a salty rinse.

Never make the mistake of both telling *and* showing.

> She was surprised to see him there. "What is he doing here?" she shouted.

If you're using too many of certain words—*is, was, were, has, made, saw, thought,* and *felt*—you might be telling (versus showing) more than you should, as in these examples.

> **TELLING:** Gerard is a talented violinist.
> **SHOWING:** The audience sat silently as they listened to Gerard play Beethoven's Moonlight Sonata, his fingers caressing the melody as if having a life of their own.

> **TELLING:** The night was cold as Trudy began the journey from her stalled car to the nearest house.
> **SHOWING:** Trudy slid out of her car and trudged through the foot-deep snow looking for a house, the frosty night air cutting into her lungs.

> **TELLING:** Harriet was impressed by the buffet table.
> **SHOWING:** Harriet made a slow, disbelieving shake of her head as she moved closer to the extravagant buffet table, momentarily forgetting the reason she was in attendance at

the event. Giddiness overwhelmed her—she couldn't wait to share the experience with her friends.

TELLING: He had bad news to tell his workers that was going to result in layoffs.

SHOWING: The news he was about to tell his workers about the first round of layoffs would undoubtedly cause stress among them, even for those who would not be directly affected, as no worker could relax knowing the next round might include them.

It helps to look for facts in your manuscript and replace them with action where appropriate.

TELLING: During the Great Depression, unemployment rose to 25 percent, housing prices plummeted 30 percent, $30 billion was lost on Wall Street, 750,000 farms were lost through sheriff sales or bankruptcy, 1.5 million men abandoned their families, and half the banks failed.

SHOWING: During the Great Depression, many people became homeless due to job loss. Unable to support themselves, people were forced to move in with family members, neighbors, and even total strangers. Children suffered from the long-term effects of poor diet and lack of medical care. Suicide rates surged, leaving families in even more desperate situations. With such widespread despair spreading across the country, soon there was no money to buy the farmer's products, and they fell even further behind the rest of the country when desperate banks called in their loans, and farmers had no money to pay them.

Long descriptive passages where there's no action or dialogue may be an indication of too much telling. Try replacing them with scenes that depict the same idea.

UNNECESSARY DESCRIPTION: They rode up the long escalator to the second floor of the mall, hurrying past the food court and its tempting array of fast food odors wafting through the air, to the mobile phone store where Randy and Todd waited for them.

BETTER: They rode up the escalator to the mobile phone store where Randy and Todd waited for them.

While showing is usually a good thing, it also has some pitfalls. Showing can be confusing because it is less precise than telling. When you show someone who is tired, for example, by having the character close his eyes, slouch in a chair, and groan, the reader may not know whether the character is exhausted, angry, ill, or irritated. Another pitfall is that showing might result in a longer narrative that some readers may not like.

The "show, don't tell" concept is an effective one, but it is not a blanket rule to be used in every sentence, paragraph, and scene. Use it wisely.

SUGGESTED READING:

Harris, Megan. Megan Harris (blog): *Show, Don't Tell and How to Make Readers Hungry for More.* http://mharriseditor.com/show-dont-tell-fiction-writing/.

McNulty, Bridget. Now Novel (blog): *Show, Don't Tell: Examples from Books Balancing Both.* https://www.nownovel.com/blog/show-dont-tell/.

Russel, Bryan (editorial quality manager). "Ten Tips to Avoid Telling in Writing Fiction." Scribendi. (No date.) https://www.scribendi.com/advice/how_to_avoid_telling_writing_in_fiction.en.html.

CHAPTER 9

Conflict, Crisis, Drama, and Tension

Conflict builds character. Crisis defines it.
—STEVEN THULON

Without conflict, crisis, drama, and tension, a story would be nothing but a string of boring facts—if every scene was peaceful, comfortable, and pleasurable, no one would read it. This may sound overly simplified, but most great stories involve a protagonist desperately wanting something but unable to get it due to something or someone getting in the way and causing trouble.

Conflict, crisis, drama, and tension define the characters and set them in motion to make choices and act in ways that reveal things about themselves, not only propelling the story, but giving power to it.

Readers prefer fiction with conflict, crisis, drama, and tension for the satisfaction and reward they can feel at the end, and in order for a writer to accomplish this, he or she has to capture the reader's attention, touch the reader's emotions, and make readers care about the protagonist. All this can be accomplished through the right amount of conflict, crisis, drama, and tension.

Some would argue that the story doesn't begin until there is conflict, crisis, drama, or tension—that they are the driving forces that move the story forward and entice the reader to keep turning pages. I tend to believe this as well.

Conflict

Two types of conflict exist that you can include in your novel: internal and external.

Internal conflict is the dilemma a character faces inside of himself or herself. For example, the dilemma might be one that requires a character to choose whether to compromise his or her ethical standards. Shakespeare was a genius in doing this, as in *Hamlet*, whose title character struggles with carrying out his father's ghost's order to kill his uncle.

External conflict is in the obstacles the character encounters during the course of the novel. An example of this is the conflict between Harry Potter and Voldemort in *Harry Potter and the Goblet of Fire.*

One way to introduce conflict into your novel is to find the main character's greatest weakness and attack it. Stomp on it. Beat it down. Then kick it. And when you're finished, kick it again one last time for good measure. Lisa Duffy does this extremely well in *The Salt House,* in which Jack and Hope Kelly, just when their emotions are explosively high following the death of their young daughter, experience a series of events that threaten their marriage and business.

Conflict can be defined as disagreement, contradiction, opposition, clash, fight, battle, struggle, strife, controversy, quarrel, discord, antagonism, collision, incompatibility, or interference. There are arguably four basic types of conflict:

MAN AGAINST HIMSELF *(internal conflict).* This may involve emotional issues, desires, difficult choices, expectations, fears, personal crossroads, addictions, and ethics. Internal conflict is featured prominently in the following novels:

The Call of the Wild by Jack London, in which the protagonist (in this case, a dog) is torn between his domesticated and wild self.

The Giver by Lois Lowry, in which twelve-year-old Jonas explores the importance of free will as he struggles with whether or not to accept the sheltered and narrow-minded beliefs of others.

HUMAN AGAINST HUMAN *(external conflict).* This is often a typical protagonist-versus-antagonist situation involving physical or emotional conflict. Human-against-human conflict is featured in the following stories:

The Wizard of Oz by L. Frank Baum, in which Dorothy struggles with the Wicked Witch of the West.

Star Wars by George Lucas, in which Luke Skywalker fights with nemesis Darth Vader.

HUMAN AGAINST SOCIETY *(external conflict).* This may include the government, culture, civil rights, religion. You will find human-against-society conflict in the following novels:

To Kill a Mockingbird by Harper Lee, in which lawyer Atticus Finch strives to prove the innocence of a young black man accused of raping a white woman.

Fahrenheit 451 by Ray Bradbury, in which fireman Guy Montag is forced to set fire to homes that are found to contain books, which have been declared illegal by the authorities.

HUMAN AGAINST NATURE *(external conflict).* This may involve natural disasters, illness, fire, environmental issues. Human-against-nature conflict is featured in the following novels:

Into the Wild by Jon Krakauer, in which young Christopher McCandless leaves a privileged life to become a back-to-nature wanderer.

The Old Man and the Sea by Ernest Hemingway, in which a Cuban fisherman engages in a tortuous battle with a giant fish in the middle of the Gulf Stream.

This is not to say the story line cannot include more than one conflict, and, in fact, a great novel will include many conflicts, both internal and external. The challenge is to make them work together to create a cohesive plot. This can be accomplished by making the conflicts oppose the protagonist's goal(s) or motivation toward reaching the goal(s). For example, if your character's goal is to beat his drug addiction (internal conflict), pressure from his druggie buddies to hang with them and his need to sell drugs in order to pay off drug debts (external conflicts) would make it difficult for him to turn things around for himself.

The central focus of a novel needs to be on how the protagonist overcomes conflict to achieve his or her goal—whether it's internal conflict, external conflict, or (more likely) a combination of the two—with each instance of conflict taking the protagonist further from the goal. Then, in the end, the protagonist needs to evolve—to grow in some way—as a result of the conflict faced. Otherwise, there is no purpose to the story.

Crisis

Crisis can be defined as a major turning point in a sequence of events, a condition that leads to a decisive change, an upheaval in a person's life, or the point at which tension is at the highest. Examples include a serious car crash intentionally caused by someone close to the protagonist, a debilitating illness, loss of a loved one, an unexpected divorce, a declaration of war.

The story's crisis is the moment when your protagonist is placed into such a tight spot that he or she *has* to make a decision from which there is no turning back—the do-or-die moment. The crisis of a story is what the reader has been waiting for. Here are some examples of compelling crisis points in fiction.

- In *Star Trek: The Next Generation* by Gene Roddenberry when the *Enterprise* is attacked by the slime monster.
- In John Steinbeck's *Of Mice and Men* when Lennie kills Curley's wife.
- In *Romeo and Juliet* by William Shakespeare when Romeo kills Tybalt and realizes he has sealed his own fate.
- In *The Color Purple* by Alice Walker when Mister separates Celie from her beloved Nettie.

If you have successfully woven crisis into your story, readers will wonder how the character will get out of the situation—what decisions are made, how the main character handles himself or herself, how other characters react, etc. Readers will have to know what happens next.

Drama

When we think of drama, we think of something intense, exciting, striking, or vivid in some way. In fiction, drama is created through dialogue, internal thoughts, character action, or the lack thereof by a series of events having an intense emotional effect.

Drama may take any number of forms—comedy, tragedy, social/political, fantasy, surprise, delight, disappointment, suspense—and may be shown by creating a single intense action-packed scene or a series of minor ones. It can be subtle or in-your-face. It doesn't have to be fast-paced—slowing down the action to create drama can be just as effective.

Creating drama in your story will serve no purpose unless you include the effect that it has on the character. Never leave the reader wondering why you included it.

Here are some excerpts that depict drama.

- From Emily Brontë's *Wuthering Heights*:
  Self-imposed incarceration and starvation is a particularly slow and excruciating way to expire, even if you do find yourself in the throes of delirium. Love hurts, Catherine, but is haunting your beloved Heathcliff until his death really the best way to appease your suffering?

- From *Appointment by Death* by Agatha Christie:
  "You do see, don't you, that she's got to be killed?" The question floated out into the still night air, seemed to hang there a moment and then drift away down into the darkness toward the dead sea.

- From Hunter S. Thompson's *Fear and Loathing in Las Vegas*:
  We were somewhere around Barstow on the edge of the desert when the drugs began to take hold. I remember saying something like, "I feel a bit lightheaded; maybe you should drive ..." And suddenly there was a terrible roar all around us and the sky was full of what looked like huge bats, all swooping and screeching and diving around the car, which was going about a hundred miles an hour with the top down to Las Vegas. And a voice was screaming: "Holy Jesus! What are these goddamn animals?"

- From David Peace's *Occupied City*:
  In the wintertime, papers in your arms, through this January night, down these Tokyo streets, you are running from the scene of the crime; from the snow and from the mud, from the bank and from the bodies; running from the scene of the crime and from the words of the book; words that first enticed and entranced you, then deceived and defeated you, and now have left you in-snared and in-prisoned—

Here are some ways to include drama in your narrative.

DON'T TELL ALL. Leave something to the reader's imagination by not giving out all the details. Tease them by alluding to (rather than revealing) something.

USE MISINFORMATION. Have a character receive some faulty information to confuse or misguide him or her.

HOLD BACK. Keep the protagonist wanting—with his or her goal just out of reach—for as long as you can.

CREATE IMPERFECT CHARACTERS. Allow your characters to make mistakes that lead them in the wrong direction.

START AT THE END. If the ending of your story contains the most drama, consider starting there. Then, pull the rest of the story into it.

CREATE A HIDDEN AGENDA FOR THE ANTAGONIST. Let the reader think in the beginning that the opposing character's purpose is something different.

CREATE OBSTACLES. Force your characters to face something unexpected to create setbacks for them.

PLAY AROUND WITH CHARACTER. Create a surprising change in values, morals, or beliefs for one of your characters—something the reader would not have expected.

AMP IT UP. Make your protagonist's goals loftier, the risks associated with them greater, and the roadblocks harder to overcome.

CONSIDER DEATH. There being no greater drama in life than death, if it enhances the story, consider fitting it in.

GIVE AND TAKE. Try giving your characters what they desire most, and then take it away.

SOW FAMILY DISCORD. Reading about happy families is boring. Family discord is always a good source for drama—try betrayal, scapegoating, favoritism, jealousy, or abuse.

Drama is a vital ingredient for all good stories—those uneasy moments that eventually crest excite readers and cause them to read on. The right balance of drama and exposition is critical to captivate your readers.

Tension

With Latin roots, the word "tension" stems from "tendere," which means to stretch. Tension in fiction occurs when something is stretched either physically or emotionally.

In the health-care industry, tension is referred to as a psychological or physical condition—associated with conflict, disparity, instability, or uncertainty—created by a need or desire to resolve a discomfort between two or more forces. Emotional tension can lead to physical tension, leading to symptoms, such as an uncomfortable feeling in the pit of the stomach, stiff muscles, or painful joints. Similarly, in fiction, tension is the element that evokes emotions, such as worry, anxiety, fear, unhappiness, uncertainty, and stress on the part of the characters, and if done well, the readers too.

Tension is most often associated with psychological or emotional factors, such as those mentioned above, but can also be associated with physical factors, such as illnesses or disorders. Tension is often driven by conflict, crisis and drama and is most effective in writing when it starts out slow and rises up to the crisis point of the story. The right balance of tension throughout the narrative will cause readers to become emotionally invested in the story and incited to keep reading.

The good thing about tension for writers is that it can manifest itself in so many different ways. Tension can occur in almost any situation—any event, conversation, or thought can inspire tension. It can be conveyed in a loud and obnoxious manner or in a quiet and restrained one. It can be obvious on the page or inferred by the narrative.

While each instance will be different depending on the situation, most tension-filled moments fit into one or more of the following five categories.

Between People

In real life, tension at some level exists in every relationship, as it's rare for people to always get along without experiencing any problems. Accordingly, in fiction, characters who have perfect, flawless relationships are unbelievable and furthermore are likely not being used to their fullest potential. (See Chapter 3 for more on character development.) Jonathan Franzen's *Freedom* is a good example of tension in fiction. In this story, the teenage son of staunch conservative parents moves in with their ultra-liberal next-door neighbors, causing extreme tension among family members as they try to find ways to get along.

Extenuating Circumstances

Tension can stem from any number of extenuating circumstances—poverty, tragedy, social/political injustice, the environment, to name just a few—causing problems for the protagonist that are beyond his or her control. Imagined circumstances can also create tension for a character, and when unknown consequences are added, tension is amped up. Social injustice, for example, is the theme in *The Girl Who Played with Fire* by Steig Larsson, in which the protagonist is accused of three murders based on extenuating circumstances, and there is tension among the accused, the investigator, and people from the accused's past.

Task-Related

Some tasks—whether dictated by other characters/circumstances or self-inflicted—can cause tension for the protagonist in multiple ways. Aside from the obvious problem(s) associated with not completing an important task, tension may also come about from not finishing a task on time, doing it wrong, or unexpected ramifications from completing it. In Kathryn Stockett's *The Help*, the protagonist's key task is to compile a book of stories about the lives of black maids in the South. The author skillfully advances the tension surrounding this task with a series of incidents that prohibit her from completing the book.

Surprises

A surprise in the narrative will undoubtedly add tension to the situation. *The Hunger Games* by Suzanne Collins shocks readers with the notion that elders in the society send their children to fight one another to the death and call it a game.

Mysteries

Mysteries—even secondary ones embedded in non-mystery genres—add tension to a story. Mysteries provide puzzles to solve and allow readers to vicariously experience the darker side of life. Richard Powers creates serious tension between siblings in his novel *The Echo Maker*, in which Mark Schluter is involved in a near-fatal accident and calls upon his estranged sister to nurse him back to health. The tension Mark feels stems from his belief that even though she resembles, acts, and sounds just like his sister, she is really someone else, and the tension she feels stems from his refusal to recognize her.

Many storytelling methods can be used to create tension:

- Foreshadowing (hinting at something that will happen later)
- Withholding information, especially in mysteries
- Creating a "ticking time bomb"
- Placing cliff-hangers at the ends of chapters
- Setting up a dangerous environment
- Separating the protagonist from his or her comfort zone

- Creating character isolation
- Showing emotional loss
- Crafting forceful dialogue
- Creating disasters
- Having characters search for or discover something difficult
- Showing unpredictable behavior
- Delaying the action, slowing the pace
- Raising the stakes
- Creating a dramatic atmosphere and mood
- Implanting flashbacks
- Inserting plot twists and interesting revelations
- Introducing unexpected characters

Tension is all about unanswered questions that keep the reader wanting to read further and well-timed moments that shake things up a bit. But once you create tension in the story, don't forget to release it at some point, acknowledging that the cause of the tension has passed.

Tension is a great tool, and the more imaginative you can be as the writer, the more effective it will be.

SUGGESTED READING:

Coles, William. Story in Literary Fiction (blog): *Drama.* https://www. storyinliteraryfiction.com/essays-on-writing/drama/.

Irving, Ian. Ian Irving (blog): *60 Ways to Create and Heighten Conflict.* https://www.ian-irvine.com/for-writers/article-5-how-to-create-conflict/.

Lekic, Natasa (founder). NY Book Editors (blog): *Tension: What It Is and How to Develop It in Your Novel.* https://nybookeditors. com/2016/10/tension-develop-novel/.

Thomas, Sophie. "How to Hook Readers with a Great Crisis." Story Grid. (No date.) https://storygrid.com/hook-readers-great-crisis/.

CHAPTER 10

Narrative Exposition

NARRATIVE—the story in itself. The entire novel is a narrative.

EXPOSITION—background information that explains a current situation. Typically used to fill gaps between active scenes and dialogue in fiction, exposition may or may not be essential to the story.

NARRATIVE EXPOSITION—exposition embedded in a novel.

N arrative exposition conveys certain factual information—that is unknown to the reader while known to the characters—that usually pertains to a character, setting, or historical event. This can be accomplished through dialogue (internal and external), flashbacks, characters' thoughts/memories, background details, or character backstory.

> Patrick reached for Helen's hand. "What's wrong?" he asked.
> "I can't help but thinking about when Billy was in the hospital and if the same thing is going to happen to Lucy."

"You have to think positive, Helen," he said, his mind drifting back to **three years earlier when their brother Billy lost his fight with cancer.**

In this example, the bolded information indicates narrative exposition—Patrick and Helen know about their brother Billy's losing battle with cancer, but readers are not aware of this because it happened before the current story began.

Every character has a past before your story begins, and some of that backstory may be crucial to the main story's development. For example, *Goldilocks and the Three Bears* begins with an introduction of the three bears, where they live, and what they typically ate for breakfast. This is important information for the reader to know before the story actually starts—when Goldilocks comes walking through the forest and smells porridge.

Writers sometimes (readers seldom) fall in love with their characters' backstories and have a tendency to provide a bit too much of it, which can slow the narration and bore readers. But unless the backstory is as much a part of the main story as the current action (for example, in *Sophie's Choice,* in which a series of Sophie's flashbacks reveals her heart-rending story that led her to Auschwitz), it is a good idea to include only those elements of the character's past that are necessary for plot development, provide an important aspect of the story, or give a better understanding of the character's current behavior or mindset.

Narrative exposition on setting, in particular—the story's time and place—is almost always needed to situate the story in a specific environment and time period in order to ground the characters to their past and present. And sometimes certain historical events are important for the reader to understand what is currently going on in the story, especially in sci-fi and fantasy stories where history is an unknown to the reader.

Understand that narrative exposition slows the momentum of the story, and too much can even bring it to a screeching halt. It's a balancing act—too little and your readers may be confused, and too much may put them to sleep. Present whatever facts you need to get across in as few words as possible—a line or two here, a short paragraph there—then return to the action as soon as you can.

Most importantly, realize you don't have to explain everything that happened in the past. In fact, most readers prefer to figure some things out for themselves, typically wanting to go on the journey with the character without being distracted by irrelevant information that interferes with the flow of the story.

Above all, don't let narrative exposition turn into an information dump…like I did with early drafts of my first novel. Here is an example of an information dump (not one of mine, thank goodness).

> Susanna retreated to the veranda, sat down on one of the high-back wicker chairs facing the water, and sipped what was left of her watered-down mint julep. The troubling conversation she had just had with her son, Harold, had lingered in her head for the past hour. It wasn't enough he was going to Brazil to join his best friend, George, to help save the Amazon rain forest, but he was leaving his wife and three small children behind to fend for themselves. George had been in Brazil before he was married and had had more than one close call with the natives who didn't want foreigners of any kind in their village. Harold knew this and still wanted to join in on what he considered to be one of the most valiant environmental efforts on the face of the earth and didn't care how dangerous it could be. And it wasn't only the natives they had to watch out for—there were also malaria-carrying mosquitoes, blood-sucking leaches, and other critters lurking in the depths of the rain forest. George had already made the arrangements for Harold's arrival, complete with an escort by local jungle police from his small plane to the nearest river and then to the campsite. Susanna stared at the sparkly surface of the calm lake while the last remnant of bourbon slid down her throat.

Readers are likely to skip over that amount of detail, and when they do, they run the risk of missing something important. In the revised version that follows, only what is essential at that point in the story remains, allowing the readers to understand the importance of what lies ahead for Harold and his family.

> Susanna retreated to the veranda, sat down on one of the high-back wicker chairs facing the water, and sipped what was left of her watered-down mint julep. The troubling conversation she had just had with her son, Harold, had lingered in her head for the past hour. It wasn't enough he was going to Brazil to join his best friend, George, to help save the Amazon rain forest, but he was leaving his wife and three small children behind to fend for themselves. She stared at the sparkly surface of the calm lake shaking her head, while the last remnant of bourbon slid down her throat.

Whether you throw away the leftovers or introduce them at a later place depends on whether they are germane to the story line. And even if they are germane, you may still want to eliminate them and let your readers fill things in on their own, forcing them closer to the action and the characters. Readers actually like that sort of thing as long as it's not too confusing or overdone.

When you catch yourself creating large amounts of narrative exposition, dole it out in small bits. Leave out explanatory details that are not essential to the story. Include only the absolute bare minimum the reader needs to know for each scene to make sense. And if you can make the same point in the main story, do it there and eliminate exposition altogether.

Some valid reasons to include narrative exposition are to:

- Explain a character's motivation
- Enhance a character's personality, psychology, what shaped them
- Make the character appear more real to the reader
- Add a strong emotion, such as irony, regret, or hope
- Educate the reader on important or relevant historical facts
- Inject clues about your character's past

• Slow the pace after a particularly dramatic scene

Here are several different ways of effectively providing background information in a novel.

Narrative summary

Narrative summary is the telling of some aspect of the story in a compressed form, most often used when the conveyance of what has transpired over a long period of time can be covered with few words.

> **EXAMPLE 1.** She grew up with an alcoholic mother and a truck-driving father who was rarely home, not even for the important events in her life.

> **EXAMPLE 2.** Garp's mother, Jenny Fields, was arrested in Boston in 1942 for wounding a man in a movie theater. This was shortly after the Japanese had bombed Pearl Harbor and people were being tolerant of soldiers, because suddenly everyone was a soldier, but Jenny Fields was quite firm in her intolerance of the behavior of men in general and soldiers in particular. (Excerpt from *The World According to Garp* by John Irving.)

Flashback

Flashbacks are interruptions in the narrative that provide background information to the current events and give insight into a character's motivation. Dream sequences, visions, and memories are methods used to present flashbacks.

> **EXAMPLE 1.** The sound of her husband's heavy work boots echoing throughout the house caused her to jump. A scene from her childhood came back to her. It was her twelfth birthday.
>
> "What's this?" her father shouted when he came home after work. He stomped into the living room where her mother

was passed out on the sofa, an empty gin bottle nestled in the crook of her arm. "Get up, you worthless piece of…"

The sight and sound of the bottle slamming against the wall caused Mary to run and hide.

"Can't you even bake a goddamn birthday cake for your kid?" he roared.

EXAMPLE 2. In Dickens' *A Christmas Carol*, Scrooge's first vision (The Ghost of Christmas Past) takes him back to his old school where he finds himself alone, abandoned by his schoolmates. As the ghost takes Scrooge and us through the journey of his past, we learn that Scrooge had been rejected by his father and sent off to school, never to go home again.

Dialogue with Another Character

Dialogue between two characters is an effective way to handle narrative exposition.

EXAMPLE 1. "My mother drank a lot," she told Gabrielle. "In fact, she was usually passed out when I got home from school. My father was a truck driver, and when he was home, which wasn't very often, he did a lot of yelling and complaining about what my mother had or hadn't done while he was gone."

EXAMPLE 2. "Voldemort… took your blood believing it would strengthen him. He took into his body a tiny part of the enchantment your mother laid upon you when she died for you. His body keeps her sacrifice alive, and while that enchantment survives, so do you and so does Voldemort's one last hope for himself." Excerpt from *Harry Potter and The Deathly Hallows* by J.K. Rowling spoken by Dumbledore to Harry.

Memories as Related through Interior Monologue

Relying on a character's recollection of something that happened in the past is another effective way to handle narrative exposition.

EXAMPLE 1. She thought back to her twelfth birthday. Her father had come home from one of his long road trips only to find her mother passed out on the sofa, her ruined birthday cake sitting on the kitchen counter.

EXAMPLE 2. I was born in the city of Bombay...once upon a time. No, that won't do, there's no getting away from the date. I was born in Doctor Narlikar's Nursing Home on August 15th, 1947. And the time? The time matters, too. Well then: at night. No, it's important to be more... On the stroke of midnight, as a matter of fact. Clock-hands joined palms in respectful greeting as I came. (Excerpt from Salman Rushdie's *Midnight's Children*.)

There are moments in the narrative that are perfect for including exposition. The trick is knowing how to spot them to achieve the right balance among the action and dialogue.

In this example from *Harry Potter and the Goblet of Fire*, J. K. Rowling used exposition in the middle of a scene for the benefit of readers who had not read her earlier books and were unfamiliar with all the characters.

Harry had been a year old the night that Voldemort—the most powerful Dark wizard for a century, a wizard who had been gaining power steadily for eleven years—arrived at his house and killed his father and mother. Voldemort had then turned his wand on Harry; he had performed the curse that had disposed of many full-grown witches and wizards in his steady rise to power—and, incredibly, it had not worked.

Rowling manages to present key pieces of information to new readers without boring those who are familiar with it.

Some authors start their novels with exposition, like Toni Morrison does in *Beloved* when she talks about the house (124 is the street number) where she and her family had lived.

124 was spiteful. Full of a baby's venom. The women in the house knew it and so did the children. For years each put up with the spite in his own way, but by 1873 Sethe and her daughter Denver were its only victims. The grandmother, Baby Suggs, was dead, and the sons, Howard and Buglar, had run away by the time they were thirteen years old—as soon as merely looking in a mirror shattered it.

When properly interspersed throughout the story, narrative exposition will boost interest and intrigue and compel readers to keep reading. Use it sparingly and keep it short. Use just enough to serve the purpose and then get back to the current story.

SUGGESTED READING:

Cox, Justin (editor). "How to Write Exposition without Boring Your Audience to Tears." The Writing Cooperative. January 11, 2019. https://writingcooperative.com/how-to-write-exposition-without-boring-your-audience-to-tears-38942f5c225f.

Ryan, Claire. Books Blog: *The Rules of Excellent Exposition—A Guide.* https://www.claireryanauthor.com/blog/2717/the-rules-of-excellent-exposition-a-guide.

Shiau, Yvonne (content marketer USA). ReedsyBlog: *Exposition in Literature: The Ultimate Guide with 19 Examples.* https://blog.reedsy.com/exposition-in-literature/.

CHAPTER 11

Moving the Story Forward

M oving the story forward is arguably the most important and most difficult aspect of good novel-writing. If someone says, "I couldn't put the book down" or "It was a real page turner," the author succeeded at engaging the reader in each chapter, paragraph, and sentence. Such expertly paced novels keep the reader always wanting to know what happens next.

The difficult part may be in that every scene must have a point to it. No matter how many car chases or dramatic screaming matches your manuscript may have, if the story stalls, you're going to lose your audience. But don't fall into the misconception that just because you have something to say that you believe is interesting, readers will be interested. Most readers are impatient and distracted by delays in the real action and will skip over the other parts to get to it. Some may even put the book down, never to pick it up again.

Here are ways to keep your readers engaged.

MAINTAIN ORDER. Keep the main action of the story in sequential order so as not to confuse readers and slow them down by having to go back and reread sections of the narrative. It's okay for you to be inspired by chaotic story-line thoughts in your head, but you must organize them for the reader.

KEEP IT FRESH. Someone who critiqued an early draft of my first novel advised, "Once you state he's a cowboy, you never have to mention it again." My book wasn't about cowboys, still I knew what she meant. In this example, to keep the cowboy image in the reader's mind, you could add cowboy-related information—such as his attire or what cowboy-related things he's doing—but stating that he's a cowboy more than once is not necessary.

ESCALATE THE ACTION. This may seem too obvious to even mention, but it's important to keep the story moving through escalation. The story needs to show an escalation of conflict, drama, conflict, and tension to drive it forward. The perfect story escalates smoothly from scene to scene, creating a sense of rising action.

FIND THE RIGHT BALANCE AMONG DIALOGUE, DESCRIPTION, AND CHARACTER INTERNAL MONOLOGUE. The right balance among these story elements will vary, as each story is different. But in all cases, they should interact so as to present the plot and characters in a narrative that consistently flows forward. Too much interior monologue and exposition may slow down the plot. Too much action and dialogue could undermine character development.

INCORPORATE SUDDEN CHANGES. A sudden change is another good way to keep the story moving forward. If your character has spent her whole life running away from something and then suddenly faces it head-on, that will keep the reader interested in what happens next. Or interject something that throws everything off balance—perhaps an obstacle for the character that forces him or her to deal with something new.

CREATE FIRSTS. You can catch a reader's attention with firsts—the first time the protagonist meets the antagonist; the first time they argue; the first time he or she feels threatened; etc. To keep the story moving, make sure the reader feels what the protagonist is feeling when these firsts occur.

BEEF UP CHAPTER BEGINNINGS AND ENDINGS. The beginning of each chapter should engage readers in some level of activity that pulls them into the story/scene, involves them with your characters, and makes them care about what's happening. Chapter endings need to close out the chapter but also open the door for the next one. Cliff-hangers, even small ones, are a great way to accomplish this at the end of chapters. Don't give readers the chance to put your book down when they finish reading a chapter.

USE BACKSTORY SPARINGLY. Backstory informs the reader about the character's past—what has shaped the character into the person he or she is. Too much and it bores the reader, too little and the reader may not understand your character's motives. Balance is key. Backstory pulls the reader out of the present, so include it only when the reader needs to know something. When you do provide backstory, avoid lengthy passages or you risk making the reader forget what is going on in the present. (See Chapter 10 for more about narrative exposition and backstory.)

AVOID THE MUNDANE. Dispense with pleasantries in dialogue and mundane information that will bore the reader. Include these only where they add to characterization or serve some other purpose in the story. For example, it's not necessary to tell the reader what the bank robber had for breakfast unless the short-order cook overheard him planning the heist and decided to taint his food to deter the robbery.

Omit unnecessary physical movements and descriptive details. It's best to keep the narrative as concise as possible to keep the story moving forward.

> He snatched her shoulder bag with his left hand before jumping off the curb and disappearing into the stream of cars heading toward the center of town.

BETTER: He snatched her purse before disappearing into the stream of heavy traffic.

She felt along the wall for the light switch and flipped it on. The many pieces of furniture in the small room—a large bed, dresser, two end tables, two bookcases and a desk—kept her from noticing the dead body at first.

BETTER: She flipped on the light switch. The furniture in the crowded room kept her from noticing the dead body at first.

START IN THE MIDDLE OF THE ACTION. Instead of starting a scene at the beginning, try starting in the middle of what's going on. Make the reader temporarily wonder what happened leading up to it.

KEEP IN SIGHT THE PROTAGONIST'S GOALS AND MOTIVATION FOR REACHING THEM. Characters who are driven to achieve their goals at any cost appeal to readers. To keep the story flowing nicely forward, don't allow readers to lose sight of the protagonist's goals, what motivates him for reaching them, what stands in his way, and what he is most afraid of losing.

Keeping the story moving forward is a common challenge for writers, especially new ones. Each scene you write must advance the story in some way with the use of dialogue, action, description, pacing, narrative, character motivation, transitional scenes, and conflict.

SUGGESTED READING:

Buggee, Carol. "Keep Your Story Moving." Gotham Writers. (No date.) https://www.writingclasses.com/toolbox/articles/keep-your-story-moving-part-ii.

Lakin, C. S. Live Write Thrive (blog): *Keys to Moving Your Plot Forward*. https://www.livewritethrive.com/2018/02/19/keys-to-moving-your-plot-forward/.

Lisle, Holly. "Writing Scenes That Move Your Story Forward." Holly Lisle: Writer. (No date.) https://hollylisle.com/scene-creation-workshop-writing-scenes-that-move-your-story-forward/.

CHAPTER 12

Descriptive Writing

Descriptive writing is the craft of portraying people, places, events, situations, thoughts, and feelings in such a manner that readers visualize what is happening and experience the scene. The skillful use of description can bring a flat, uninteresting sentence to life.

Consider this excerpt about tea from a *Houston Chronicle* article by Jessica Danes.

> It tastes like the earth. Pungent and loamy and more real than anything you've ever tasted in a while. A sip and the daydreaming starts—of high-peaked mountains and the tender plants that prized leaves were plucked from. Tea can do that to you.

She could have saved a lot of verbiage and said it this way:

> One of the world's oldest beverages, tea is also one of the most enticing.

But it wouldn't have been as interesting or as engaging. Good descriptive writing uses well-chosen words and an artful ordering of the words.

The Five Senses

Since the five senses (sight, sound, taste, touch, and smell) play a key role in how human beings understand the world around them, it makes sense for a writer to use them to increase the feeling of authenticity in a story. Incorporating the five senses into the narrative draws readers into the story and allows them to experience the same sensations the characters are experiencing. When writing descriptions, you may find it helps to form a mental picture first, putting yourself in the scene, and then describing what is seen, heard, smelled, tasted, or felt.

For you baby boomers out there, my favorite example is from an old *I Love Lucy* episode when Lucy tries to describe to Ethel what Charles Boyer looks like. "It's like he just walked into a room where a big pot of cauliflower is cooking," she said. Say no more.

For my younger audience, Patrick Suskind focuses on a character who has a very acute sense of smell in his novel *Perfume: The Story of a Murderer.*

> In the period of which we speak, there reigned in the cities a stench barely conceivable to us modern men and women. The streets stank of manure, the courtyards of urine, the stairwells stank of moldering wood and rat droppings, the kitchens of spoiled cabbage and mutton fat; the unaired parlors stank of stale dust, the bedrooms of greasy sheets, damp featherbeds, and the pungently sweet aroma of chamber pots. The stench of sulfur rose from the chimneys, the stench of caustic lyes from the tanneries, and from the slaughterhouses came the stench of congealed blood. People stank of sweat and unwashed clothes; from their mouths came the stench of rotting teeth, from their bellies that of onions, and from their bodies, if they were no longer very young, came the stench of rancid cheese and sour milk and tumorous disease.

With more than 40 novels and countless poems and short stories published, Joyce Carol Oates has a reputation for her mastery of descriptive writing, often appealing to the senses. In the following excerpt (originally published in *Washington Post Book World* and reprinted in *Faith of a Writer: Life, Craft, Art* [HarperCollins, 2003]), Oates describes the one-room schoolhouse she attended in grade school.

> Inside, the school smelled smartly of varnish and wood smoke from the potbellied stove. On gloomy days, not unknown in upstate New York in this region south of Lake Ontario and east of Lake Erie, the windows emitted a vague, gauzy light, not much reinforced by ceiling lights. We squinted at the blackboard, that seemed far away since it was on a small platform, where Mrs. Dietz's desk was also positioned, at the front, left of the room. We sat in rows of seats, smallest at the front, largest at the rear, attached at their bases by metal runners, like a toboggan; the wood of these desks seemed beautiful to me, smooth and of the red-burnished hue of horse chestnuts. The floor was bare wooden planks. An American flag hung limply at the far left of the blackboard and above the blackboard, running across the front of the room, designed to draw our eyes to it avidly, worshipfully, were paper squares showing that beautifully shaped script known as Parker Penmanship.

The lack of one or more of the senses can also be used in descriptive writing—for example, describing how others perceive someone with a hearing loss can add depth to a scene, as in this excerpt from Carson McCullers's *The Heart Is a Lonely Hunter.*

> People felt themselves watching him even before they knew that there was anything different about him. His eyes made a person think that he heard things that no one else had ever heard, that he knew things no one had ever guessed before. He did not seem quite human.

Using the five senses in descriptive writing helps readers develop a better understanding of the fictional world that the author has created by allowing them to imagine the world as experienced by the characters.

Word Choice

Choosing the right descriptive words will help to capture the reader's attention and emotions and create a picture in the reader's mind by adding life to characters, places, objects, actions, and setting.

> **FLAT:** Stella liked her new home.
> **DESCRIPTIVE:** Stella treasured her new country cottage.

> **FLAT:** The man ran quickly through the crowd.
> **DESCRIPTIVE:** The thief slithered his way through the tangle of holiday revelers.

> **FLAT:** She listened to them talking about their plans.
> **DESCRIPTIVE:** She eavesdropped on the coterie of tattoo-covered teens as they one-upped each other with chilling plans.

> **FLAT:** Ben walked through the mud to get to his damaged car.
> **DESCRIPTIVE:** Ben trudged through the mud to reach the pile of metal that had previously been his car.

> **FLAT:** She saw a large rock fall on his head.
> **DESCRIPTIVE:** She watched in horror as a boulder bashed in his head.

A thesaurus can be a valuable tool for finding the right word, but you need to use it with caution. Just because the thesaurus says a word is a synonym for another word doesn't mean it is a good replacement, so check the definition in the dictionary to make sure it's the right word for the meaning of the sentence.

A thesaurus is also a place where you can find big words—be careful about using big words when shorter, more common ones will suffice.

Word Arrangement

The organization and order of words matter. It is important to arrange words within sentences and sentences within scenes in chronological order, i.e., in the order in which things actually happen. Without a clear organizational pattern, important detail can be lost, and then your readers can become confused and eventually lose interest.

Words written in a confusing chronological order make the meaning of the following sentence ambiguous.

> Police arrested a twenty-five-year-old man from Littlefield, Colorado, stopped by police the previous year on suspicion of drunk driving and had charges against him dropped due to lack of probable cause for the arrest when no objective, factual evidence was presented in court.

This is confusing. When had the charges been dropped—in the previous year or now? By putting the verb closer to the subject, the sentence has obvious meaning.

> Police arrested a twenty-five-year-old man from Littlefield, Colorado, the charges against him dropped due to lack of probable cause for the arrest when no objective, factual evidence was presented in court. The man had been stopped by police the previous year on suspicion of drunk driving.

In this excerpt from Vonda Sinclair's *My Rebel Highlander*, the author does a good job keeping things in chronological order.

> Rebbie stepped closer, tipped her chin up and stroked his fingers along her cheek. With fathomless eyes, he watched her

beneath lowered black lashes. With a simple touch and a look, he could strip away her resistance…not that she'd ever had much where he was concerned. Nay, the first time she'd seen him, she'd set out to seduce him. Though she'd been terrified at the time, it had turned into the most enjoyable task of her life.

When he leaned down and brushed his lips across hers, she drew in a sharp breath of his delectable scent—clean soap and man—and kissed him back. All the nerve endings in her body tingled and yearned for him. There was no way in Hades she could resist him. Her body was so sensitized to his kiss, his touch, she already ached for him.

The kiss deepened and she opened for him, savoring the spicy, mulled wine flavor of his kiss. Eager for more, she wound her arms around his neck. His moan vibrated against her lips.

Writing with spatial order—where the words used to describe a subject are arranged in the same order as the subject's physical location—can also help readers better visualize the subject matter. This can be especially important in mystery writing, in which the order of items located in a crime scene are critical evidence in the story. On which side of the right-handed corpse the revolver was found, for example, could be important.

Pacing

Sometimes the pace of a scene will dictate how much detail to include. If it's a fast-paced scene, too much detail will bog it down—no one wants to be bothered with little details when there's action going on. For example, you probably wouldn't want to write about the gorgeous sunset on the western horizon while the off-duty policeman is chasing an armed robber down a dark alley. You could save that detail for the scene where the policeman's wife is sitting on their back porch, sipping a glass of wine, wondering why her husband isn't home yet from his trip to the 7-Eleven for a carton of milk.

Historical fiction may be the exception as it usually requires more detail than other types of fiction in order to educate (or remind) readers of what was going on in that time period. Let's say a novel set in 1950 contains a scene in which a character talking on the phone suspects someone is listening in on the "party line." If you don't explain what a party line is, readers born after 1955 may say, "Huh?" In this case, more detail would be helpful, perhaps with dialogue, such as, "Hello? Is there someone listening in on this line?"

The Urge to Explain

Renni Browne and Dave King coined the phrase "Resist the urge to explain" (R.U.E.) in their book *Self-Editing for Fiction Writers*. Simply stated, it means don't over-explain things.

New writers in particular are often tempted to explain every detail of the story on the assumption that the reader needs them to understand what's going on. But this underestimates readers who are generally smart and catch on quickly. Not only *can* readers figure things out for themselves, they *want* to figure out things for themselves. In short, if you need to explain something instead of allowing the action to speak for itself, you likely haven't done a good enough job showing the action. Now, reread the last sentence—it's that important.

Here are three examples of R.U.E. issues.

> **EXAMPLE 1.** The narrow end of a baseball bat sticking out from beneath the bed caught Emily's attention. She picked it up and cringed at the red stain on the other end. Could it be blood? She'd seen dried blood before, and it had been similar in color.
>
> In this example, the last two sentences are unnecessary— readers do not need to have the red stain explained to them.
>
> **EXAMPLE 2.** Bernard sat across the restaurant table opposite his blind date, praying the beads of sweat that had formed on his

forehead wouldn't run down his face. He read aloud items from the menu and watched her face for some sign of interest—first the appetizers, then the main courses, and finally the desserts. When he saw no change in her facial expression, he returned to the appetizers. Maybe she didn't want him to choose what they ate, he thought. Maybe she wanted to choose for herself. Being it was their first date, he wanted to do the right thing, follow the right protocol, make her think he knew what he was doing. The stress was killing him. "I think I'll have the cod. Do you see anything you like?" he finally asked her.

> The fact that it's a blind date and there are beads of sweat forming on his forehead says a lot, so there is no need to explain his nervousness further. Nor is it necessary to describe the menu sections, as most readers are familiar with menus. Here is a better paragraph.

Bernard sat across the restaurant table opposite his blind date, praying the beads of sweat that had formed on his forehead wouldn't run down his face. He read aloud items from the menu and watched her face for some sign of interest. When he received no indication from her as to what she would like to eat, and wanting to make her think he knew what he was doing, he said, "I think I'll have the cod. Do you see anything you like?"

EXAMPLE 3. She ran to her room to retrieve her gun from the nightstand, so she could confront the intruder.

> Readers don't need to know where she kept her gun, and why else would she retrieve it but to confront the intruder? In this example, the sentence could end with the word *gun* and still provide all the information needed.

To avoid excessive explanations in your manuscript, be on the look-out for the following:

- Sections that make use of narrative summary, where the narrator tells the reader what happened in a condensed form.
- Long stretches of narrative that contain no dialogue or action.
- Backstory that could be woven into the present.

As part of your editing process, review each sentence for the right amount of description. For example, it may add to the story if the reader was told the character grew up in a twenty-room mansion in Beverly Hills rather than merely a house in southern California, or drank a tankard of Dortmunder rather than a can of beer, or drove a 1936 Auburn Boattail Speedster convertible, dark blue with a tan interior rather than an older, classic car. Still, if it doesn't add to the story, if it doesn't move it forward in some manner, leave it out.

Adding the right amount of description is a balancing act, and everyone has a different opinion as to what is the right balance. And what complicates the matter is that different readers want different levels of detail—what will satisfy one reader's need for extensive detail will annoy another. You'll have to decide this for yourself—as you know the most about the characters and the story—and, of course, rely on your editor for help. Just keep in mind, though, that editors are also human, so they will have differing opinions as well. It's a matter of taste, and as we all know, you can't please everyone.

All that said, eliminating details doesn't mean the narrator should forget what they are—his or her knowing all the details and backstory is helpful in creating what is important in conveying the rest of the story to the readers.

SUGGESTED READING:

Conrad, Jordan. Live Write Thrive (blog): *How to Make Your Sentences More Descriptive.* https://www.livewritethrive.com/2018/06/18/how-to-make-your-sentences-more-descriptive/.

McNulty, Bridget (Co-founder). Now Novel (blog): *Writing Descriptive Sentences: 6 Simple Rules.* https://www.nownovel.com/blog/descriptive-sentences-writing-rules/.

Strathy, Glen. "The Key to Descriptive Writing: Specificity." How to Write a Book Now. (No date.) https://www.how-to-write-a-book-now.com/descriptive-writing.html.

CHAPTER 13

Setting, Tone, and Mood

E stablishing the setting, tone, and mood for your book is an essential element—without these things, the story will feel incomplete to readers. If you search these literary terms on the Internet, you'll find lots of different definitions, some of them contradictory. I found the following definitions the most consistent.

> **SETTING**—the time and location of the story. For the purpose of this discussion, it also includes weather and political/social/cultural environment.

> **TONE**—the narrator or character's attitude toward the subject matter.

> **MOOD**—the element(s) that evokes specific feelings, emotional tones, frame of mind, or attitude in readers.

Setting

One of the first things the reader needs to get a sense of is setting—in particular, the time and place in which the events take place. Setting not only serves as a backdrop, but the time and place of the story can also give it context that sets it apart from other stories.

Establishing setting is more than just inserting a time and place. The right setting has the ability to bring life to the story.

> At 7 pm, she drove down the back road that led to his house.

In this example, the setting (time, 7 pm; place, a road) has been established, but it's rather mundane and uninteresting.

> The sun had recently disappeared over the western horizon—later in the day than she had wanted to meet up with him—and when she turned onto the desolate dirt road, she saw his house looming in the distance.

This rewrite includes the same setting—same time and place—but now brings life to the scene that the first one didn't offer.

Some stories—especially those in historical and fantasy novels—are almost as much about setting as they are about characters or plot. In George R. R. Martin's *Game of Thrones,* setting is central to the story. The various settings—castles and war camps—affect how the characters act. Well-constructed settings evoke images, establish mood, and can supplement characters' motivations and feelings in the moment. While paragraphs of description can establish a setting, other techniques may also be used to bring readers into a story world. Here are some things to consider when creating the setting.

TIME: calendar date, season, era, clothing styles, car models, lingo/slang, mannerisms, moralities, music, theater

He climbed into his 1936 Boattail Speedster and turned on the radio. Glenn Miller was crooning the last few lyrics of "Fools Rush In." He looked in the mirror, adjusted his fedora, and headed for the Roosevelt rally.

LOCATION: surroundings, people, animals, landscape, scenery, nature, actions, obstacles, threats

Hundreds of people had gathered in Times Square to watch the demonstration. Police inched their way toward scores of protesters who had blocked the candidate's motorcade. Some demonstrators cursed at the occupants of the longest limo in the procession. Others hurled eggs at it. A steady chant persisted throughout the demonstration—"Hey, hey, ho, ho. This S.O.B. has got to go!"

WEATHER: heat, cold, wind, precipitation, fog, sun, clouds

Without warning, the rain came down in sheets. Marie ran back to the car with Richard close behind her. But instead of opening the door for her, he gently pushed her against the vehicle and kissed her. Heat from their bodies rose like steam in the moist air.

POLITICAL, SOCIAL, AND CULTURAL SURROUNDINGS: cultural influences, economic classes, religious beliefs

He walked past abandoned cars, boarded-up houses, and barefoot children playing kickball in the street. His heart pounded as he headed up the crumbling concrete stairs to his father's home, not knowing what to expect if his dad actually opened the door and invited him inside.

When setting is used solely to establish a time and place for the story or scene, it may not have to be referred to again. However, if expanding on it is essential to the story, or it's been a long stretch since the time or place has been mentioned and you deem it necessary to remind readers of it as to not get confused, the setting bears repeating.

The following excerpt from *The Summit* by Harry Farthing is an example of when the effects of weather are pertinent throughout the scene where sixteen-year-old Nelson Tate ascends the highest summit of Mount Everest.

> Denying the bitter, tooth-cracking cold; the racing, freezing wind; the rattle of snow crystals it carried, his addled brain was telling him instead that he was in a beautiful garden of his parents' house.

And then, later in the chapter…

> Pushing the kid's ski goggles up off the bridge of his nose and unhooking the straps of his oxygen mask, he pulled it away. The edges ripped from the teenager's beardless cheeks, taking ice and a little skin with them.

And again…

> He shivered as he felt the bitter cold of the frozen fingers touch his warm skin.

Tone

Tone in writing refers to the narrator's attitude toward the subject matter. There are two aspects of tone in narration—the overall tone of the narrator, and the different tones required for specific scenes. In either case, tone will affect how the reader receives the message being communicated and hopefully deepen the reader's connections to the story or events of the scene.

Establish the overall tone of the book early on, in the first few sentences, and continue with it throughout the book, changing it only to signal a change in the character.

Tone may be expressed in many ways: through specific words, through the arrangement of the words, or through description. When done effectively, a character's tone (attitude toward a certain subject matter) will evoke an intended emotion in the reader. If you're familiar with the expression "It's not *what* you said but the way you said it," you know what tone is. Or if you have listened to a teenager mumble indiscernible words with unmistakable tone, then you get it as well.

Following is an example of the emotionless tone created in the first paragraph of Chapter 1 in Kurt Vonnegut's *Slaughterhouse-Five*.

> All this happened, more or less. The war parts, anyway, are pretty much true. One guy I knew really was shot for taking a teapot that wasn't his. Another guy I knew really did threaten to have his personal enemies killed by hired gunmen after the war. And so on. I've changed all their names.

Your writing can take on many different types of tone. Here are just a few:

HUMOROUS: "I don't know how other men feel about their wives walking out on them, but I helped mine pack."—from *Breaking Up* by Bill Manville

DETACHED: "Many years later, as he faced the firing squad, Colonel Aureliano Buendía was to remember that distant afternoon when his father took him to discover ice."—from *One Hundred Years of Solitude* by Gabriel García Márquez

SUSPENSEFUL: "A sudden hush fell on the crowd as Mr. Summers cleared his throat and looked at the list. 'All ready?' he called. 'Now, I'll read the names—heads of families first—and the men come up and take a paper out of the box. Keep the paper folded in your hand without looking at it until everyone has had a turn. Everything clear?"—from *The Lottery* by Shirley Jackson

PEACEFUL: "It was very late, and everyone had left the cafe except an old man who sat in the shadow the leaves of the tree made against the electric light. In the daytime the street was dusty, but at night the dew settled the dust and the old man liked to sit late because he was deaf and now at night it was quiet and he felt the difference."—from *A Clean, Well-Lighted Place* by Ernest Hemingway

NERVOUS: It was a low, dull, quick sound—much such a sound as a watch makes when enveloped in cotton. I gasped for breath, and yet the officers heard it not. I talked more quickly, more vehemently but the noise steadily increased. I arose and argued about trifles, in a high key and with violent gesticulations; but the noise steadily increased. Why would they not be gone?—from *The Tell-Tale Heart* by Edgar Allen Poe

SARCASTIC: I notice the food. The rolls and apples are untouched, but someone's definitely picked away part of the cheese. "And you ate without me!" I really don't care, I just want something else to be mad about.

"What? No, I didn't," Peeta says.

"Oh, and I suppose the apple ate the cheese?" I say.—from *The Hunger Games* by Suzanne Collins

To test your writing for the appropriate tone, read it aloud, or have another person read it to you. Make sure the tone matches the essence of the story or individual scene.

Mood

Mood (sometimes called atmosphere or ambiance) in literature refers to the overall unsaid feeling or emotion an author creates for the reader through descriptive writing—an intangible presence that creates an emotional response in the reader and allows for greater understanding of what the author is trying to convey.

In this excerpt from *Brokeback Mountain*, author E. Annie Proulx shows what kind of characters the two cowboys are and the isolation in which they live. This atmosphere alludes to the way each man approaches life.

> They were raised on small, poor ranches in opposite corners of the state, Jack Twist in Lightning Flat, up on the Montana border, Ennis del Mar from around Sage, near the Utah line, both high-school drop-out country boys with no prospects, brought up to hard work and privation, both rough-mannered, rough-spoken, inured to the stoic life. Ennis, reared by his older brother and sister after their parents drove off the only curve on Dead Horse Road, leaving them twenty-four dollars in cash and a two-mortgage ranch, applied at age fourteen for a hardship license that let him make the hour-long trip from the ranch to the high school. The pickup was old, no heater, one windshield wiper, and bad tires; when the transmission went, there was no money to fix it. He had wanted to be a sophomore, felt the word carried a kind of distinction, but the truck broke down short of it, pitching him directly into ranch work.

Atmosphere determines the emotional experience the reader will have. I believe the example above would leave most of us feeling sympathetic.

Many different elements contribute to mood: a character's diction; the setting; and the descriptions of people, places, and things. Writer/producer Paul Shapiro may have said it best: "The mood is the aura created by many sentences. It exists nowhere on the page. It exists everywhere around the page."

The established mood—whether it leaves the reader feeling joyful and content or angry and frustrated—should always be there. Creating the right mood in fiction is an important and powerful tool to use to engage readers and make them feel like they are part of the journey.

Alice in Wonderland is a fitting example to illustrate mood changes in fiction. Overall, the mood is whimsical, lively and cheerful, often innocent and childlike. Other times, the mood is curious and inquisitive, or satirical and sarcastic, or fearful and scary—all brilliantly shown through fantastical imagery, setting, and Alice's actions and conversations.

- **WHIMSICAL/CHILDLIKE**—as shown in the unprejudiced and innocent way Alice approaches everything she encounters once she enters Wonderland.
- **BIZARRE**—when Alice sees a white rabbit carrying a watch and wearing a waistcoat, she decides to follow him.
- **SCARY**—not only does Alice continuously find herself in situations that scare her or threaten her life, but she also meets the Queen of Hearts, whose famous catchphrase is "Off with their heads!"

Sometimes just the title of a book creates a certain mood. Think about HP Lovecraft's titles—*At the Mountains of Madness, The Crawling Chaos, The Dunwich Horror,* and *The Whisperer in Darkness.* Even without knowing anything about these stories, one can guess the mood.

Mood evokes emotional responses in readers, thus ensuring an attachment to the story. Once readers are emotionally connected to the story, they can better understand the message you are trying to convey.

SUGGESTED READING:

Chapman, Harvey. "How to Build Your Story's Setting." Novel Writing Help. (No date.) https://www.novel-writing-help.com/story-setting.html.

Literary Devices Editors. "Definition and Examples of Literary Terms – Tone." Literary Devices. 2019. https://literarydevices.net/tone/.

Literary Devices Editors. "Definition and Examples of Literary Terms – Mood." Literary Devices. 2019. https://literarydevices.net/mood/.

CHAPTER 14

Body Language

BODY LANGUAGE: *the nonverbal communication of emotion, state of mind, or state of physical well-being.*

R esearch shows that people convey thoughts, emotions, and feelings in three different ways:

7 percent verbal—what is said
38 percent vocal—how it is said
55 percent nonverbal—facial expressions, posture, gestures, etc.

Since most communication between people in real life is nonverbal, authors must incorporate this into their character interactions in order to make a story feel authentic. But it takes skill to create visuals of a character's movements in the reader's mind, to make the characters seem like real people rather than stick figures moving around on a stage. Weaving in body language can make characters come alive, adds physicality to the story, and reveals things about the characters that can't be conveyed in any other way.

Types of body language include gestures (the positioning of a hand, arm, body, head, or face that is expressive of an idea, opinion, or emotion), posture (the physical carriage of the body), movement (a change of place, position, or posture of a person or part of a person), and facial expressions (movement of any part of the face). Here are some examples of characterization through body language.

- She put her hands on her hips and stood firm without saying another word.
- He snapped his fingers. "Get my dinner, woman," he shouted.
- She bowed her head so as not to have to look at his face.
- He slammed his fist on the table. "I've had enough!"
- He sat at a slight angle across from the interviewer with his arms folded and legs crossed.
- She waited for the officer to arrive as she sat with her son slumped in the chair next to her.
- He locked his arms across his chest. "No way!"
- She leaned away from him. "This isn't working."
- Her eyes narrowed. "You expect me to believe this?"
- His cheeks turned red. "What do you mean you hurt her?"
- "I'm sorry." She stared at the floor. "I didn't want it to be this way."
- The corners of his eyes crinkled. "Really?"

Don't be afraid to use every part of the body when showing body language—head, hair, forehead, face, eyebrows, eyelashes, eyes, ears, nose, nostrils, mouth, lips, teeth, jaw, chin, neck, shoulders, arms, hands, fingers, hips, legs, feet, and toes. The tricky part is to create the motion as though the character is doing it unconsciously. Here is a good example from *Runaway* by Alice Munro.

> She didn't do anything to avoid Sylvia's look. She drew her lips tight over her teeth and shut her eyes and rocked back

and forth as if in a soundless howl, and then, shockingly, she did howl. She howled and wept and gulped for air and tears ran down her cheeks and snot out of her nostrils and she began to look around wildly for something to wipe with.

Describe body movements and facial expressions sparingly—be careful not to decelerate a scene and shift the reader's focus away from the action. Instead, blend it in with the rest of the narrative so that it's subtle. Use it to reveal a person's intentions, feelings, or mood when words aren't enough or instead of words, which is sometimes better.

The following paragraph contains the right amount of body language indicated with bolding.

Danny drove at a leisurely pace south on Highway 1 just outside of Santa Monica when a red, older-model Mustang that had been parked on the side of the road pulled out in front of him, causing him to slam on his brakes and swerve. Once he caught up to the reckless driver and **made eye contact with him** in the driver's rearview mirror, Danny recognized him as his sister's ex-boyfriend Carl. The two drove within ten feet of each other for a quarter mile or so, and then **Carl's arm jerked up to flip him the bird.** Enraged by Carl's behavior, **Danny returned the gesture.** Carl decelerated to 15 mph, slow enough for Danny to catch **Carl's sneer** in his mirror. **Carl threw his head back and laughed** as he sped up, but as soon as Danny reached him, he slowed down again, this time to a crawl. Incensed, Danny pulled around him, only to see the toddler, his niece, in the back seat, **her mouth wide open, arms flailing, and eyes so wide open he could see her blue irises.**

Following are a few examples of ways to convey body language.

ANGER/AGGRESSION: Contracted brows, chin up, chest out, clenched teeth/fist/jaw, tight lips, frown, clasped hands behind head, tense mouth, flared nostrils, high-pitched voice, facial/neck flush, hands on hips, staring, sneering, loud voice, rapid speech, brow muscles moved inward, slamming things, bared teeth, legs apart, finger pointing.

BOREDOM: Legs crossed with slight foot kick, head resting on hand, eyes downcast, yawning, hand supporting chin or side of face, hands in pockets, consistently looking around, doodling, tapping toes, repeatedly looking at clock/watch, slouching, leaning against wall.

CONFIDENCE: Brisk direct walk, direct eye contact, palms down, standing tall, hands clasped behind head, legs crossed, controlled voice, head held high, chest forward, shoulders back, hands behind back, feet apart, chin up.

FLIRTATION: Looking at a person from head to toe, continual glancing, running hands through hair, eye catch and then look away, eyelash flicker, shoulder glance, moistening lips, parted lips, flicking hair, head tilt, self-touching, leaning forward, chest out, shoulders back, stomach in, cowboy stance (thumbs in belt loops, fingers pointed toward genitals), room scanning, mutual smiling, smiling with tilted head, foot touching, preening, leaning in.

NERVOUSNESS: Crossed arms, Adam's apple jump, biting nails, increased blinking, forced laugh, one arm across body clasping other arm by side, handbag/briefcase held in front of body, adjusting things, looking to sides, clenched hands, stuttering, voice cracking, fidgeting, fumbling, locked ankles, jiggling money/keys in pocket, tugging on ear, clutching object tightly, pacing.

SURPRISE: Flashbulb eyes, widened eyes, raised (curved up) eyebrows, open mouth, sudden backward movement/jump, backward head tilt, head jerk, hand clasped over mouth, dropped jaw, tense muscles, wrinkled forehead, shrieking, screaming.

Sometimes all that is needed is body language, like when your female character takes two steps backward before she picks up a heavy candlestick during an argument with her abusive husband. Nothing has to be said—the message is in her body language. Or having your character sit in a chair with one arm on the arm rest, the other one draped along the chair's back, and one ankle crossed over the opposite knee. Only a confident person would sit like that.

The best place to find authentic body language for specific occasions is within yourself. Imagine yourself in the scene. How would you react? What expression would be on your face? What movements would you be making? Immerse yourself in the scene to determine what fits.

SUGGESTED READING:

Haggerty, D. E. Storm Writing School Blog: *The Pitfalls of Emotional Body Language in Your Writing.* https://blog.stormwritingschool. com/body-language/.

Hall-Wilson, Lisa. "The Body Language of Fear." Writers in the Storm. October 31, 2108. https://writersinthestormblog.com/2018/10/the-body-language-of-fear-beyond-lions-and-tigers-and-bears-oh-my/.

Vicino, Anthony. Anthony Vicino (blog): *Use Body Language to Tell a Better Story.* https://www.anthonyvicino.com/use-body-language-tell-better-story-writing-workshop/.

CHAPTER 15

Dialogue

When done well, dialogue advances the story and fleshes out the characters while providing a break from exposition. But writing well-crafted, realistic dialogue doesn't come easily to everyone—it takes time to develop the skill.

Content

For dialogue to be meaningful, it needs to flow naturally for each character, giving each one a distinctive voice. Some will use slang. Others will swear. More formal characters may actually speak in grammatically correct sentences. Think about your family members and friends. It's implausible that two people speak exactly alike.

Characters can be differentiated by the number of words they say. Some people say very little, but when they do say something it's important. Others ramble on and say nothing.

And don't forget about the age factor. Consider these three distinct personalities coming through as they comment on the same serving of brussels sprouts.

Four-year-old boy: "Mommy, I don't like these slimy green things."

Forty-four-year-old husband: "Maybe if they had been cooked a little longer…dear."

Eighty-four-year-old curmudgeon: "What…are you tryin' to kill me with these things?"

Choose dialogue content carefully. Eliminate boring chit-chat. Omit dialogue if it doesn't work toward developing the character, establishing the mood for a scene, moving the plot forward, or depicting the character's feelings.

Readers will be able to picture a scene better if you replace "telling" with dialogue.

INSTEAD OF: She threw the remote at him and stomped out the door.
TRY USING: She threw the remote at him. "I'm outta here," she said on her way out.

INSTEAD OF: His hand gesture made it seem to her that he didn't care.
TRY USING: He flapped his hand in her direction. "Whatever."

INSTEAD OF: She gaped in disbelief, wondering why he purposely broke the vase her mother had given to them.
TRY USING: "How dare you!" she said when he purposely broke the vase her mother had given to them.

INSTEAD OF: She was too upset to go out with her friends.
TRY USING: "Go on without me. I'll see you later."

Style

Varying the style in which characters speak will help to differentiate them from one another. For example, some people talk in run-on sentences. Others pause between their thoughts.

Use sentence fragments, especially when the tension is high. Or when children are speaking…teens in particular. And preoccupied husbands. In fact, sometimes a grunt will do just fine.

Don't be afraid to let the character trail off in thought, interrupt someone else, or lose his or her train of thought altogether. That's natural. Just don't overdo it, unless it helps to define the character.

Before a character speaks for the first time in the story, consider describing his or her voice. Is it baritone, gravelly, or lilting? Does the character have a lisp? Do they talk fast, or do you have to drag the words out of them?

Keep dialogue as brief as possible. Lengthy exchanges between characters—unless they are categorically essential to the story, mood, or character—will bore or frustrate most readers.

And avoid telling the reader what the character is about to say before he or she says it. In the following example, the dialogue speaks for itself. The lead-in sentence should be eliminated.

> John decided to put a stop to it. "Stop your fighting, or I'll put you in a time-out."

I have found it helpful when writing dialogue to just let it flow. Later, when editing, I clean it up with the goal of creating speech that sounds natural to the ear.

Creating good dialogue takes a certain skill, but once you've mastered it, it will come much more easily.

Common Pitfalls

Regardless of genre, dialogue is essential to a good story. Without effective dialogue, even the best storytelling will fall flat. Readers pay attention to dialogue. While speaking is a natural part of our lives—something we do without much thought—when we are writing dialogue, we need to take the time to reread what we've written to make sure it's what we want the character to say and how we want him or her to sound. Some common pitfalls follow.

Too Formal or Casual

Dialogue that is either too formal or too casual for the situation will not sound realistic.

> **FORMAL:** "Hello, Martin. I was considering going to the Rusty Bucket this evening for a glass or two of beer. Would you care to join me?"

> **CASUAL:** "Hey, Mart. I was thinking about going to the Rusty Bucket later for some brewskies. Want to come?"

> **VERY CASUAL:** "Yo, dude. Wanna throw back a few cold ones tonight at the Bucket?"

Misused Dialogue Tags

A dialogue tag is a small phrase inserted before, after, or in between the spoken words to identify the speaker. For example:

> "Did you pick up the dry cleaning?" Kathryn asked.

The phrase "Katherine asked" is the dialogue tag in this sentence.

Dialogue tags are purely functional. You need to use them only when it is unclear who is doing the speaking.

It is possible to have too many tags:

The three of them sat squished together on the sofa in front of the television—Sylvia, her boyfriend Ralph, and her ten-year-old son Marty.

"Look at that fish!" Marty shouted. "I wish I could catch one like that," he said.

"Can you keep it down?" Sylvia asked. "I'm trying to read," she said.

"What are you reading?" Ralph asked.

"One of my aunt's wonderful novels," Sylvia answered. "Do you mind?" she asked.

"I guess not," said Ralph. "Would you like me to pour you a drink?" he asked.

"You didn't see that fish?" Marty said.

And it is possible to have too few tags:

The three of them sat squished together on the sofa in front of the television—Sylvia, her boyfriend Ralph, and her ten-year-old son Marty.

"Look at that fish!" Marty shouted. "I wish I could catch one like that."

"Can you keep it down? I'm trying to read."

"What are you reading?"

"One of my aunt's wonderful novels. Do you mind?"

"I guess not. Would you like me to pour you a drink?"

"You didn't see that fish?"

This would be the right number of tags:

The three of them sat squished together on the sofa in front of the television—Sylvia, her boyfriend Ralph, and her ten-year-old son Marty.

"Look at that fish!" Marty shouted. "I wish I could catch one like that."

"Can you keep it down?" Sylvia asked. "I'm trying to read."

"What are you reading?" Ralph asked.

"One of my aunt's wonderful novels. Do you mind?"

"I guess not. Would you like me to pour you a drink?"

"You didn't see that fish?" Marty said.

Another mistake I often see is when writers use dialogue tags stylistically, as in this example:

"Get out of my store!" he demanded loudly.

"No," she retorted.

"I'll call the police," he said threateningly.

"Go ahead," she blurted. "I'll tell them you owe me child support," she added.

Better:

"Get out of my store!" he shouted.

"No," she replied.

"I'll call the police."

"Go ahead. I'll tell them you owe me child support."

Overuse of Characters' Names

In real life, people don't use a person's name very often when speaking directly to them. Nor should authors in writing fiction.

OVERUSED NAMES:

"Where are you going, Samantha?" he asked.

"To the store, Richard, but I can't find my wallet. Did you take it again, Richard?"

"You're really going to see *him*, aren't you Samantha?"

"No, I'm not, Richard. Not this time," she said. "Now, give me back my wallet."

BETTER:

"Where are you going?" he asked her.

"To the store, but I can't find my wallet. Did you take it again, Richard?"

"You're really going to see *him*, aren't you?"

"No, I'm not. Not this time," she said. "Now, give me back my wallet."

Too Much or Too Little Descriptive Narrative

Scenes that weave in dialogue with descriptive narrative tend to engage the reader at an emotional level much more effectively than scenes that are only descriptive narrative. Finding the balance is key. As with so many other rules in writing fiction, include only that which moves the story forward.

TOO MUCH DIALOGUE, NEEDS MORE DESCRIPTIVE NARRATIVE TO EXPLAIN THE ACTION:

"I'm going to get behind the bar where it's safe," Eleanor said to her date.

"Watch out for flying bottles!" he told her.

She joined another woman behind the bar who was crouched in between two beer kegs. "Are you all right?" she asked the woman. "You have a black eye, and your cheek is swollen."

"I think so. Did you just see that chair come flying over our heads?"

"How about those two swinging at each other over there? Can you believe this? I hope they don't bring their brawling over here where we're sort of safe."

TOO MUCH DESCRIPTIVE NARRATIVE, NOT ENOUGH DIALOGUE:

To avoid flying bottles and anything else the unruly patrons had decided to throw, Eleanor joined another woman who had ducked behind the bar. Crouched in between two beer kegs, the woman sported a black eye and swollen cheek. Eleanor sandwiched herself in next to her just as a chair flew over their heads and came crashing down behind them. At the end of the bar where there was an opening, the man who had started the fight was throwing punches at another man, mostly missing him. Eleanor prayed they wouldn't take the fight behind the bar where she felt relatively safe.

BETTER BALANCE BETWEEN DIALOGUE AND DESCRIPTIVE NARRATIVE:
To avoid flying bottles and anything else the unruly patrons had decided to throw, Eleanor joined another woman who had ducked behind the bar and was crouching between two beer kegs. Not missing the woman's black eye and swollen cheek, Eleanor sandwiched herself in next to her just as a chair flew over their heads and came crashing down behind them.

"Are you all right?" she asked the woman.

"I think so."

At the end of the bar where there was an opening, Eleanor saw the man who had started the fight throwing punches at another man, mostly missing him. She prayed they wouldn't take the fight behind the bar where she felt relatively safe.

When I first started writing fiction, someone advised me to eavesdrop on peoples' conversations to learn to write realistic dialogue. Sounds lame, doesn't it? It did to me, until I tried it. Not that you would ever write dialogue that exactly replicates how people talk—real people speak in fragments, talk about mundane topics, talk over each other, and trail off quite often. And most people don't speak in complete or grammatically correct sentences either. But if you tweak it some, real dialogue can become credible dialogue for your characters. Dialogue in fiction has to be a blend of what goes on in real life and completely proper dialogue. Strike the right balance, and you'll satisfy the reader and the integrity of your characters and the story.

There are times when it is appropriate to craft dialogue that mimics the way people speak in real life. Take *Same Kind of Different as Me*, for example. The first-person narration in this book alternates from chapter to chapter between two characters: Ron Hall, a well-educated art dealer, and Denver Moore, a homeless drifter. In this scene, Denver is standing over Ron's wife's grave talking to her.

> "You was the onlyest person that looked past my skin and past my meanness and saw that there was somebody on the inside worth savin. I don't know how, but you knowed that most a' the time when I acted like a bad fella, it was just so folks wouldn't get too close. I didn't want nobody close to me. It wadn't worth the trouble. Besides that, I had done lost enough people in my life, and I didn't want to lose nobody else."

In this example, Moore's distinct dialect is imperative to the story.

SUGGESTED READING:

Chapman, Harvey. "Writing Dialogue: 10 Rules for Sounding Like a Pro." Novel Writing Help. July 16, 2019. https://www.novel-writing-help.com/writing-dialogue.html.

Jenkins, Jerry. Jerry Jenkins (blog): *How to Write Dialogue That Captivates Your Reader.* https://jerryjenkins.com/how-to-write-dialogue/.

Lekic, Natasa (Founder). NY Book Editors (blog): *Guide to Writing Better Dialogue.* https://nybookeditors.com/2017/05/your-guide-to-writing-better-dialogue/.

CHAPTER 16

Scene Development

S cenes carry the novel. Whether you write romance or mysteries, fantasies or literary fiction, the key to keeping readers' attention is creating effective scenes.

The basic elements of a story have been commonly defined as plot, character, setting, theme, and conflict. These elements come together and have meaning through the creation of scenes. Without scenes, a writer would tell the entire story in one long descriptive narrative rather than show the action and let the reader absorb and interpret what is happening.

Sans an actual scene, descriptive narrative will generally serve as a reporting of events, as in this example.

> After Rachael woke up and neared the kitchen, the smell of what her mother was cooking made her turn around and run for the bathroom, where she immediately threw up.

Alternatively, a scene takes place in real time and shows the action.

> The smell of hickory-smoked bacon wafting into her bedroom was enough to wake Rachael, bringing back sweet memories of when she was a child and her mother made pancakes and

bacon Sunday mornings before church. The cold water she splashed on her face jolted her body out of its groggy state.

As she got closer to the kitchen, she inhaled a deep breath of the sweet-smelling air. Without warning, nausea hit her. She clasped her hand over her mouth as she ran into the bathroom, reaching the toilet just in time. The sour stench of vomit quickly replaced the savory aroma of bacon. While her stomach lurched, she counted on her mother never finding out what she had done the night before.

Each scene in a novel should contribute to the story in some way, whether through characterization, atmosphere, or plot progression. Scenes are the framework of a novel—care should be given to writing them with purpose.

The Five Ws

Each scene should contain enough information to answer the who, what, when, where, and why of the action.

Who
Readers need to know enough about each character in each scene for it to make sense. What emotions are running through their heads? What is their mood? How does the scene change them? Only as much information as is needed should be included and not anything the protagonist doesn't know, if you're writing in third-person limited. (See Chapter 4 for more on narrative tense.)

What
What is happening in the scene should be shown through action, using more nouns and verbs than adjectives and adverbs. Include conflict, suspense, and tension. And then add the character's reaction to it.

Where
The setting of the scene can be important. A fistfight that takes place in

a church during a wedding ceremony will have a different impact on the reader than if it takes place in the middle of a secluded wooded lot. If it adds to the story, talk about the atmosphere, the smells and the sounds, nearby buildings, the weather, plant and animal life. Ask yourself what the protagonist sees while the scene is taking place. Add enough detail so readers feel they are actually there, but not so much that they become bored and skip over parts.

Why

Most scenes occur due to someone's motivation. What is their goal? What is it they want? What drove them to take the action? This doesn't necessarily need to be spelled out, but make sure the reader has some clue as to the *why* of the scene.

When

When the action is occurring may be important to the scene. Is it morning, noon, or night? Is it connected to some other event? Does it take place before, during, or after another event?

Purpose

Every scene must have a purpose that relates back to the goal(s) of the protagonist. Scenes should serve one or more of the following purposes in order to move the story forward:

- Create atmosphere
- Introduce a character
- Reveal something about a character
- Introduce plot
- Heighten plot
- Develop setting
- Solve a problem
- Inform the reader
- Entice the reader

To keep on track when writing a scene, make sure it serves at least one of these purposes. Otherwise, leave it out as it likely doesn't serve to move the story forward.

Beginning, Middle, and End

Consider each scene (even the short ones) in your book as a mini novel in itself, with a beginning, middle, and end. A scene needs to build to a peak of intensity and then have some form of resolution.

The beginning of the scene should contain sufficient background information for the reader to understand what takes place later in the scene. What the character wants should be clear by the middle of the scene. The scene's middle is also where the conflict occurs—the meat of the scene. The end should include a resolution that provides some sense of how the scene caused the character to change or get closer to or farther from his or her goal.

The following short scene is from *Killing Floor* by Lee Child and occurs after protagonist (and narrator) Jack Reacher is arrested for murder.

> We pulled up at the front doors of the long low building. Baker got out of the car and looked up and down the frontage. The backup guys stood by. Stevenson walked around the back of our car. Took up a position opposite Baker. Pointed the shotgun at me. This was a good team. Baker opened my door.
>
> "OK, let's go," he said. Almost a whisper.
>
> He was bouncing on the balls of his feet, scanning the area. I pivoted slowly and twisted out of the car. The handcuffs didn't help. Even hotter now. I stepped forward and waited. The backup fell in behind me. Ahead of me was the station house entrance. There was a long marble lintel crisply engraved: Town of Margrave Police Headquarters. Below it were plate glass doors. Baker pulled one open. It sucked against rubber seals. The backup pushed me through. The door sucked shut behind me.

This scene's distinct beginning, middle, and end make it understandable and complete.

Scene Problems

Be aware of some of these common scene problems:

Not everything in the scene helps to move the story forward.

> She walked into the kitchen expecting to find Jim. When she didn't see him there, she retrieved items from the refrigerator to make a ham and cheese sandwich, poured a glass of milk, and then sat down to eat. Not knowing Jim's whereabouts made her uneasy. As she glanced around the kitchen for any sign that he had been there, she noticed a knife missing from the knife block—bottom left slot, one of the big ones. She stared at the slot for the missing knife. No longer hungry, she put down the sandwich.

Details about retrieving items from the fridge and pouring the glass of milk don't add anything that helps to move the story forward. But the fact that she made the sandwich and then couldn't finish it is important to the story as it shows that something was bothering her.

> REWRITE: She walked into the kitchen expecting to find Jim. When she didn't see him there, she made herself a sandwich and sat down to eat. As she glanced around the kitchen for any sign that he had been there, she noticed a knife missing from the knife block—bottom left slot, one of the big ones. She stared at the slot for the missing knife. No longer hungry, she put down the sandwich.

The character's scene goal isn't clear or is revealed too late in the scene.

> As soon as Trudy learned the address of the place where her daughter's captor might be hiding out, she threw on a hoodie,

> jumped in her car, and drove there. The lead hadn't been
> that solid, but she didn't care—her precious daughter had
> been missing for a month. Once she arrived at the address
> she had been given, she parked her car, slumped down in
> the seat, and stared at the small, run-down bungalow with
> the crooked green awnings.

What was Trudy's goal once she arrived at the address? What did she expect to achieve? Even if she didn't know herself what her goal was, that needs to be stated.

The character's motivation isn't clear.

Using the above example, Trudy's motivation for going to the address where she thinks her daughter is being held would be love for her daughter, but it may not always be as clear in other stories. Sometimes it's hidden, even to the character (sometimes called unconscious motivation) and is revealed subtly in the character's behavior as in the following example.

> After Allie broke up with Kenneth, her best friend
> reminded her that he was the fourth boyfriend she had kicked
> to the curb in as many months for no good reason.
> "He wasn't right for me," she said. Has it really been
> four? she thought.
> "Maybe you need to figure out why you keep doing
> this, Allie."
> "Hmm?" Allie said, failing to remember her rationale
> for breaking up with any one of them.

The scene lacks focus on the character's actions and internal thoughts.

> WEAK: A man in a black hoodie appeared from behind
> the parked car and came toward him. Jack pretended he
> had a gun.

BETTER: A stream of adrenaline shot through Jack's veins as he caught a glimpse of a man in a black hoodie approaching him from behind the parked car. When the man was within several yards, Jack reached in his pocket for a make-believe gun. "Come any closer, and I'll shoot," he said.

Here is an example of a scene from John Grisham's *The Testament* that shows great character insight and detailed action.

> I grit my teeth and remind myself of how badly I want to die. I slide the envelope across the table to Stafford, and at the same instant I rise from my wheelchair. My legs are shaking. My heart is pounding. Just seconds now. Surely I'll be dead before I land.
>
> "Hey!" someone shouts. Snead I think. But I'm moving away from them.
>
> The lame man walks, almost runs, past one of my portraits, a bad one commissioned by my wife, past everything, to the sliding doors, which are unlocked. I know because I rehearsed this just hours ago.
>
> "Stop!" someone yells. No one has seen me walk in a year. I grab the handle and open the door. The air is bitterly cold. I step barefoot into the narrow terrace which borders my top floor. Without looking below, I lunge over the railing.

The action in the scene is too short or too long.

The length of a scene depends on your goal for the scene. Long scenes tend to work better when you want to slowly build to the height of the action, highlight the climax of the story, or intentionally slow the pace after action takes place. Short scenes work best when you need to pick up the pace right after a long scene, build suspense, or create a sense of intrigue by doling out small bits of information at a time. Too many long scenes one after another may exhaust some readers. Too many short scenes one after another can make the flow of the reading feel choppy and disrupt the continuity of the story.

The reader doesn't know what's going through the character's mind during the action.

When characters' internal thoughts are revealed, readers are allowed to better understand them and/or their actions. Including the right amount (as with so many other aspects of writing good fiction) is a balancing act. Too much and the story gets lost under all that thinking. Too little and readers may be confused about the character's motivation. Include only inner thoughts that advance the plot. Avoid those that readers can deduce from the story's narrative or the characters' dialogue and action.

Scenes are the fundamental building blocks of your story. They drive it forward, build suspense, develop characters, and intensify conflict. Scenes help to develop plot from beginning to end. Crafted correctly, scenes take readers into a crucial moment in time of the character's story, engaging them as if they were actually there.

SUGGESTED READING:

Coles, William H. Story in Literary Fiction (blog): *Writing in Scene: A Staple for Reader Engagement in Fiction.* https://www.storyinliteraryfiction.com/essays-on-writing/writing-in-scene/.

Edwards, Sue Bradford. Women On Writing (blog): *Creating Scenes— Fiction's Building Blocks.* https://www.wow-womenonwriting.com/40-FE4-CreatingScenes.html.

Johnson, Emma. "6 Tips for Writing Gripping Scenes." Writer's Edit. (No date.) https://writersedit.com/fiction-writing/6-tips-writing-gripping-scenes/.

CHAPTER 17

Transitions

Transitions are the words and phrases that make for a logical connection between sentences, paragraphs, and chapters in your book. Good transitions allow readers to follow the sequence of events and understand the relationship between two or more slices of narrative.

If your writing seems choppy or lacking in flow, it may need better transitions. Here is an example of a paragraph with poor transitioning.

> The driving rain beating down on the skylight in her bedroom prevented Marguerite from sleeping. Being awake for hours on end enabled her to rethink her relationship with Brian.
>
> Unable to face her mother-in-law as planned, Marguerite opted to go to the movies instead.

This revision ties the second paragraph to the first.

> *The driving rain beating down on the skylight in her bedroom prevented Marguerite from sleeping. Being awake for hours on end enabled her to rethink her relationship with Brian.*

> *The next morning, too exhausted after her sleepless night to face her mother-in-law as planned, Marguerite opted to go to the movies instead.*

Here are ways to create graceful transitions in different situations.

THROUGH TIME: Transitions in time must be accounted for in fiction—readers need to know how much time has lapsed within and between scenes. This can be accomplished by using:

- **THE POSITION OF THE SUN.** A glint of sun rising above the shoreline greeted Captain Richards as he resumed his watch over the canyon the next morning.
- **THE CALENDAR.** Weeks later, a glimmer of life shone through the rubble.
- **NATURE.** The bright yellow daffodils in her garden were a sure sign of spring.
- **A PERSON'S CONDITION.** Now looking as though she was about to deliver her baby any day, Mary waddled across the parking lot to her car.
- **HOLIDAYS AND OTHER SPECIAL EVENTS.** Seeing the lit Christmas tree in Rockefeller Center brought a tear to her eye as she thought of happier times.
- **REFERENCES TO THINGS THAT HAPPEN AT A SPECIFIC TIME EVERY DAY.** The sound of the neighbor girls shouting "good-bye" to their father as he left for work told her she'd overslept.
- **THE CLOCK.** Nine o'clock! Where did the day go? she wondered.

FROM ONE SCENE TO ANOTHER: Moving from one scene to another without a good transition can be confusing for the reader. Here are two ways to effectively make these types of transitions:

- Use setting to distinguish a change from one place to another where the action is taking place.

As David made his way back down the hill for the second leg of his hike, something caught his eye—a dark cloud of black smoke billowing from the Tylor-Perlman building where his father-in-law Ambrose was general manager. As he approached the parking lot of the building, the all-too-familiar toxic smell of burning polystyrene polymers unnerved him. He had previously warned Ambrose about the illegal burning. Once inside the building, David asked the receptionist to see the general manager and mentally prepared himself to confront his father-in-law.

- State a shift in the time of day.

He stared at the night sky, wondering if she was outside too, looking at the same stars, regretting their purposeless fight as much as he was.

After a night of fitful sleep, the early morning sun caused him to squint and realize that any chance of her calling him had long since gone.

CHANGING POV: If you choose to write from multiple points of view (POVs), in order to avoid confusion, it is essential to inform the reader of the POV shifts, and the more POV characters you use, the more work you'll need to do to make the transitions smooth. Transitions can be accomplished by maintaining the same POV for the entire chapter or by separating POVs with section breakers, such as extra white space or three centered asterisks or dots. Ideally, you'll keep the same pattern throughout the story—the last thing you want is for readers to be confused about whose head they're in. When transitioning from one POV to another, it's good to use the perspective character's name as soon as possible after the change, so readers do not have to guess at the identity of the POV character for very long.

ZOOMING IN FROM A GENERAL SITUATION TO A SPECIFIC MOMENT: "When not done properly, it's like zooming the camera lens in too quickly from a long shot to a closeup," my editor once explained to me. Consider this example of a problematic transition:

> She spent the days preceding Labor Day in the kitchen preparing a lavish Jamaican-style buffet from her mother's handed-down recipes.
> The first of her guests arrived at noon.

The first paragraph is general, and the transition to the next paragraph, which is specific, is too abrupt.

REVISED EXAMPLE:
> She spent the days preceding Labor Day in the kitchen preparing a lavish Jamaican-style buffet from her mother's handed-down recipes.
> After decorating the patio with red, yellow, and green streamers and lanterns, she placed bowls of bananas, mangos, and pineapples on the brightly colored tablecloths. Jamaican folk music played in the background.
> The first of her guests arrived at noon.

The added paragraph helps to transition from a general narrative that describes activities that occur over a period of several days in the immediate past to a specific now-in-the-moment scene.

SIGNALING FLASHBACKS: It is important that readers realize they're reading a flashback and not present action. Try these methods of signaling a flashback:

- Talk about something that triggers a character's memory (a smell, an object, certain words, etc.).
- Change the tense of the flashback.

- Show the character coming in and out of the flashback by using internal dialogue.
- If the flashback is short—a sentence or two—use a change in formatting to indicate the flashback—indention, font, italics, etc.

Poor transitions in your manuscript are often an indication of uncertainty. If the narrative leaves the reader confused, it may have to do with poor flow. Good transitions will help the reader connect the dots.

SUGGESTED READING:

Hardy, Janice. Janice Hardy's Fiction University (blog): *Writing Transitions: How to Move Smoothly through Your Novel.* http.// blog.janicehardy.com/2009/09/re-write-wednesday-next.html.

Hill, Beth. The Editor's Blog: *Mastering Scene Transitions.* http:// theeditorsblog.net/2010/12/16/mastering-scene-transitions/.

Luke, Pearle. "Transitional Words and Phrases in Fiction: 4 Writing Tips." Be a Better Writer. (No date.) https://www.be-a-better-writer.com/transitional-words.html.

CHAPTER 18

Adjectives, Adverbs, and Clichés

ADJECTIVE: a word that describes, modifies, or clarifies a noun by giving some descriptive information about it.

ADVERB: a word that modifies or provides greater description to a verb, another adverb, an adjective, a phrase, a clause, or an entire sentence.

CLICHÉ: a trite, overused, or stereotyped phrase or expression.

A problem that new writers often have is the overuse of adjectives, adverbs, and clichés. And the reason is because it's easier to throw one of them into a sentence than to construct a powerful, effective sentence that skillfully links events, actions, and objects in a purposeful and persuasive manner.

Adjectives and Adverbs

There is no shortage of famous quotes on the use of adjectives and adverbs in writing.

> *I believe the road to hell is paved with adverbs.*
> —Stephen King

> *Cross out as many adjectives and adverbs as you can.*
> —Anton Chekhov

> *Adverbs are a sign that you've used the wrong verb.*
> —Annie Dillard

> *Write with nouns and verbs, not with adjectives and adverbs.*
> —Strunk and White

The inclination to use adjectives and adverbs seems to come naturally for most of us as an element of description and a way to spice up sentences. But using bland nouns and verbs modified by adjectives and adverbs is usually second best to finding stronger nouns and verbs that don't need adjective and adverbs to intensify them. For example, instead of being "really mad," you should be "furious." Instead of a "difficult problem," try using "dilemma." The following examples show the advantage of omitting the adverb or adjective and replacing a weak verb or noun with a stronger one—using fewer words overall.

> **WEAK:** She walked softly toward the door.
> **BETTER:** She tiptoed toward the door.

> **WEAK:** He will be very glad to see you.
> **BETTER:** He will be delighted to see you.

> **WEAK:** A huge rock came very fast down the mountainside.
> **BETTER:** A boulder tumbled down the mountainside.

WEAK: He walked angrily toward the front door.
BETTER: He stormed through the front door.

Sometimes using more words to replace an adjective better conveys the message. Consider these sentences.

BLAND: She gave him a flirtatious look.
BETTER: She batted her lashes and smiled with her eyes.

BLAND: The baby was adorable.
BETTER: The baby's wide innocent eyes and toothless grin made everyone in the room smile.

In both of the previous examples, the better version contains more words but makes the point by bringing it to life for the reader.

Many adverbs end in *ly*. During the self-editing process, search your manuscript for these words. In almost every case, you will be able to replace them with better descriptors.

BEFORE: She walked slowly toward the window.
AFTER: She took her time walking to the window.

BEFORE: He was excessively afraid of the big dog.
AFTER: He was terrified of the dog poking his head over the four foot fence.

Listed below are some of the more commonly overused adverbs that can be replaced with better descriptors or omitted altogether.

The celebration was **actually** for her.
The celebration was for her.

Hopefully, he would come for a visit.
She longed for him to visit.

He was **perfectly** sure.
He was sure.

She **really** liked him.
She adored him.

The dog **suddenly** lunged at her face.
The dog lunged at her face.

The two of them were **totally** in sync.
The two of them were in sync.

She was a **very** interesting person.
She was a fascinating person.

With respect to adjectives, use them only when the noun by itself isn't enough, as in these examples.

The **scariest** villain of all time is Darth Vader.
Please pull out the **three red** roses and put them in another vase.
I'm looking for a **young, good-tempered** dog for a pet.

Avoid redundancy. If the adjective doesn't add value to the sentence, it will clutter up the writing and cause readers to skip over it. And if readers find themselves skipping over too much text, they may put the book away unfinished.

Free gift—If it's a gift, it's free.
Serious danger—All danger is serious.
Cold snow—There is no such thing as warm snow.
The bull bellowed loudly—How else would a bull bellow?

There are times to use and times to avoid adjectives and adverbs. The point is to not *overuse* them. Include them only if you can't convey the same meaning without them. Adjectives and adverbs are fine in moderation, but strong nouns and verbs will make your writing more engaging.

Clichés

As much as I am aware of the need to avoid clichés in my writing at all costs, my editor will still red flag one here and there that I've inadvertently managed to include. They come so naturally, and that's the problem.

Clichés degrade your writing, take away from your creativity, and therefore can weaken the dramatic effect of the story.

Here are just a few clichés you need to avoid *(like the plague)*:

- better safe than sorry
- bring to the table
- but at the end of the day
- dead as a doornail
- every dog has its day
- giving 110 percent
- if only walls could talk
- ignorance is bliss
- it's an uphill battle
- like a kid in a candy store
- low-hanging fruit
- no-brainer
- out of left field
- play your cards right
- plenty of fish in the sea
- raining cats and dogs
- read between the lines
- take the tiger by the tail
- the grass is always greener on the other side
- the pot calling the kettle black
- thick as thieves
- think outside the box
- you can't judge a book by its cover

Here are examples of alternative ways to get the same point across for a few of the overused clichés.

Giving 110 percent
Putting forth the maximum possible amount of effort

Out of left field
Unexpected, surprising, erratic, peculiar

Think outside the box
Expand your thinking, examine from a different perspective

A no-brainer
Easy, simple, cinch, uncomplicated

There are tens of hundreds of clichés to avoid, too many to list here. For a more comprehensive list, refer to the third resource listed in the "Suggested Reading" section of this chapter.

SUGGESTED READING:

Darwin, Emma. The Itch of Writing: The Blog: *Cut All the Adjectives and Adverbs.* https://emmadarwin.typepad.com/thisitchofwriting/ 2017/11/cut-all-the-adjectives-adverbs-why-its-nonsense-and-why-it-isnt.html.

Donovan, Melissa. Writing Forward (blog): *Abolish the Adverbs.* https://www.writingforward.com/writing-tips/avoid-adverbs.

Lepki, Lisa. ProWritingAid (blog): *The Internet's Best List of Clichés.* https://prowritingaid.com/art/21/List-of-Clich%C3%A9s.aspx.

Telfer, Jonathan (Editor). "Cut the Clichés!" Writers Online. (No date.) https://www.writers-online.co.uk/how-to-write/creative-writing/ cut-the-cliches.

CHAPTER 19

Theme

Theme is difficult to define in that unlike other elements of writing—plot, characterization, and conflict, for example—it is abstract in nature. The theme of a story refers to its main topic or central idea, its underlying concept. Theme can usually be stated in the form of a message, lesson, key idea, or morals.

Themes can often be expressed in one or a few words. Here are some common themes in fiction:

- Ambition
- Betrayal
- Coming of age
- Courage and heroism
- Death
- Deception
- Discovery
- Escape
- Fear
- Freedom
- Good versus evil
- Individual versus society
- Isolation
- Jealousy
- Loss
- Loneliness/alienation
- Love
- Lust
- Power and corruption
- Prejudice
- Security
- Spirituality
- Suffering
- Survival

A book's theme is the main idea that flows through the narrative and connects the components of the story. The events in your story may be intriguing, but without some connection via a central theme, they run the risk of disengaging readers. Theme is the pulse of the story that happens beneath the surface—something the reader shouldn't notice but would miss if it wasn't there.

The following examples show how theme can manifest itself in a story.

LOVE

- Shakespeare's *Romeo and Juliet*—the classic tragic tale of forbidden love.
- Nicholas Sparks's *The Notebook*—a "love conquers all" story involving a common laborer and a wealthy young socialite.

DEATH

- Alice Sebold's *The Lovely Bones*—a story told from the perspective of a dead girl trying to come to terms with her own death.
- John Green's *The Fault in Our Stars*—the story of teenagers coming to terms with terminal illness.

GOOD VERSUS EVIL

- Tolkien's *The Lord of the Rings*—pits men, hobbits, and elves against an army of evil creatures.
- Charles Perrault's *Cinderella*—features pure and innocent Cinderella having to deal with her cruel stepmother and stepsisters, who treat her like a servant in her own home.

POWER

- George Orwell's *Animal Farm*—involves animals taking over their human oppressors. The more power the animals get, the more human-like they become.
- J.R.R. Tolkien's *The Lord of the Rings*—Characters compete for a ring that has been lost in a riverbed for more than two

thousand years. The ring's power over the characters creates the theme.

Establishing a theme before you start writing and maintaining it throughout the story are important. Not only will this keep readers engaged, it will also help to keep you focused and on track as you write.

It is not always easy to identify the theme of your story, especially since most stories contain more than one. Here are some questions to ask yourself to help identify the theme.

- What is your main character passionate about? If it's another person, the theme may be love. If it's about making money, it may be power.
- What type of conflict is keeping your main character from reaching his or her goals? If it's an abusive spouse, the theme may be survival. If it's a parent, it may be alienation.
- How does the main character change? If it's in a physical way, the theme may be loss. If it's internal, it could be spirituality.
- How does the main character affect other characters? If it's in a positive way, the theme may be heroism. If it's in a negative way, it may be betrayal.
- What message do you hope to send to your readers? If it's surviving one's youth, the theme may be coming of age. If it's about overcoming low self-esteem, it may be self-discovery.

Theme adds dimension to the story and, when done effectively, will result in a peeling away of the layers to reveal people, places, and/or events for what they truly are, leaving readers with something to think about after they've finished the final chapter.

Symbols and Motifs

Symbols and motifs can be used to strengthen the theme of your story.

A symbol is a concrete image, character, object, or figure that represents something beyond whatever is just on the surface. *The Wizard of Oz* is chock full of symbols: the yellow brick road symbolizing one's journey through life; the ruby red slippers symbolizing Dorothy's unrealized potential; the cyclone representing things in this world that are beyond our control. The list goes on.

A motif, on the other hand, is a recurring, usually abstract idea that provides clues that contribute to the theme of the story. In *Oz*, the primary characters—Dorothy, the lion, scarecrow, and tin man—each has a mission, and they feed off each other in their individual quests. The recurring motif element in this story is the courage one needs to continue the quest for something he or she desires.

Following are examples of symbols and motifs for some well-known stories.

> *The Notebook* by Nicholas Sparks—Birds symbolize freedom. Water represents life. Allie's painting represents her independence to do what she wants to do. Noah's house on the water symbolizes Allie.

> *The Lovely Bones* by Alice Sebold—The reference to bones throughout the beginning of the novel represents destructive behavior but later shifts to healing.

> *Lord of the Rings* by J. R. R. Tolkien—The motif of hope is illustrated with both the character Aragorn, who can rightfully use the seeing stone, and Estel, whom he affectionately calls his queen. The temptation motif of the ring is the motivating force behind most of the characters—fighting temptation, nurturing it, denying it, or preventing someone else from giving in to it.

> *Animal Farm* by George Orwell—The farm symbolizes the Soviet Union under Communist Party rule with a government (the pigs), a police force (the dogs), and a working class (the

other animals). The barn, on whose outside walls the pigs paint the Seven Commandments, represents the collective memory of a modern nation.

Symbols and motifs can give your story a sense of structure and continuity by creating patterns that recur throughout the work. Weave them in throughout the story to subtly remind the reader of certain ideas you want to get across in your story telling.

Integrating Theme into the Story

Theme is almost always character-driven, so the first thing to do is ask yourself these questions about the main character:

- How would you describe the main character at the beginning of the story?
- What are his or her flaws, fears, excuses, or history that keeps goals out of reach?
- How do the events of the story change the character?

Once you've answered these questions and identified the theme that arises, the question then becomes how to weave the theme into the story. Characterization for sure—dialogue, internal thoughts, and actions as well as how they change throughout the story define the theme. Incorporating motifs and symbols also help to develop theme. Taken together, these three things are powerful tools when it comes to making sure the theme is easily understood and constantly present in your story.

It's best to establish the theme before you start writing, but if you can't, it's better to start writing and let it come later naturally. In other words, don't get so caught up in trying to develop the theme that you neglect good storytelling.

Theme can be a powerful tool in writing, as it makes a statement about the topic(s) your book addresses without being preachy about it. And by making good use of theme in your novel, you create an emotional connection between the characters and your readers that hooks them into the story. A well-incorporated theme will provide readers with something to think about, something that will stay with them long after they've finished the final chapter. That is the power of theme.

SUGGESTED READING:

Atwood, Margaret. "Complete Guide to Literary Theme in Literature." Masterclass. September 11, 2019. https://www.masterclass.com/articles/the-complete-guide-to-narrative-theme-in-literature-definition-examples-and-writing-how-to#quiz-0.

Chapman, Harvey. "What Is Theme and Why Does It Matter?" Novel Writing Help. August 16, 2018. https://www.novel-writing-help.com/what-is-theme.html.

Weiland, K. M. "How to Write Unique Themes." Helping Writers Become Authors. July 16, 2018. https://www.helpingwriters becomeauthors.com/how-to-write-unique-themes/.

PART 3

The Final Stretch

Starting something can be easy, it is finishing it that is the highest hurdle.

—ISABELLA PORETSIS

CHAPTER 20

Budget

O ne of the first things you will want to determine after you've finished the epic journey of writing your book (or long before you've finished if you're a devout planner) is how much it's going to cost to get it published. Well, that depends on how much you are willing to invest in your business (writing books is a business, by the way), and the amount of profit you wish to earn. Quality sells, and quality costs money. I urge you to embrace quality in everything you do with your book, because if you go cheap, you run the risk of ending up with a book that doesn't sell well.

In addition to production costs, other costs crop up for writers who want to become successful authors—education expenses, reference materials, dues/subscriptions, office supplies and equipment, and postage. Here is a breakdown of the cost of goods and services you will likely incur to self-publish a 60,000-word (200-page) book.

Editing
There are arguably five levels of editing: manuscript assessment, content editing, line editing, copy editing, and proofreading. Not all authors require all five. My books go through three levels of editing—manuscript

assessment, line editing, and copy editing. (I also have my books beta-read, but there is no cost involved.) The number of levels of editing you will need for your book depends on your writing-skill level and budget restrictions. (Learn more about the editing process in Chapter 21.)

Following are the costs associated with the five levels of editing for a 60,000-word book. The ranges are wide as cost depends on the editor's expertise and the condition of the manuscript.

- Manuscript assessment: $600–$3,000
- Content editing: $3,600–$6,000
- Line editing: $1,800–$4,800
- Copy editing: $600–$3,000
- Proofreading: $600–$1,800

Cover Design

The good news for self-publishers is that you can find a cover designer for just about any budget—you can pick up a decent pre-made, full-color cover for $50 or have one designed that will compete with books published by Penguin, Harper Collins, and Random House for up to $1,200.

These are factors that impact how much designers charge.

- Specifications
- Time frame
- Number of variations (different options shown to the author)
- Number of changes allowed following initial design
- Whether the designer outsources the work
- Geographic location of the designer (cost of living)
- Demand for the designer's services
- Their experience and level of expertise

Here are typical price ranges for different types of covers.

- Pre-made: $50–$100
- Designed using stock photographs: $125–$400
- Custom designed: $500–$1,200

Formatting

If you have the expertise, you can obviously format your book your-self. It's not that complicated. But there are so many things that can go wrong in book formatting that I think it pays to have a professional do it. There are differing processes and requirements for formatting books in paper, digital, and Kindle formats—the formatting that looks good in print isn't necessarily the best or easiest to read for Kindle readers, for example. Here are the price ranges for formatting services for three different formats in a novel.

- Print: $80-$120
- E-book (EPUB & Kindle): $75-$100

Printing

I currently use IngramSpark to order print copies of my novels (6x9, black-and-white interior, full-color cover, no illustrations) and pay on average $0.015 per page. For a 200-page book, that adds up to $3 per copy. I think they are in line with other printers. I use these copies to gift to family, friends, and reviewers; sell at book fairs; and donate to libraries and other not-for-profit organizations.

Distribution

Today, more than half of all book sales (regardless of format) take place online, and self-published authors have the same access to online retail distribution as the major publishers and without many up-front costs. If you choose to sell your book on Amazon—the number one retailer of books in both print and digital formats—there is no cost involved in the distribution of your books. Or you can choose to work with any number of distribution services for a nominal fee or percentage of your profits. For example, IngramSpark charges a $49 set-up fee per title, and there is no additional distribution fee. If you want your book eligible to be placed in bookstores, libraries, or with wholesalers, it will need an International Standard Book Number (ISBN) assigned to it. If purchased individually from Bowker, the current cost is $125.

Paid Promotion and Advertising

In most cases, self-published authors have limited money to spend on promoting their books. (See Chapter 31 to learn about free ways to promote your book.) But free promotional opportunities go only so far in helping your book gain the exposure it needs to become profitable. The amount of money you budget for book promotion and advertising really comes down to how much you can afford to spend, and the figure I hear very often is $100 per month. This may be too high or too low for you, but it's a starting point. See how far it will go, track results, and modify it as needed. (See Chapter 35 for paid advertising sites.)

Education

You can learn a lot about writing and the publishing industry for free, but there will be times when you will want to take a class or attend a webinar that isn't free. My education expenses last year were under $50—the cost of one webinar. Education expenses for me were higher in previous years when I was more of a novice.

Reference Materials, Dues, and Subscriptions

Expenses in this category include how-to books; software licenses; website domain fees; online subscriptions, such as *Chicago Manual of Style* and *Merriam-Webster Dictionary*; trade journals; and writing association dues. My budget for this last year was $300.

Office Supplies and Equipment

Don't forget to budget for things like business cards, mailing envelopes, printer ink, and anything else you might need in the way of office supplies. If you need to purchase computer equipment specifically for the purpose of writing books, include the associated cost in your budget as well as the cost to maintain it.

Postage

You will probably send out copies of your printed book to friends, family, and reviewers. I usually budget at least $50 for this.

As in other aspects of our lives—personal and business—having a budget in place before the spending begins is a wise thing to do to keep on a good financial track. Expenses required to promote books can get out of hand quickly if not properly managed, so it's beneficial to take time early on in the process to prepare a budget.

SUGGESTED READING:

Bolt, Chandler. The Book Designer (blog): *Book Cover Trends Through the Decades.* https://www.thebookdesigner.com/2019/09/book-cover-trends-through-the-decades/

Max, Tucker. "How Much Does It Cost to Publish a Book?" Scribe. (No date.) https://scribewriting.com/cost-publish-book/.

Shiau, Yvonne (Content Marketer USA). Reedsy blog: *How Much Does It Cost to Self-Publish a Book in 2019?* https://blog.reedsy.com/cost-to-self-publish-a-book/.

CHAPTER 21

Editors

Contrary to popular belief, editors don't exist to make your life miserable—they exist to help you make your work accurate, clear, credible, and marketable.

Here are my reasons for hiring a professional editor:

- Most writers don't possess complete editorial skills like editors who have a bachelor's or master's degree in English, creative writing, communications, or journalism and have been educated in all aspects of writing and editing.
- Editors are likely to catch errors that authors miss, since it's easy for authors to inadvertently skip over errors when they know what they meant.
- After living and breathing the manuscript for months, writers often become too attached to be critical. Editors are more objective and don't have this problem.
- A good editor will challenge you to take your manuscript to the next level.
- An opinion from someone who knows what sells can be invaluable.

- A poorly edited book is distracting to many readers and lessens an author's credibility.
- Your future writing will benefit when you incorporate the editor's changes and suggestions into your work.

There is substantial work involved when it comes to shaping a manuscript into a market-ready book, and one of the most important aspects of this process is in the editing. If you are traditionally published, the publisher will either assign an editor to your project (the larger houses do this) or require you to hire one (the smaller houses may do this). But if you self-publish, the choice is yours to make. That said, if you want to be respected as a serious author, you'll choose to have your work professionally edited.

There is a certain amount of self-editing you can and should do (see Appendix B, Self-Editing Checklist). Once you get the manuscript as polished as you can, given the skills you possess, a professional editor will ensure the finished product is comparable to traditionally published books.

Even well-established, successful authors benefit from an editor, as writers are often too close to their work to clearly see what needs to be done in order to take the book from good to great. That's where an editing staff comes into play. I specify staff because there are many levels of editing.

Levels of Editing

There are arguably five different levels of editing.

> Manuscript assessment
> Developmental editing
> Line editing
> Copy editing
> Proofreading

I say arguably because there appear to be no industry standards for what is included in each of these categories. Talk to one publisher, and he'll list ten different things his line editors look for in a manuscript. Talk to another and she'll list six of the same things in addition to three more of her own.

This is what I most often see differentiating the levels of editing:

MANUSCRIPT ASSESSMENT (OR CRITIQUE OR CONTENT EDITING): The most basic level of editing—the big-picture evaluation of your manuscript—is a manuscript assessment. The content editor points out the strengths and weaknesses of the manuscript, usually in a multi-page report. The elements assessed may include all or some of the following.

- Story line
- Character development
- Setting
- Narrative flow and style
- Plot structure
- Scene development
- Point of view
- Organization
- Pacing
- Format
- Suitability for intended audience
- Marketability
- Accuracy of facts
- Clarity
- Tone
- Voice
- Dialogue
- Book and chapter titles

DEVELOPMENTAL EDITING (OR STRUCTURAL EDITING): A developmental editor provides fixes or suggested fixes for the manuscript (chapter by chapter, paragraph by paragraph, scene by scene) that will correct the deficiencies identified in the assessment. This intensive edit is ideal for writers who have been made aware there are problems with their work but don't know how to fix them.

LINE EDITING: A line editor analyzes and then polishes each sentence with respect to clarity and style. Some or all of the following elements may be taken into consideration.

- Sentence and paragraph
  structure and flow
- Syntax
- Clarity
- Repetitiveness
- Transitions
- Paragraph breaks
- Vocabulary level
- Use of clichés and
  undesirable verbal tics
- Diction
- Grammar
- Punctuation
- Spelling

COPY EDITING: Copy editing focuses on technical errors, including the following.

- Subject-verb agreement
- Verb tense
- Diction
- Grammar
- Spelling
- Punctuation

PROOFREADING: The proofreader does a final check of the manuscript before it gets published for any remaining technical errors (spelling, punctuation, typos, and formatting).

Because there are no precise definitions that describe the different types of editing, it's important that when an editor quotes a fee for a particular level of editing, you ask what exactly is included.

Fees

Most editors charge by the word. I've listed below some typical fees (2019) for each level of the editing process. That's not to say you can't find lower or higher rates out there, but these are the ranges I most often encounter.

Manuscript assessment: 1 to 5 cents/word
Content editing: 6 to 10 cents/word
Line editing: 3 to 8 cents/word
Copy editing: 1 to 5 cents/word
Proofreading: 1 to 3 cents/word

The ranges are wide due not only to the experience level of the editor but also to how much work the manuscript requires. An editor will charge more for a manuscript containing significant errors than one the author has effectively self-edited.

Experienced editors who work on an hourly rate charge between $40 and $80 per hour, depending on the level of service they are providing. Again, you might be able to find less expensive ones, as I'm sure they exist.

My advice is to not skimp on editing—as with most things, you get what you pay for.

How to Choose an Editor

If you decide to self-publish, you will definitely need an editor. Okay, so that's not entirely true—many authors publish their work without having had it professionally edited. But it's what I (and other successful authors I know) recommend, so for the purpose of this book, let's consider this to be a truth. Even if you attempt to secure a traditional publisher to publish your work, and you know an editor comes with the deal, you will still need an editor to get your manuscript in good enough shape to submit it to an agent/publisher, as manuscripts submitted with errors are often discarded. A good editor is crucial to either process.

Be sure to find an editor who is comfortable with your genre. Editors who specialize in a particular genre are more likely to know its idiosyncrasies, the market, and reader expectations.

I would not recommend looking to social media or some search engine for an editor unless you are prepared to weed through thousands of search results that include everyone from a *New York Times* best-selling editor to someone's next-door neighbor who got an A in English back in the fifth grade.

Referrals are good if the person with the first-hand experience has written a book similar to yours. Questions to ask a fellow author about his or her editor are:

- What type of project did you work on together?

- Did you sign a written contract that detailed the editor's services, fees, and deadlines?
- Was there anything the editor did that you didn't like?
- Did the editor meet agreed-upon deadlines?
- Was the editor responsive to your phone calls, e-mails, text messages?
- Were there any hidden or additional costs you weren't expecting?
- Did the editor help you become a better writer?
- Would you rehire this editor?

Here is a list of sites with directories of editors.

> book-editing.com/book-editors/—Offers a relatively small, select group of editors who are vetted by a network coordinator who keeps track of customer satisfaction.

> the-efa.org/membership-directory—Requires that editors have some professional experience as a writer, proofreader, or editor, but they are not vetted or evaluated.

> naiwe.com/member-search/—Lists anyone who identifies himself or herself as an editor. There is no vetting process.

Once you narrow down the list of potential editors to three or so, it's acceptable to ask them for a sample edit on one of your chapters. Most editors will do this free of charge. This will give you a good idea of what they will provide for the services offered and give them an idea if they want to take on your project. Be sure to ask competing editors to edit the same chapter so you are making sensible comparisons.

Seasoned editors understandably charge more for their services than newbies in the field. That's not to say you can't find good, inexperienced editors—it's just trickier to qualify them because they have little or no track record. But if you have a limited budget and can only afford an inexperienced editor, you should be able to make an informed decision based on the comparison of the young editor's sample edit to that of a more seasoned one.

When you have selected an editor, be sure to ask what their lead times are, and don't be surprised if they are months long. With this in mind, you'll want to get on their schedule far in advance, and then work with a mutually agreed upon deadline for you to get your manuscript to them. This is very important because if you the author miss a deadline, you will likely be charged a percentage of the editor's fee for service anyway. Read your editor's terms of agreement to see how he or she handles missed deadlines.

Editors are like any other service provider you might hire—some will be more compatible with your needs and requirements than others, so it pays to spend time vetting them before making a contractual commitment with them.

Working with an Editor

Some of you may have concerns about what an editor will "do" to your manuscript. After spending months writing what you believe to be a great piece of work, you may fear the editor will tear it apart. While the editing process may initially feel a bit discouraging, especially if you're not accustomed to getting objective feedback, the fact is that good editors do help you improve your writing. They work for you by giving you insight and options. They do not (should not) change your work simply to suit their liking.

But working with an editor does require you to have a thick skin and an open mind. You must be prepared for the editorial feedback you've paid for, especially the high-level feedback. While it's easy to accept someone telling you to use a semicolon instead of a comma in a particular sentence, it's quite another thing to be told your character isn't believable or lacks depth. Keep in mind an experienced editor has been down this road many times before and knows what readers want. Be open to criticism. Get the most out of the process.

Please don't be like some authors who think they can throw a messy draft at an editor and expect him or her to fix it—that's not how it works. Do all you can before you send your manuscript out for editing. There's a lot of work to be done between pounding out a first rough draft and knowing when it's time for an editor to take over. (See Appendix B, Self-Editing Checklist.)

Finally, if you put trust in an editor, but you feel strongly that a particular suggestion isn't on target, do not feel compelled to make the change to suit the editor. After all, it's your name on the cover, not the editor's. But when this happens, I suggest that you don't reject the suggestion immediately. Try to look at it objectively. Question him or her about it—good editors are happy to discuss their reasoning with you. If you still think the suggested changes would negatively affect the story, go with your instincts. My only advice is to really (and I mean really) try to be as objective as possible before abandoning the suggestion. If an editor is recommending a change, it's likely there is a good reason.

Pitfalls in Choosing Not to Work with an Editor

I've talked about the reasons I think you *should* work with an editor, but if that hasn't convinced you yet, here are some consequences of choosing *not* to do so:

- Books that are not professionally edited are at higher risk of getting bad reviews. That's not to say they definitely will—some readers care only about the story and not the quality of the writing. But keep in mind that writers are readers too, and if a writer reads your book, and your book contains errors, you can bet it won't get a good review, and all it takes are a few bad reviews immediately following your book launch to kill its success.
- Some book-vetting organizations will filter out books that have obviously not been professionally edited, so in these cases, your book will not be completely reviewed and vetted.

Vetted self-published books have a better chance of selling than non-vetted ones.

- Without an editor pointing out your mistakes, you will continue to make them and therefore will not develop the skills required to become a better writer. I feel that each book I write is better than the previous one, and I owe much of this to my editor.

Whether your motivation in hiring an editor is to improve your book's marketability, to grow as a writer, or to get closer to a publishing deal, be prepared to invest a significant amount of money in the process. Your manuscript is something in which you have invested much of your valuable time, your heart, and your soul—it deserves a professional edit.

SUGGESTED READING:

Hamilton, Chantel. Jane Friedman Blog: *The Comprehensive Guide to Finding, Hiring, and Working with an Editor.* https://www.janefriedman.com/comprehensive-guide-to-finding-working-with-editors/.

Poisso, Lisa. Lisa Poisso (blog): *The Author's Guide to Finding and Hiring an Editor.* http://lisapoisso.com/find-an-editor/.

Teymour, Shahabi. Jane Friedman Blog: *How to Find an Editor As a Self-Published Author.* https://www.janefriedman.com/how-to-find-an-editor/.

Touch, Craig. The Book Designer (blog): *Beta Readers Vs Editors Vs ARCs.* https://www.thebookdesigner.com/2018/05/beta-readers-vs-editors-vs-arcs/

CHAPTER 22

The Publishing Process

Publishing has been around for a long time—one might argue ever since clay tablets and papyrus scrolls. Let's start with some definitions.

By most definitions, **PUBLISHING** is the dissemination of literature, music, or information for the purpose of making it available to the general public.

TRADITIONAL PUBLISHERS purchase the right to publish your manuscript and assume most or all of the costs associated with cover design, editing, formatting, promoting, printing, and distributing your book. Because they rely on book sales for revenue, they are highly selective about who they represent. The book becomes the property of the publisher. The author receives payment in the form of an advance and modest royalties based on sales. Traditional publishers vary in size from the so-called Big Five, which dominate the industry, to small regional publishers, which have modest staffs, pay small advances, and offer limited services other than marketing and distribution.

It wasn't until the onset of the World Wide Web that so many authors considered **SELF-PUBLISHING** rather than going through traditional publishers to promote their work. When an author decides to self-publish, he or she essentially becomes the publisher and is responsible for all aspects for publishing the book, including cover design, formatting, editing, printing, promoting, and distribution. Authors contract with companies or individuals that offer self-publishing services to handle what they cannot do for themselves. The finished product is usually, but not always, the sole property of the author, who has complete control over the process including royalties and publishing rights.

Traditional Publishing

Most authors start out hoping to secure a deal with a traditional publisher. Going the traditional publishing route means the publisher assumes all the up-front costs and does much of the legwork required to get books to the marketplace. An author's dream would be to have one of the Big Five—Penguin Random House, Harper Collins, Hachette, Simon & Shuster, and Macmillan—publish their book, but there are numerous smaller publishers that can do the job as well. I found these three publishers listed on more than one list of recommended publishers that specialize in general fiction. See the Recommended Reading section at the end of this chapter for complete lists.

Overlook Press, New York NY (abramsbooks.com/imprints/overlookpress/)

Steerforth Press, Hanover NH (steerforth.com)

Workman Publishing Company, New York NY
(workman.com) (Also owns Algonquin Books of Chapel
Hill, Storey Publishing, Timber Press, Artisan Books, and
HighBridge Audio)

Most traditional publishers (definitely the larger ones) will accept submissions only through agents. These agents are like gatekeepers: they have established connections with publishers and know how to pitch to them far better than the average writer. Publishers trust the agents' judgment and taste. Agents save publishers a lot of work by finding quality material for them to consider.

Before you even think about contacting an agent, you must be able to produce a near-perfect manuscript—one that is free of errors, well suited to its genre, and marketable. If you cannot afford a professional editor, hire a professional proofreader at the very least. If you don't, it is unlikely you will be able to find a reputable agent to represent you.

Finding an agent who is right for you and willing to represent your work is not easy, as most agents receive thousands of inquiries a week and accept only a small percentage of them.

Once you have identified an agent (or better yet, a list of agents) who will accept your type of literary work, you will want to contact them with a query letter—a well-crafted one-page letter that pitches your work. Elements of a query letter that is more likely to get attention include:

- A salutation line that includes the agent's name. "To whom it may concern" is inappropriate and may lead to immediate rejection.
- A brief summary of the book's story line in the form of a hook. For fiction, this means including what your character wants, why he or she wants it, and what keeps him or her from getting it. You want the agent to think *Wow, I've got to see more of this!*
- The book's title, genre, and word count.
- Identification of your target audience and why they will love your book.
- Your writing credentials.

- An offer to send a proposal, a few chapters of the book, or the full manuscript. "I look forward to hearing from you" isn't strong enough.
- A "thank you" for their consideration.
- Your full name, e-mail address, phone number, and applicable social media and website links.

The query letter—a compelling, passionate letter that shows off your writing skills—must pique the agent's interest right away. If it doesn't, then it won't matter how amazing your novel is, because the agent likely won't pursue it further. The letter should be error-free. Proofread it ten times if you have to. Have someone else proofread it. While one typo or misplaced modifier won't necessarily kill the deal, it's important to come across as thoroughly professional in every way.

It is advisable to always follow the agent's submission guidelines before sending them anything—ignoring them will typically lead to immediate rejection. And if you have room, it's not a bad idea to include in the body of the message a few paragraphs from the beginning of the book. (This is obviously easier to accomplish if your query is sent via e-mail where there are no defined page lengths.) If the writing in that snippet grabs the agent's attention, you're in a good place.

Sometimes, an agent will like a query letter enough to ask for the full manuscript. Other times they will request more information in the way of a proposal—a longer, more detailed version of a query letter—before they decide whether to accept your project. Here are key elements to include in a proposal:

- **AUTHOR INFORMATION:** previously published works, social media links and stats, website or blog link, connections with the publishing industry, relevant education, and anything else that gives credibility to you as an author
- **HOOK:** an attention-grabbing sentence or two that captures what your book is about
- **SYNOPSIS:** a full synopsis of your book, spoilers and all
- **GENRE:** which genre(s) your book best falls into

- **TARGET AUDIENCE:** description of the audience you are trying to reach
- **COMPETITION:** list of successful books similar to yours and why yours is competitive
- **SAMPLE CHAPTERS:** one to three sample chapters
- **MARKETING:** details of your ideas and plans for promoting the book

---

SCAM ALERT: Stay away from agents who ask for a fee to read your manuscript or any other up-front fee. Reputable agents earn money by enjoying a percentage of your royalty.

The major publishers generally do not consider unsolicited manuscripts—they rely on agents, their literary connections, or their own stable of writers for new books. However, many of the smaller presses and regional publishers that focus on specific markets do accept submissions from the public without agents as middlemen. If you decide to go this route, refer to their websites for submission guidelines. Also be aware that if you send your un-agented manuscript to publishers and later decide to go the agent route, many agents will not resubmit to a publisher you have already contacted.

Here is a list of places to find agents and publishers.

> Duotrope.com. Database for finding publishers. Paid subscription required.
> PublishersMarketplace.com. A place to research literary agents. Paid subscription required.
> AgentQuery.com. About 1,000 agent listings. Free subscription.
> QueryTracker.net. About 200 publisher listings and 1,000 agent listings. Basic service is free.
> WritersMarket.com. Thousands of agent and publisher listings. Basic service is free.

> Firstwriter.com/Agents/. More than 2,500 listings. Basic
> service is free.

Finding a traditional publisher is what most writers imagine when they think about getting published, but due to the enormous amount of competition, the odds of finding one are slim. For most writers, self-publishing is the more feasible option.

Self-Publishing

Publishing a book is an arduous process—one that traditional publishers have perfected over decades. That's why they get such a big cut of your earnings—they do the heavy lifting. Self-publishing is no different—contrary to popular belief, it involves much more than uploading a document to the web and hitting the PUBLISH button. Know that while empowering, self-publishing a successful book is also challenging and labor-intensive.

When you take on the role of publisher and become responsible for all aspects of publishing your book and associated costs (the definition of self-publishing), you can choose to do as much or as little of the work as you wish, engaging a company or individual service providers for the work you elect not to do. The good news is there are many options available. The bad news is that the abundance of these options complicates the process.

The Self-Publishing Evolution

Starting in the early 1990s, more and more authors began opting for self-publishing rather than give up on their book after being rejected by traditional publishers. Since then, the self-publishing industry has exploded. Here is a condensed timeline on how self-publishing has progressed since then.

> **1997**—Lightning Source, one of the largest print-on-demand
> (POD) companies, is founded, eliminating the need for large

print-runs and opening up the market to authors who want to self-publish. (Print-on-demand, which was made possible by digital printing, allows books to be printed one at a time based on orders received as opposed to producing large, costly pre-order print runs).

2000—Stephen King self-publishes his novel *The Plant* on the Internet, calling it "Big Publishing's worst nightmare." He publishes it as an e-book in six installments available for purchase on his website. Self-publishing on the Internet takes off.

2011—Twenty percent of the U.S. population own an e-reader of some kind, and the *New York Times* adds the new category "E-Book Best Sellers" to their lists. Companies like BookBaby and Smashwords make it easy for writers to self-publish and distribute books worldwide. Books published in .txt, .mobi, and .doc formats become commonplace. E-books outsell printed books on Amazon.

CURRENT—In April 2019, Amazon CEO Jeff Bezos reveals that over a thousand self-published authors each surpassed $100,000 in Kindle Direct Publishing (KDP) royalties in 2018. And according to a recent report from Bowker (a leading provider of bibliographic information), self-publishing titles grew at a rate of more than 28 percent in 2017 (up from an 8 percent increase during the prior year), surpassing the million mark for the first time. "Self-publishing shows no signs of slowing down and continues to grow at a steady rate," according to Beat Barblan, director of Bowker's Identifier Services. "We don't expect any decline in self-publishing."

While earning statistics for the top self-published authors are impressive, the median income for this group is anything but. According to the 2018 Authors Guild income survey, self-published authors' median annual income jumped from $1,000 in 2013 to $1,951 in 2017—a remarkable

95 percent increase, but still meager. In contrast, traditionally published authors' median income decreased by 32 percent, falling from $4,950 in 2013 to $3,360 in 2017. (For the full report, go to authorsguild. org/industry-advocacy/six-takeaways-from-the-authors-guild-2018-authors-income-survey/.)

I recite these statistics to alert you to the grim reality of trying to make a living writing books. Is it possible? Yes, it is. Is it easy? No, it isn't. Savvy, motivated self-published authors can succeed in the current publishing environment—it takes hard work, dedication, and the willingness to spend money to make money.

Overcoming the Stigma

After self-publishing had been around for a while, at some point, probably in the 1920s, the term "vanity publishing" came into common use. Authors who couldn't find a traditional publisher—someone who valued their book enough to front the costs to publish it and then pay the author an advance against royalties—would pay a company to print it. Such companies were often referred to by outside observers as "vanity presses" because they were perceived to cater to the vanity of untalented writers.

It has been a slow process, but fortunately, the public image of the self-publishing industry has improved significantly in recent years with the addition of numerous award-winning and otherwise successful books to its inventory, rendering the term "vanity press" outdated. In contrast, today's "self-publishing service providers" are based on a few different business models. Some of them offer printing only; others offer à la carte services and/or packages that might include editing, cover design, formatting, printing, distribution, and promotion. Some have content requirements; others do not. Some hold the rights to the book; others allow the author to keep the rights. Sadly, some are scammers who mislead authors (inexperienced ones, in particular) about what they provide, charge exorbitant fees, promise more than they deliver, and offer substandard services.

The self-publishing stigma may not have gone away entirely—there are indeed thousands of poor-quality books available online that no agent or publisher would ever consider representing. But it has receded substantially as more and more quality self-published books—especially best-sellers and those vetted by organizations like Awesome Indies and indieBRAG—infiltrate the current marketplace. Today, as long as your book has been properly edited and formatted, you should be able to say with pride that you are a self-published author.

Unassisted Self-Publishing

Not many writers have the requisite skills to do *all* the work involved in self-publishing a book. While a completely DIY approach can be self-affirming and exhilarating for some, it is overwhelming and daunting for most. Consider the following skill sets required to publish a book.

- Content editing—determining the strengths and weaknesses of the manuscript, story line, character development, setting, narrative style, plot structure, point of view, clarity, tone, voice, manuscript organization, pacing, format, and marketability
- Line editing—sentence and paragraph structure, transitions, word usage, diction, grammar, punctuation, spelling, and syntax
- Copy editing—grammar, spelling, punctuation, diction, subject-verb agreement, and verb tense
- Proofreading—catching typos and performing a second check for obvious problems
- Cover design
- Formatting (paperback and e-book)
- Printing
- Marketing and promotion
- Distribution

Obviously, the more you can do yourself, the less money you will need to invest in production costs. I would caution you that if your book does not appear to be professionally edited, designed, formatted, and printed, you may not be taken seriously as a writer, and sales will likely suffer. I've seen this happen…a lot.

Assisted Self-Publishing

Authors needing to utilize the services of others to self-publish have many approaches to consider. There are numerous companies offering packages that may include editing, formatting, cover design, title setup, printing, distribution, and marketing. Others are more limited in their service offerings. Some will claim a portion of the royalties based on sales. Some will actually hold the copyright for your work. Some offer a print-on-demand model, while others produce large print-runs. The number of different approaches these service providers offer is mind-boggling, especially for new authors.

As you research service providers, you will come across labels such as "hybrid," "subsidy," "print-on-demand," "co-publisher," and "fee-based." I choose not to provide definitions for these because there is too much interpretational disagreement. When you are considering a service provider, what should be most important to you are the terms of their contract and whether you are getting the specific services you need, not how they label themselves.

I cannot emphasize strongly enough how important it is to understand all the terms of a publishing contract before signing it—in this arena of so many disreputable service providers, you need to be extra cautious. Do your due diligence. Don't have regrets afterward for the path you chose.

So, which assisted self-publishing companies should you use? It depends on which one(s) best suits your needs, objectives, budget, and timeline. But while I can't advise you which company is most advantageous for you, I can at least offer some information about the service providers that most frequently make the top self-publishing companies lists. Each of the service providers named below has made such a list and has been rated "Excellent" or "Recommended" by Alli (The Alliance of Independent Authors) and/or has an "A" rating by the Better Business Bureau.

Aaxel Author Services
aaxelauthorservices.com/
Services provided: Manuscript evaluation, marketing,
publishing plans
Alli's rating: Excellent
Better Business Bureau rating: None

Blurb
blurb.com/trade-books
Services provided: Printing
Alli's rating: Recommended
Better Business Bureau rating: A+

BookBaby
bookbaby.com/
Services provided: Cover design, formatting, editing,
marketing, distribution
Alli's rating: Excellent
Better Business Bureau rating: None

Dart Frog Books
dartfrogbooks.com/
Services provided: Cover design, formatting, editing,
marketing, and promotion
Alli's rating: Excellent
Better Business Bureau rating: None

Draft2Digital
draft2digital.com/
Services provided: Formatting, distribution
Alli's rating: Excellent
Better Business Bureau rating: None

Emerging Ink
emergingink.com/
Services provided: Cover design, editing, formatting,
ghostwriting
Alli's rating: Excellent
Better Business Bureau rating: None

Heddon Publishing
heddonpublishing.com/
Services provided: Editing, formatting, cover design
Alli's rating: Excellent
Better Business Bureau rating: None

iBooks (Apple)
apple.com/ibooks-author/
Services provided: Distribution
Alli's rating: Recommended
Better Business Bureau rating: None

Ingram-Spark's Lightning Source
ingramcontent.com/publishers/print
Services provided: Distribution, printing
Alli's rating: Excellent
Better Business Bureau rating: A+

Kindle Direct Publishing
kdp.amazon.com/en_US/
Services provided: Formatting, distribution, promotion
Alli's rating: Excellent
Better Business Bureau rating: None

Kobo
kobo.com/us/
Services provided: Distribution
Alli's rating: Excellent
Better Business Bureau rating: None

Mindstir Media
mindstirmedia.com/
Services provided: Cover design, editing, marketing,
distribution
Alli's rating: None
Better Business Bureau rating: A+

PublishDrive
publishdrive.com/
Services provided: Distribution, promotion
Alli's rating: Excellent
Better Business Bureau rating: None

Smashwords
smashwords.com/
Services provided: Distribution
Alli's rating: Excellent
Better Business Bureau rating: A+

StreetLib
streetlib.com/
Services provided: Cover design, formatting, printing,
distribution
Alli's rating: Excellent
Better Business Bureau rating: None

XinXii
xinxii.com/
Services provided: Distribution
Alli's rating: Recommended
Better Business Bureau rating: None

One-stop assisted self-publishing companies may be an especially good option for first-time authors. Until I learned my way around the industry, I used CreateSpace (the former publishing arm of Amazon) for everything. Having one source for cover design, editing, formatting, printing, and distribution made the process relatively easy.

Freelance Service Providers

If you are in a position to pay a little more and have the time and knowledge to hire individual freelance providers and coordinate everyone's services, this may be a good option for you. Choosing single-service providers à la carte requires you to draw on the skills of various vendors that, when combined with your own competencies, will serve to maximize creativity, financial freedom, and control.

There is no shortage of individual freelancers and companies who provide these services, and hiring them independent of each other gives you the opportunity to handpick the ones who will work best for your particular project. What has worked well for me has been to hire an independent editor, book cover designer, and formatter. Then I use Kindle Direct Publishing (KDP) for publishing and distributing e-books, and IngramSpark for printing and distributing print copies (using POD technology). I use Amazon and my own website to promote my books, and Amazon to sell them.

When you go the freelance route, I believe referrals from other authors are the most effective way to find reputable service providers. One way to do this is to join one or more online discussion or social media groups where authors freely share their experiences. (See Chapter 31 for a discussion on online chat groups.) Another method is to check the acknowledgements pages of books from authors you admire to see whom they are using for an editor, cover design, etc.

In addition to relying on referrals, the assisted self-publishing companies listed in the previous section that offer à la carte services, and online discussion groups that exist for each discipline, you might want to make use of the following list of sites that will help you find freelancers to handle your publishing needs.

COVER DESIGN:
99designs.com
aipponline.org
fiverr.com
freelancer.com
guru.com

thebookcoverdesigner.com
upwork.com

EDITING:
aipponline.org
book-editing.com/book-editors
fiverr.com
naiwe.com/member-search
newyorkbookeditors.com
the-efa.org/membership-directory

FORMATTING:
aipponline.org
authorems.com
fiverr.com
formattedbooks.com

PRINTING:
fcidigital.com
wbsusa.com

MARKETING AND PROMOTION:
aipponline.org
allauthor.com
amarketingexpert.com
smithpublicity.com

Know Your Rights

If you decide to perform all of the tasks involved in publishing the book yourself, there is no question as to who owns the legal rights to print, publish, distribute, and make changes to the book—*you* do. But if you hire one or more service providers to assist you in the process, you could lose some of these rights depending on the service provider's terms.

Here are some questions to ask when considering contracting with a book publishing service provider.

1. Who owns the rights to the book?
2. Who makes the final decision on cover design and book content?
3. Are royalties part of the terms of agreement and, if so, what are they?
4. Are the books printed via print-on-demand? If not, who houses the printed books?
5. How much control do you have over the production process?
6. Who handles marketing, promotion, and distribution?
7. What are the author's costs?

It is so important to read and understand all the terms in the contract you sign with every service provider. The last thing you want is to be surprised later upon finding out what you can and cannot do with your own book.

Traditional Versus Self-Publishing

The following sums up the most significant differences between traditional publishing and self-publishing.

- A traditional publisher handles most, if not all, of the up-front costs and production work. Self-publishers take all of this on themselves.
- When you work with a reputable publisher, you are pretty much guaranteed a high-quality, marketable product. Self-publishers must figure this out for themselves.
- Traditional publishers control content, title, cover and interior design, price, distribution channels, marketing, and timing. Self-publishers have control over all of this.
- Since publishers assume both costs and risks, they (along with the agents and bookstores) take in most of the money. Typical

royalty rates for authors are 7 percent to 8 percent for trade paperbacks and 5 percent for e-books. Self-publishers have control over their royalties, receiving 100 percent if they have done everything themselves.

- If you are a first-time author, you will likely make more money in royalties with a traditional publisher than by self-publishing. Using conservative industry estimates from 2017, you would earn less than $2,500 over the lifetime of your book (assuming 75 percent e-book sales and 25 percent paperback) with a traditional publisher and less than $300 if you are self-published.
- Traditional publishers sometimes have broader distribution channels available to them (although this is rapidly changing) including in bookstores.
- Because publishers are in charge, it may be difficult for an author to make changes to the manuscript along the way. As a self-publisher, you have this option.
- Most publishers will print a certain number of books when the book is launched, and the author may have to buy the copies that don't sell. Self-publishers have the print-on-demand option that allows them to avoid excess inventory.
- Self-publishing still holds a stigma for some. In the past, self-publishing was often dismissed as "vanity publishing." It still holds somewhat of a stigma today but not to the same extent as more and more best-selling and award-winning self-published books are released.

Most of the time, the choice of whether to self-publish or go with a traditional publisher is not in our hands, as less than one percent of proposals sent to agents and traditional publishers are accepted. But if you choose to self-publish, know that you are in good company and part of a growing trend!

SCAM ALERT: Whether you choose a traditional publisher, an assisted self-publishing company, a small independent publisher, or any other type of service provider to publish your book, you must be diligent when it comes to vetting them. Beware of the following:

- Fast-talking, hard-selling, slick salesmen.
- Service providers who make unrealistic promises (like TV and film rights) or guaranty success.
- A publisher who claims to be a traditional publisher and asks for up-front money from you—traditional publishers do not ask you for money.
- Verbal promises not in writing.
- Publishers that offer contracts with exclusive rights to publish.
- Publishers that charge a fee (reading fee, separate publishing fee, fee to list your book on Amazon) in addition to the cost of producing the book.
- A service provider that claims to be something it is not (for example, one that claims to be selective about the books it publishes but in reality is not).
- Publishers that require all fees be paid up-front.
- Publishers that refuse to provide the terms of agreement in writing.
- Publishers that require authors to buy back the books that don't sell.
- Service providers who falsely claim you keep 100 percent of the royalties.
- Providers who advertise, "We want to help new writers," or "Get published for free," or "None of our books have resulted in failure."
- Convoluted contract language.

- Service providers who seek you out and tell you they are impressed with your work and recognize a success story when they see it.
- Publishers that claim they have large numbers of sales-people who spend all their time selling clients' books.
- Exorbitant fees for design, editing, formatting, and printing your book.

E-book, Paperback, Audiobook, or Hardcover?

The more formats in which your book is available, the more readers you will attract. But most often, the format choices you make will depend on cost and return on investment (ROI).

E-books are, by far, the most popular format chosen by readers today. I can attest to that—at least 95 percent of my book royalties come from e-books. Today, anyone with a computer—notebook, laptop or desktop—can read an e-book: specific readers such as Kindle are no longer required. E-book production is also, by far, the least expensive method of publishing, with the cost only a small fraction of that of producing a paperback.

A paperback version of your book (also called soft cover or perfect-bound) is required for readers who have not migrated to e-books. While this category of reader has dwindled drastically in past years, their numbers are still worth considering. You will also need a paperback version of your book if you want to give out autographed copies, display the book at book fairs and conferences, or see your book in bookstores or on library shelves. Bookstores are tough to get into—I have found the smaller independent bookstores much easier than the larger chains. With regard to libraries, I have never been turned down when offering to donate my books. If they do well, the library manager will order more copies from a distributor.

To reach an even broader audience, you may want to consider producing an audiobook in addition to the other formats. But it's not cheap, so try to estimate the ROI before investing in it. I've seen narrator rates range from $50 to $350 per hour. Seasoned audio-book narrators average 1.5 to 2 hours of work to produce 1 hour of reading. Assuming they read 9,000 words per hour, that would result in your spending between $675 and $4,725 for an 80,000-word book. Quite the range. Be aware that the less expensive narrators are not necessarily less qualified—they may be just starting out. So the advice here is to listen to their auditions, vet them, and then take price into consideration.

Hardcover (also called case-bound, hardback, and hardbound) is the least popular format in books due to their high cost to produce. Consider hardcover if any of the following is true:

- Presentation and durability are of utmost importance (photography and other art forms, cookbooks, some children's books).
- You can afford it (it costs more than double to print a hardcover book than a paperback).
- The high price-point will not deter consumers.
- It is expected because you are a celebrity.

The more formats you make available, the wider the audience you will reach. Estimate the ROI and make your decisions accordingly.

ISBN, ASIN, and LCCN Numbers

You've seen them listed here and there and wondered what they were and if you need them for your book. Here are their definitions and purposes in publishing.

An ISBN is an International Standard Book Number, ten digits in length up to the end of December 2006 and thirteen digits since January 1, 2007. The ISBN identifies the registrant as well as the specific title, edition, and format of your book and is essentially a product identifier used by publishers, booksellers, libraries, Internet retailers, and other supply-chain participants for ordering, listing, sales records, and stock control purposes.

The publisher of the book is the one who applies for the ISBN. For this purpose, the publisher is the group, organization, company, or individual responsible for initiating the production of the publication. Normally, it is also the person or entity who bears the cost and financial risk in making the product available. It can be the author of the book if the author has chosen to self-publish.

An ISBN is assigned to each edition and variation (except reprintings) of a book. Paperback, e-book, and hardcover versions of the same book require separate ISBNs.

You can purchase ISBNs from an affiliate of the International ISBN Agency, such as Bowker. (See myidentifiers.com.) Bowker's current cost is $125 if you purchase a single one and $295 if you purchase ten.

An Amazon Standard Identification Number (**ASIN**) is a unique block of ten letters and/or numbers that Amazon uses to identify items sold on their website. You can find the ASIN on any Amazon item's product information page at Amazon.com alongside further details relating to the item, which for books includes information such as number of pages, publication date, and sales ranking. Once you submit your book for sale on Amazon, it will be assigned an ASIN for each version of the book available (paperback, e-book, audio, hardcover).

The Library of Congress Catalog Control Number **LCCN** is a unique identification number that the Library of Congress assigns to the record created for each book in its cataloged collections. Librarians use it to locate a specific record in the national databases and to order catalog cards from the

Library of Congress or from commercial suppliers. When printed inside the book, the LCCN facilitates access to the bibliographic record for that book and thereby expedites book processing by libraries and book dealers who obtain copies of the book. (See loc.gov/publish for more information.)

SUGGESTED READING:

Feuerberg, Nathan. San Miguel Writers' Conference and Literary Festival (blog): *Self-Publishing vs Traditional Publishing.* https://sanmiguelwritersconference.org/self-publishing-vs-traditional-publishing/.

Friedman, Jane. Jane Friedman (blog): *The Complete Guide to Query Letters.* https://www.janefriedman.com/query-letters/.

Jenkins, Jerry. Jerry Jenkins (blog): *How to Publish a Book.* https://jerryjenkins.com/how-to-publish-a-book/.

Penn, Joanna. The Creative Penn (blog): *Pros and Cons of Traditional Publishing versus Self-Publishing.* https://www.thecreativepenn.com/self-publishing-vs-traditional/.

CHAPTER 23

Book Titles, Covers, and Innards

> *When you boil it down, a book title is a business decision.*
> — BETHANY ATAZADEH

New authors in particular are so anxious to get their book published after they have written the final chapter that they rush through the title-selection process, cover design, and the interior pages required before and after the main text of the story. While it's understandable you want to publish your book as soon as possible, I advise giving these components of your book considerable attention to make your book all that it can be.

Titles

Your title—the book's calling card, so to speak—introduces readers to the world of your book and can have a significant impact on the book's success.

Consider these book titles:

Beloved
Blood Dazzler
Brother, I'm Dying
The Catcher in the Rye
The Da Vinci Code
The Dressmaker's Gift
The Eagle Has Landed
The Girl with the Dragon Tattoo
Harry Potter and the Deathly Hallows
Jonathan Livingston Seagull
Little Voices
The Lord of the Rings
A Message to Garcia
A Naked Singularity (self-published)
She
Slammed (self-published)
Sophie's World
Still Alice (self-published)
Switched (self-published)
And Then There Were None
To Kill a Mockingbird
Valley of the Dolls
War and Peace
Watership Down
Where the Crawdads Sing

What do they all have in common? They're intriguing, I would argue, and they each represent an award-winning book. Was the title the reason they won an award? Maybe not entirely...but I'm sure it helped.

You get only one shot at stimulating interest for book browsers at first glance, so it is important to create a title that catches their attention. You want your book to jump off the shelf (or web page) ahead of the competition.

Here are some concepts for finding the right title.

EMOTION. Readers love emotional stories, and what better way to let them know that yours is full of emotion than by giving it an emotion-laden title, like William Faulkner's *As I Lay Dying.*

GENRE. Diehard, one-genre readers will gravitate to titles they know is within their area of interest just by reading the title. Consider *Murder on the Orient Express* by Agatha Christie, for example.

TONE. Determine the tone of your book and use it for the title. Elif Batuman's title for his novel, *The Idiot,* hints at the wry tone of the narrator.

MEMORABILITY. Since word of mouth is still one of the most effective marketing tools, you want readers to remember your book so they can talk about it with others. Who could ever forget the title of George Orwell's *1984* after hearing it?

ONE WORD. One-word titles can be very effective, as in *Less* by Andrew Sean Greer and *Milkman* by Anna Burns.

PHRASE FROM THE BOOK. A phrase from your book, especially from a pivotal scene, will potentially draw in the reader, as in *Much Ado About Nothing* by William Shakespeare or *Catch-22* by Joseph Heller.

PLAY ON WORDS. Many books have included a clever play on words, such as *Czech Please.* (There is no book by this title—I just made it up.)

INTRIGUE. Create intrigue with your title, as in *The Girl Who Fell from the Sky* by Heidi W. Durrow.

A CLICHÉ. Clichés, while not recommended in writing, can make good titles, as in *Still Waters* by Viveca Sten and Marlaine Delargy.

HIDDEN MEANING. Keep your readers guessing at the meaning of your title with something like *Lost Roses* by Gunter Grass.

A PERSON'S NAME. Many authors have been successful with the protagonist's name in the title. *Eleanor Oliphant Is Completely Fine* by Gail Honeyman, for example.

THE NAME OF A PLACE. A place name might work well as a title, especially if it has other connotations. Consider *Cemetery Road* by Greg Iles.

THE NAME OF AN EVENT. *The Reckoning* turned out to be a memorable title for John Grisham's book.

SHORT AND CATCHY. This is another way to keep people remembering your book. Just think of *Butterfield 8* by John O'Hara.

CONTRASTING TERMS. Contrasting terms can be effective, as in *Dangerous Liaisons* by Peirre Choderlos De Laclos. Or *Big Little Lies* by Liane Moriarty.

SPUNKY/FUN. Or just make it fun, like Catharina Ingelman-Sundberg did with *The Little Old Lady Who Broke All the Rules*.

Here are some ways to come up with a good title for your book:

MAKE A LIST. Select several of the nouns and verbs from the synopsis or plot points from your story, make a list of them, and go from there. For example, consider these key words:

cowboy	shoot
Oklahoma	trick
rodeo	aim
gamble	murder

Now consider this list of possible combinations for a title:

Murder in Oklahoma
His Last Rodeo
The Rodeo Shooting
A Cowboy's Gamble
Taking Aim at the Cowboy

BRAINSTORM WITH FAMILY AND FRIENDS. Write down every title that is thrown out by them, even those that initially sound wrong. Then narrow down the list by process of elimination. Once you think you have a viable title, do an Amazon search for similar titles—when people are searching for your book, you don't want them to pull up twenty other books with similar titles.

USE AN ONLINE TITLE GENERATOR. There are many online book-title generators, such as the ones listed in this article writerswrite.com/bookpublishing/title-generators/. If you don't find an auto-generated one you like, perhaps you'll be inspired by the ones that come close.

Here are some more tips when it comes to choosing a book title:

• Don't be too wordy. Book browsers tend to lose interest after five words.
• Be unique.
• Don't give away the plot or too much of the story with the title.
• Avoid cutesy and trite titles unless your story line fits it.

- Before you announce it anywhere, live with the title for a while. See how it feels, how it sounds in a sentence. Make sure it's the right fit.
- Don't rush the process. It's too important.

Your book's title should complement the cover image—they work hand in hand to show what genre the book is in. If they don't, you run the risk of disappointing or confusing readers.

Always get feedback on your chosen title from others who have read a draft copy of the book. A fresh pair of eyes can often confirm your choice or provide inspiration for a new one.

Front Covers

The cover of a book provides potential readers with a first impression and is therefore one of the most important aspects of marketing the book as a product. Ideally, it signals something about the book that will make readers want to buy it, so you would be wise to spend time developing just the right one. If you want to test this theory, just ask readers how they choose the books they buy. If they're typical, they look at the front cover for no more than a few seconds, and then if their interest has been piqued, they go to the back cover. Some will go on to read the opening paragraph. If readers aren't hooked by then, they are not likely going to buy the book.

In addition to providing a visual image that relates to the book's content, a well-designed front cover is usually the first indication the reader has that the book is of high quality. It behooves you to take time to create a high-quality front cover that stands out in the crowd—bad or cheap-looking covers are a turnoff to most book browsers. When they see a bad cover, they immediately equate it to the contents of the book and wonder just how much time the author has put into the book itself—an unprofessional cover may be a sign of unprofessional writing.

You can design your own cover, but I warn you that most readers can spot homemade covers a mile away. Just as you should not be your own final editor, my advice is to not be your own cover designer. If your book is professionally written, it deserves a professional-looking cover.

You can spend anywhere from $50 to $1200 for a book cover, depending on how much creativity and detail you desire and the experience and knowledge of the designer. Most designers these days work with existing photography to create a cover, using images and photo-manipulating them to make the cover unique to your story. But there are other designers who do custom illustration by taking your idea and either hand-drawing or digitally illustrating the cover, making it completely unique. And then there are also designers who use both techniques by taking existing photos and digitally painting over them to customize the design further.

If you can't afford a professional designer, look into pre made pro fessionally designed covers, which are available for as little as $50. The challenge would be to find one that reflects your story.

Here are some general guidelines about cover design.

FONT SIZE NEEDS TO BE READABLE. For printed books, the font size used for the title and author name on the front cover should allow easy reading from eight feet away. Picture your book on the shelves in a busy bookstore. You want people to be able to read the title even if they aren't right in front of the shelf. The font should be easy on the eyes so it can be read quickly. Author name and other text should be set in a more standard serif or sans serif font that complements the title. The title and author name should be placed on a plain background for easy readability. (Since you will likely use a thumbnail-size image of your cover for various promotions, make sure the cover image and title are still visible when reduced to a smaller size.)

For e-books, the title must be readable on a person's smartphone, notebook, or computer screen.

FONT COLOR IS IMPORTANT. The font color shouldn't clash with the background color, the cover art, or the theme of the book, and it shouldn't stand out so much that it takes away from the other cover elements.

CONSIDER THE LITERARY GENRE. The font style, size, and color for the title should suit the genre of the book. Mystery readers expect to see something intriguing on the cover. Romance enthusiasts expect something heartfelt or sexy. Vampire lovers will expect to see blood...well, maybe. I don't read books about vampires, so I really don't know. Anyway, you get the idea. Draw them in with an illustration with which they can identify.

THE COVER IMAGE SHOULD REFLECT THE BOOK. We know the human eye is drawn to images, so having the right image on your cover is important. For fiction, the cover image should be a reflection of what is inside—giving the reader a quick idea of what to expect from reading the book—and the focus should be on the genre, tone, and emotion the reader is supposed to feel. (I know of one book-cover designer who will not create a cover without first reading the book. Most designers will at least ask for story highlights from the author and go from there.) An effective cover image will set the tone for the story line and entice the reader to turn the book over to read the back cover.

COLOR SCHEME SHOULD SET THE RIGHT MOOD. The overall color scheme of the cover can be instrumental in the feeling you convey to a prospective reader.

> Cool colors (green, blue, purple)—calming
> Pastels, bright and warm colors (yellow, orange, pinks, red)—happiness
> Bright colors—energizing
> Dark and muted shades—sadness, darkness

And did you know that of all the colors, in general more people choose blue as their favorite?

AVOID CLUTTER. When it comes to book-cover images, less is often better than more. Clutter will only frustrate the reader and send him or her off to look for something more concise and easier to interpret.

Here's the link to one cover designer's website (TugboatDesign.net) where you can view many professionally designed custom covers as well as a gallery of pre-made ones.

Back Covers

If an effective front cover serves to grab readers' attention and entice them to find out more about the book, an effective back cover—the 100 or so words that describe the story to the reader—will clinch the deal. What is on the back cover, if written well, will hook readers and convince them they *have* to buy your book. This sales pitch needs to live up to the same standard as the front cover.

There are several elements to consider.

Headlines
Headlines are immediate attention-grabbers. Keep them short and tight. Consider one or two, no more than three, short abrupt sentences.

> She thought she had met her Prince Charming. He had other plans.

> Most people would have called the police. Mary didn't.

> He treated her badly. She treated him worse. Revenge is sweet.

The Synopsis
Keep the synopsis of your story on the back cover short, no more than 100–150 words. Make it long enough for readers to understand the basic story line but short enough not to exceed their attention span or give away too much of the story.

Include the setting for your story, time period, basic plot, and what conflict the reader can expect for the protagonist. I include setting because many readers clearly do not like certain settings. For example, I know someone who will not read a book that takes place outside of the U.S., and I know someone else who does not like to read stories that aren't fairly current. Some readers look for these things, and if they are not clear from the back cover, they will not buy the book, or worse yet, they'll buy the book and be disappointed.

Now that the reader knows what the basic story line is, focus on what they will gain from reading the book. In the last line of the synopsis, talk about the essence of the book. What will they learn? What will they come away with? What emotion will they experience alongside the protagonist? Stir up their emotions. Leave readers wanting more. Give them a sense of what they'll walk away with, but never promise them something you don't deliver inside the book.

Keep the synopsis tight and make every word count. And never, ever give away the ending.

Here are a few synopses from back covers of successful, award-winning books.

Harry Potter and the Philosopher's Stone by J. K. Rowling

Till now there's been no magic for Harry Potter. He lives with the miserable Dursleys and their abominable son, Dudley. Harry's room is a tiny closet beneath the stairs, and he hasn't had a birthday party in eleven years.

But then a mysterious letter arrives by owl messenger: a letter with an invitation to an incredible place called Hogwarts School of Witchcraft and Wizardry. And there he finds not only friends, flying sports on broomsticks, and magic in everything from classes to meals, but a great destiny that's been waiting for him … if Harry can survive the encounter.

Message in a Bottle by Nicholas Sparks

Divorced and disillusioned about relationships, Theresa Osborne is jogging when she finds a bottle on the beach. Inside is a letter of love and longing to "Catherine," signed simply "Garrett." Challenged by the mystery and pulled by emotions she doesn't fully understand, Theresa begins a search for this man that will change her life. What happens to her is unexpected, perhaps miraculous—an encounter that embraces all our hopes for finding someone special, for having a love that is timeless and everlasting....

The Girl on the Train by Paula Hawkins

Rachel takes the same commuter train every morning and night. Every day she rattles down the track, flashes past a stretch of cozy suburban homes, and stops at the signal that allows her to daily watch the same couple breakfasting on their deck. She's even started to feel like she knows them. Jess and Jason, she calls them. Their life—as she sees it—is perfect. Not unlike the life she recently lost. Until today. And then she sees something shocking. It's only a minute until the train moves on, but it's enough. Now everything's changed. Unable to keep it to herself, Rachel goes to the police. But is she really as unreliable as they say? Soon she is deeply entangled not only in the investigation but in the lives of everyone involved. Has she done more harm than good?

Killing Floor by Lee Child

Ex-military policeman Jack Reacher is a drifter. He's just passing through Margrave, Georgia, and in less than an hour, he's arrested for murder. Not much of a welcome. All Reacher knows is that he didn't kill anybody. At least not here. Not lately. But he doesn't stand a chance of convincing anyone. Not in Margrave, Georgia. Not a chance in hell.

The book description on your back cover is the pitch to the reader about why they should buy your book. It is sales copy to get them to see that the book is for them (or not) and then make a purchase decision. Take time to do it right. Treat it the same way you do the inside story—get feedback from others and have it professionally edited. Or even better, seek assistance from a professional copywriter. It's that important.

Reviews

Positive reviews sell books. If you have room, include on the back cover a few one-sentence excerpts from reviews you've received, especially if they are from credible reviewers or people who relate to your book in some way. Avoid quotes from friends and family members—if that's all you have at the time of publication, best to include none. I generally don't have any bona fide reviews before my books are published, so I publish the book without them at first and then pay a small fee to have the back cover revised to include them at a later date.

Author Bio

If you don't have reviews before your book goes to print, and you have room, you may want to include your bio and professional head shot on the back cover instead of elsewhere in the book. Readers like to have a visual image of the author, and what better place to put it than on the back cover. Include writing achievements and interesting facts about yourself. Do not include education unless it is related to writing, or hobbies unless they are related to the story.

E-books

While e-books don't typically include a back cover, I recommend you design and post an image of one (Amazon allows you to do this and possibly other booksellers), as there is no reason to miss out on this valuable sales tool. If you publish in both paperback and e-book and use Amazon to market them, you can link the two formats so that the back cover from the paperback is easily attainable for the e-book readers.

Book Innards

So now you have your front and back cover designed and the story sandwiched in between. There's more.

Paper Color

Most printers will offer at least two color options for the print version of your book—white and ivory. I prefer white for contemporary books and ivory for historical ones, but there is no right or wrong choice.

Font Size

Choosing a font size for the print version of your book is a bit of a balancing act. You want it small to keep the number of pages down (and printing costs lower), but you don't want to frustrate readers by making them strain to read the words. I am told by professional formatters that font size 12 is pretty standard.

E-books are a little different in that most e-readers have the ability to adjust the font size, but size 12 tends to be standard here as well.

Page Headers/Footers

There are several combinations of ways you can format the pages with headers and footers. For novels, I personally like my name on each left-hand page header and the title of the book on the right-hand side. And I like page numbers in the footers, close to the outer edge of the page. There's no rule on it—whatever you prefer.

Title Page

Keep the title page simple—the title of the book and your name are all that are required. Use this page for your autograph in your paperback and hardcover formatted books.

Copyright, Product Identifier, and Disclaimer Page

Years ago, copyright law required writers to register their work with The U. S. Copyright Office for the work to be protected. This is no longer the case. As soon as you put your writing into any type of form (whether it is handwritten, or on a pad of paper, hard drive, smart phone, or any other recording device) you own the copyright to that work and are protected by copyright law. Being protected by copyright law means you have the exclusive right to promote and distribute the work, reproduce it in other forms, and create derivative works from it (adaptations, sequels, translations, and abridgements).

You are no longer required to identify your work as copyrighted, but it's a good idea to do this as an added protection. Include the following information when declaring copyrighted work:

> The symbol © or word 'Copyright'
> Year of first publication
> Name of copyright owner
> The phrase "All Rights Reserved"

While not a requirement to be legally protected, you may still want to register your work with The U. S. Copyright Office, as it establishes a public, searchable record of your work. Registration only becomes a requirement in the event you wish to file an infringement lawsuit against someone.

Next come the ISBN and LCCN numbers and your disclaimer statement, which should look something like this:

> ISBN-13: XXX-X-XXXXXXX-X-X
> ISBN-10: X-XXXXXXX-X-X
> LCCN: XXXXXXXXXX

> This is a work of fiction. Names, characters, places, and incidents are either the product of the author's imagination or are used fictitiously. Any resemblance to actual persons (living or dead), business establishments, events, or locales is entirely coincidental.

Acknowledgements Page

Writing a book often involves assistance from others—people who were the source of valuable information that you used, editors, graphic designers, illustrators, beta readers, formatters, proofreaders, as well as those whose support during the process was greatly appreciated.

An acknowledgements page gives you the opportunity to show your appreciation for their help and give them credit for their contribution.

Keep it short and sweet—one page is usually enough. Take a look at the acknowledgement pages of other books in your genre to get a feel for how they are typically crafted.

Dedication Page

There are times when a dedication page is appropriate, most often when there is someone extraordinarily special in your life without whom you wouldn't have been able to write the book. Or you may want to dedicate your book in memory of someone. Dedications can be sentimental, funny, cryptic, or touching. Dedications are typically just one sentence in length.

Review Request

I like to include a review request on the page immediately following the end of the story—when the story is still fresh in the reader's mind. Feel free to use the one I composed for some of my books:

> I hope you enjoyed reading TITLE OF BOOK and will consider posting a short review on Amazon and/or Goodreads. Reviews and word-of-mouth referrals play an important role in helping authors promote their books, and your help in this regard is much appreciated.

Other Books

Your current book is a good opportunity to promote your other books. I do this after the review request. For each book, I include a brief synopsis, an excerpt from my favorite review, and purchase information.

About the Author

A page that tells readers a little about you can have a big impact. Include a photo so they can put a face to your name. Keep it short and light. Include humor and interesting facts about yourself. Include your contact information and links to your website, blog, Amazon and Goodreads author pages, and social media pages. I've seen author pages at the beginning of books and at the end. I prefer to place mine on the last printed page of the book.

SUGGESTED READING:

Chesson, Dave. "Seven Tools for Creating Superb Best-Selling Book Titles." Write to Done. (No date.) https://writetodone.com/bestselling-book-titles-2/.

Chesson, Dave. Kindlepreneur (blog): *How to Create a Back Book Cover That Sells.* https://kindlepreneur.com/back-book-cover-blurb/.

Penn, Joanna. The Creative Penn (blog): *Book Cover Design.* https://www.thecreativepenn.com/bookcoverdesign/.

Sansevieri, Penny. Author Marketing Experts (blog): *Book Cover Design Tips for Your Next Release.* https://www.amarketingexpert.com/10-book-cover-rules/.

Shiau, Yvonne (Content Marketer USA). Reedsy Blog: *Generating Book Titles—10,000 Book Titles to Inspire You.* https://blog.reedsy.com/book-title-generator/.

CHAPTER 24

Elevator Speeches, Blurbs, and Synopses

I f you are an author who wants to sell books, then you also need to be a salesperson, and as a salesperson it is important to have a few brief "commercials" readily available to promote your product. You need to know how you'll respond to someone who says, "Tell me about your book" because that someone could be in a position to help you promote it, write a review for it, choose it for their book club, or tell their big-time screenwriter brother-in-law about it (hey, it could happen). You never know when or where your next valuable connection will present itself, so be prepared.

First, some definitions:

> **ELEVATOR SPEECH:** A twenty- to thirty-second verbal statement about your book—taking no longer than your average elevator ride between two floors—that provokes interest in your work and solicits questions about the story line.

BLURB: Used for promotional purposes to entice readers, a blurb is a brief written description of the story line including one or more of the following: hint of the plot; theme of the story line; mood of the story line; setting; potential problems facing the main character; and insight into the main character. A blurb is what is typically found on the back cover of a book and on promotional sites.

SYNOPSIS: A summary of the major points of the story line.

Elevator Speech

When I was writing my first book, a friend of mine asked me what it was about. I clumsily went on and on about the story line until even I began losing interest. Lesson: It's never too early to have your elevator speech ready.

When creating your pitch, keep in mind that when someone asks you what your book is about, what they're really asking is, "Why would anyone be interested in your book?"

Authors will tell you it's far more difficult to write an elevator speech than the book itself—it's challenging to condense the essence of the story into a few sentences that will make the listener both grasp the story line and be enticed by it. I've written and rewritten my elevator speeches numerous times until I thought they were just right.

Here are some things to take into consideration for your elevator speech:

- Keep it short—one or two simple but powerful sentences.
- Use more nouns and verbs in your sentences than adjectives and adverbs.
- Introduce the protagonist (main character) and his or her initial situation.
- Add what the protagonist wants, his or her goal(s).
- Include an interesting roadblock, challenge, or conflict the protagonist faces.
- End with a hook—what is unique about the book, why people should be interested in it.

- Speak enthusiastically, with believability and a smile.
- Practice your speech in front of a friend, family member, or mirror. The words should roll off your tongue in a natural way. Then memorize it until you are reciting it in your sleep.

After you have delivered your elevator speech, stop talking. If you've done a compelling job with it, your audience will ask a question or make a comment. If you haven't, they will look at you as if to say, "So what?" If you get the latter reaction, it's time to go back and revise your speech.

Here are three examples of effective elevator speeches.

> **Example 1:** The title of my book is *Looking for Meinhard*, and it's the story of a terminally ill woman who searches for her long-lost brother, even though she's resentful of what he did to her years earlier.

> **Example 2:** *In My Shoes* is about a foreign-born young man coming to America searching for freedom, only to discover that freedom in America for an immigrant from Iran comes at a very high price.

> **Example 3:** *Safety Net* is the story of two sibling orphans who escape being rescued by the authorities during their year-long adventure on the seamier side of Chicago. What they learn is that being out on the streets of Chicago may be safer than living in someone's home, where they find more than just their lives are at stake.

Blurbs

Like an elevator speech, a written blurb is key to catching someone's attention and interest in your book. The blurb will showcase not only your book but also your writing style. Whether you're pitching to agents, editors, or readers, an effective blurb is a very important selling tool.

You will use all or part of your blurbs everywhere, and I say blurbs (plural) because you'll need more than one. You'll use them in your press release, on book-promotion sites, in interviews, on your website and social media pages, on the back cover of your book, and with agents and publishers. Your book blurbs should be ready to go as soon as possible—it's never too early.

I suggest starting with four blurbs, each containing the same general information but in varying lengths and level of detail.

> **400–500 WORDS** — This would be an appropriate length to send to agents and publishers.
>
> **150–200 WORDS** — You will find this length suitable for most promotion sites and interviews.
>
> **100–150 WORDS** — This one is about the right length for your back cover.
>
> **50 WORDS OR LESS** — This one will typically be one sentence, even shorter than your elevator speech, and is the one you can use in advertisements.

It will make things easier if you start with the longest one, because once it's written, all you have to do to create the shorter ones is delete and tighten. If you are asked to submit a blurb that is somewhere in between, it will be very easy to shorten or lengthen an existing one to suit that need.

You might think it's impossible to boil down your several-hundred-page book to a single page, let alone one sentence, but it's not. Here are some tips:

1. Check out movie blurbs on movies.com or any other movie site. They do a good job at reducing the essence of a two-hour movie to a few well-written sentences.
2. Get ideas from the back covers of books in your genre. Take note of what captures your attention.
3. Without giving away too much, include the following in your blurb:
   • The setting (time period and place)
   • Thumbnail description of the major characters

- What the protagonist wants and why he/she wants it (the bare bones of your story)
- Conflicts, roadblocks, or challenges the protagonist may encounter along the way
- What's at stake for the protagonist
- The change that occurs for the protagonist between the beginning and the end

The writing style for your blurb should be clean and tight. Focus on action, not descriptions of things. Avoid writing about the sequence of events. Instead, write about the main character—his or her emotions, fears, and excitement. Include twists and turns without giving away the whole story.

Be sure to include the incident that gets things moving, without giving away the whole story or the ending. And talk about the protagonist's conflicts—interior and exterior.

Try to make the blurb interesting, intriguing, and compelling.

Synopses

A book synopsis—a summary of the major points of the story—is most often requested by an agent, publisher, or book-cover designer because they are interested in knowing the story from beginning to end, spoilers and all.

Just like you need several different blurbs, you also need several different synopses. But unlike blurbs, I don't think you need four. I would write two, and if you need one of a different length later, you can edit down one of them. I would start with creating one with 400–500 words and another with 100–150 words.

A synopsis tells the story in a condensed form by touching on the major points of the story including the ending. Synopses do not include hooks, themes, conclusions, or the promise of anything. Just the facts.

Here is an example of a book synopsis that includes just the plot points of the book.

The Goldfinch by Donna Tartt

At age thirteen, Theodore Decker goes to the Metropolitan Museum of Art with his mother to see an exhibit of Dutch masterpieces. He especially likes a painting, *The Goldfinch* by Carel Fabritius, but a young redheaded girl named Pippa also catches his eye.

An explosion hits the museum and kills his mother. While Theo stumbles around in the rubble, an old man gives him a ring and encourages him to take *The Goldfinch* with him.

After finding the man who gave him the ring and returning it, Theo goes to Las Vegas to live with his dad and his dad's girlfriend, bringing with him the painting but telling no one about it. There, he befriends Boris. When his dad is killed in a drunk driving accident, Theo heads to New York, still hiding the painting, where he contacts the old man's business partner, Hobie, who invites him to stay with him.

Theo becomes partners in Hobie's antiques business, with plans to marry his old friend Kitsey, although he cannot get Pippa out of his mind. In an effort to save the antique business, Theo sells fake antiques and is faced with blackmail over one of his dishonest deals. The blackmailer connects *The Goldfinch* painting with Theo and threatens him further. Theo falls apart when he discovers his fiancée is in love with someone else and his friend Boris has stolen *The Goldfinch* and traded it away.

Theo and Boris go to Amsterdam to retrieve the painting. Things go awry when they steal the painting only to lose it again. In the process, Theo kills a man, and Boris is shot. Boris returns after saving the painting for the museum, and shares the reward with Theo.

Theo returns to New York and connects with his true love Pippa.

If properly written, elevator speeches, blurbs, and synopses leave people feeling desperate to read the whole story. Do your book justice by spending the time to write the most effective statements possible, so you can share the end product of all your hard work with as many people as possible.

SUGGESTED READING:

Atwood, Margaret. "How to Write a Novel Synopsis—A Step-By-Step Guide." MasterClass August 13, 2019. https://www.masterclass.com/articles/how-to-write-a-novel-synopsis-step-by-step-guide#quiz-0.

Bumgarner, Lori. "The Best Way to Write an Elevator Speech." The Writing Cooperative. (No date.) https://writingcooperative.com/the-best-way-to-write-an-elevator-speech-b8a708e863fa.

Shiau, Yvonne. Reedsy Blog: *How to Write a Book Blurb: A Guide for Novelists.* https://blog.reedsy.com/write-blurb-novel/.

CHAPTER 25

Reviews, Assessments, and Testimonials

REVIEW: a descriptive and critical evaluation of the book's content, style, and merit that gives prospective readers an indication of what the book is about and the reviewer's opinion as to its quality.

ASSESSMENT: an evaluation of the book provided by a qualified assessor based on preestablished assessment criteria. Criteria may include but is not limited to story/plot structure, characterization, writing style, and technical accuracy.

TESTIMONIAL: a recommendation given by a satisfied reader, voluntarily or upon the author's request, that affirms the value of the book.

P ositive reviews, assessments, and testimonials of your book can be your best sales tools as you can periodically post excerpts from them on your website, blog, social media sites, and anywhere else you have exposure. I wrote this article for The Book Designer website back in 2015 about what professional book reviewers look for when rating a book. It still holds true. thebookdesigner.com/2015/09/florence-osmund/

Listed below are ways to secure reviews, assessments, and testimonials for your books, both paid and unpaid.

Trade Publication Reviews

Trade publication reviews are the ones taken seriously by booksellers, librarians, and others who make book-buying decisions based (in part) on reviews. The top four trade publications that offer reviews are *Kirkus Reviews, Library Journal, Publishers Weekly,* and *Midwest Book Review.* With the exception of *Midwest Book Review,* all of these publications charge a fee, some of them hefty, so think about the potential ROI before you decide to go this route. *Kirkus,* for example, currently charges between $475 and $575 for a review. A positive book review by a prominent reviewer such as *Kirkus* may help you gain exposure and credibility for your book, but be aware that you aren't guaranteed a positive review. In the case of a negative review, some publications give authors the option of not having the review published in their book review section or posted on their website and other places, while others publish and post all reviews regardless of the outcome. Currently, *Kirkus Reviews* and *Publishers Weekly* will not publish or post a review without author consent. *Library Journal* and *Midwest Book Review* publish and post reviews without seeking author consent.

Amazon and Goodreads Reviews

The largest groups of book reviews exist on Amazon and Goodreads (Amazon has owned Goodreads since 2013), so when readers tell you they enjoyed your book, it behooves you to ask them if they would write a short review on one or both of these sites. A positive book review on Amazon, in particular, is invaluable. Potential book buyers read reviews! If you can get ten or more positive, impartial reviews immediately following your book launch, your book will benefit from it. Consider reviews a gratuitous marketing tool—the life of a positive review is much longer than any content you could create.

Goodreads states its mission as "to help people find and share books they love." Readers can search this site for the types of books they like and, based on reviews and other factors, decide to purchase them. It's that simple. According to Goodreads, reviews on their site help your book stand out in two ways—by helping new readers discover your book and by re-posting reviews on sites such as Powell's, Google Books, and the Sony Ebook Store. They claim that books with no written reviews are added to an average of only seven readers' Want to Read list, while books with just five written reviews are added by more than forty people.

My goal for each of my books has always been to have more five-star reviews than four-star ones, more four-star reviews than three-star ones, etc. So far, I have been able to accomplish this. I believe it's a reasonable goal to have for an author.

Testimonials

Equally as effective as reviews, testimonials are a powerful, free marketing tool to spread the word about your book. Consumers tend to believe other people over the "seller" of the product, and because a testimonial means that the person giving it is putting their own reputation on the line, potential readers are able to hear from an impartial person about the book's merits. In an industry with so many choices for readers, books with one or more testimonials included on the back cover have a competitive advantage over books without them, especially if the testimonial comes from someone well-known and/or credible in the industry.

Testimonials are generally short—one or two sentences usually suffice. Here are three examples of effective testimonials:

> *Memoirs of a Geisha* by Arthur Golden—*Memoirs of a Geisha evokes all the delicate steel of Kyoto's geisha culture with such uncanny fidelity that, after you've finished, you feel as if you've entered not just another world, but an extraordinary and foreign heart.*—Pico Iyer

The Pact by Jodi Picoult—*Anyone who doubts that there is any more vivid, original fiction being written must read The Pact. Jodi has written a truly fine book, a piece of total contemporary America.*—Anne Rivers Siddons

Bufflehead Sisters by Patricia J. DeLois—*A mesmerizing coming-of-age tale, Ms. DeLois has gotten it just right.* —Lesley Kagen

To get the most from testimonials, publish them on the back cover of your book, post them on social media, and include them on your Amazon and Goodreads book description pages.

Freebie in Exchange for a Review or Testimonial

It is acceptable to offer a free book to someone in exchange for a review. What you hope for is a reviewer who highlights the things you did well and constructively states where they think the book needs improvement. But you don't always get that, so be aware that you may get back something that you don't want others to see. Technically referred to as ARCs (Advanced Review Copy), the practice of giving away a book in exchange for an honest review was originally established by publishers who sent free copies of books to booksellers, librarians, and journalists for review in advance of publication. Today, individual authors do this. Unfortunately, some authors abuse this free-book-review process to influence the review—*"I'll give you a free book if you give me a positive five-star review."* Because of this, Amazon requires reviewers who have received a free copy of the book in advance to state this up-front in their review. So if you use this method, be sure to advise the reviewers that you are seeking honest, unbiased reviews and they are under no obligation to leave a positive review, or taking it a step further, that they are under no obligation to leave a review at all.

Another common practice to get books into readers' hands is to conduct giveaways and contests. As with ARC campaigns, if the contest obligates a reader to review the book in order to participate or the winner to review the book, then the reviews are biased and the campaign viewed as unethical. So, make it clear to the winner that while you certainly appreciate a review, they are under no obligation to post one.

Free Review Sites

Numerous sites exist that will post an honest review for your book free of charge. Here is one link that lists quite a few of them. publishersweekly.com/pw/by-topic/authors/pw-select/article/73538-the-indie-author-s-guide-to-free-reviews.html. I like local sites like Windy City Reviews in Chicago. Google your town to see what's available. The same precaution exists as for paid sites—you are never guaranteed a good review. And if you are, do not consider them.

Reader Reviews from Individual Paid Readers

There are independent readers who charge a fee to write a review for your book. Amazon considers it unethical to pay for reader reviews and is actively trying to curb this practice. I do not recommend paying a reader to write a review.

Blatantly Fake Reviews

There used to be quite a few services that guaranteed a certain number of positive reviews for a price. While these scam services have dwindled now that Amazon has taken a hard line against paid reviews by removing them and suing such unethical services, some scam companies still exist and are willing to take your money in exchange for a positive review. Paying for fake reviews is not only deceptive and unethical, it is illegal in that they defraud customers by encouraging them to purchase a product they otherwise might not. Don't do it.

Book Vetting Services

You can get reviews and/or assessments from organizations that specialize in book-vetting services and often provide authors with exposure for their books as part of their campaign to support self-published authors. Examples: indieBRAG, Awesome Indies, Ascribe, and The indiePEN-dents. Some charge an administrative fee for an assessment/review, and others do not.

The not-for-profit indieBRAG organization brings together a large group of readers—both individuals and book clubs. With reviewers located throughout the United States, Canada, and the European Union, BRAG (Book Readers Appreciation Group) states its mission as "recognizing quality on the part of authors who self-publish both print and digital books." Books submitted are read and evaluated by a number of reviewers and judged using a proprietary list of criteria—the single most important criterion being whether or not they would recommend the book to their best friend. Once a book unanimously meets this standard of quality from at least three reviewers, they award the book their B.R.A.G. Medallion. Less than 15 percent of books submitted receive this honor, so if you submit your book and become an honoree, you can use it proudly to help promote your book. They currently charge an administrative fee for this service.

Awesome Indies is a not-for-profit accreditation service that approves independently published works of fiction that meet the same standards as books published by mainstream publishers (in the opinions of publishing industry professionals who evaluate them). "We aim to showcase books that meet a specific set of standards for fiction writing so readers can browse for indie books knowing they will be buying well-crafted works." They currently do not charge a fee for this service.

Ascribe allows self-published authors to submit their books that include a recommendation from somebody who is acknowledged as an expert by their peers (literary agents, consultants, editors, or certain other published authors). They then post details of the novel for others to consider for purchasing. They currently do not charge a fee for this service.

The indiePENdents recognizes the increasing number of low quality books tarnishing the reputation of authors who chose to self-publish and awards a "seal" to those in which the writing, editing, and presentation are equal to or above the standards found in traditional publishing. They currently do not charge a fee for this service.

Receiving a Bad Review

Every book, even best-selling ones, receives some bad reviews. It is inevitable—there is no way you can write a book that will please everyone's taste. If you accept this premise, you'll save yourself a lot of anguish. My advice is to ignore the one-off criticisms of your work. But if you receive repeat criticisms, consider them blessings in disguise. Learn from them so you don't make the same mistakes in your next book.

Always resist the urge to respond to a bad review. I have heard horror stories about authors getting completely hammered on certain sites for reacting to a bad review. It's a jungle out there—don't set yourself up for a possible massacre.

Bogus Reviews

Whatever you do, do NOT pay someone to post bogus reviews on Amazon or any other site. Not only is this dishonest and less than honorable, but you'd only be fooling yourself about the quality of your writing.

SUGGESTED READING:

Craig, Emerson Rose. "Why Are Book Reviews Important for Authors?" This Is Writing. (No date.) https://thisiswriting.com/why-are-book-reviews-important-for-authors/.

Penn, Joanna. "Book Marketing: 10 Ways To Get Reviews For Your Book." The Creative Penn. (No date.) https://www.the creativepenn.com/2017/07/29/how-to-get-book-reviews-as-an-unknown-author/

Thorn, Patti. "How to Get Book Reviews for Your Self-Published Book." IngramSpark. (No date.) https://www.ingramspark.com/blog/book-review-checklist-what-to-do-before-submitting-for-review.

PART 4

Marketing and Promotion

Unless you're a celebrity, famous author, or just an average writer who caught some lucky breaks, in order to be successful, know that you will have to spend as much time marketing your books as you did to write them.

CHAPTER 26

Fundamentals of Book Marketing

I f you thought writing a novel was hard, wait until you see what is involved in getting people to notice it. Even the best-written book will not succeed if no one knows it exists and where to purchase it. With hundreds of thousands of new titles published each year, authors need to focus on effective marketing and promotion more now than ever. So remove your writer hat, under which you were allowed to be somewhat reclusive with your brilliant thoughts, and put on your marketing and promotion hat to test your public persona and salesmanship skills.

Many of the approaches discussed in the succeeding chapters are cost-free, except for your time, so try as many as you can. Keep in mind that it's difficult to predict which of the strategies will pay off for you—sometimes book sales happen as a result of a combination of two or more different strategies. And if you've implemented many different strategies simultaneously, like most of us do, it's not always obvious which ones had the most effect. I personally find this to be the most frustrating aspect of selling books.

I learned in business school about the four elements of marketing: product, place, price, and promotion. This holds true for us authors.

Product = our books
Place = where our books are available for purchase
Price = that sweet spot where we'll earn the most profit
Promotion = everything we do to reach prospective readers

I mention this because being an author is like running a business. You have to produce a quality product, let people know it's for sale for a reasonable and competitive price, and promptly deliver it.

While this part of author life may not seem as exciting or creative as the writing part, it is essential. You can't succeed without it.

There are five elements most fundamental to a successful book promotion.

1.   Good-quality product
2.   Well-targeted audience
3.   Title and cover design that draw attention
4.   Back-cover blurb that entices readers to buy the book
5.   Competitive pricing

Good-Quality Product

Unlike with traditionally published books, self-published titles have no quality-control mechanisms in place, and some authors are merely uploading a Word document to Amazon to get published. That's unfortunate, as it puts many poor-quality books out there and gives self-published authors in general a bad name. Please don't be one of these authors. The successful self-published authors I know work hard to write and rewrite a manuscript until it is as polished as they can make it, and then they hire professional editors and cover designers.

The traditional publishers expect that only a handful of the titles they publish each year will be big sellers. They publish a manageable number of books in the hope that one or two will take off and generate a nice profit. The situation is similar with self-published titles—only a few will go on to be best-sellers. A book that is badly written, unconventionally structured, poorly proofread, and full of technical errors and typos has little chance becoming a big success and will most likely fail altogether.

I can't emphasize this enough—all the marketing in the world will not sell a badly written book. At the very least, I recommend investing in a professional proofreader. But if you're serious about writing, you'll hire an editor. (See Chapter 21 for more on editors.) Strive to make your finished product flawless—one you're proud to call your own.

Target Audience

Knowing your target audience is extremely important. Forget the notion that you've written a book everyone will love—it's never been done and never will be. Without a solid grasp of who will read and like your book, you will waste time, energy, and money promoting your work to the wrong market. Or worse yet, you will receive negative attention and reviews from people who had no chance of ever liking it.

Once you have a description of your ideal reader, it becomes easier to please them—both in your writing and marketing. Start by understanding genres, as they each appeal to a different set of readers. Even if your book falls within multiple genres, you can still narrow your target audience to a more manageable number. If you're not certain of your genre, find a comparable book online or in a bookstore to see where it has been categorized.

There doesn't appear to be a nice, neat chart of who reads which genres, but after perusing many articles and opinions on the subject, I can offer the following compilation of reader demographics I found for a few of the current most popular genres.

- Crime/Thrillers—A fairly even split between male and female readers with more males reading books written by males with male protagonists, and females reading books written by females with female protagonists. Reader age range is typically 15 to 40 years old.
- Literary Fiction—Twice as many females as males. 30 to 55 years old.
- Fantasy—Slightly more females than males. 15 to 35 years old.
- Science Fiction—Slightly more males than females. 15 to 35 years old.

- Historical—Twice as many males as females. 18 to 40 years old.
- Horror—Twice as many males as females. 18 to 40 years old.
- Romance—Primarily females. 30 to 55 years old.
- Books in General—Three times as many female readers as males. 18 to 29 years old seems to be the largest group (a surprise to me—I would have thought older).

The size of your target audience is important, as it is difficult to write a book with wide appeal. Even very successful authors don't attempt to write overly broad books. The old adage that trying to please everyone leads to pleasing no one is particularly relevant here. With readers having access to virtually any book at any time, it's hard enough to make a single book stand out to people who are interested in your genre, let alone to the masses. If you write for and create your marketing campaign toward a targeted group of people, they will purchase enough copies of your book to make it successful. Anyone else who happens to purchase your book is a bonus. The goal is to reach people who will become loyal fans. Write for an audience that is too broad, and you wind up writing something that is generic and will have to face a lot of competition.

Trying to appeal to the masses instead of understanding the needs, wants, and desires of readers of a particular genre usually doesn't work. Authors tend to do well with a narrow niche audience—one that gives them a better chance of finding loyal fans and the most effective channels for reaching them.

Title and Cover Design

I talk more about the creation of title and cover design in Chapter 23. The front cover is the first impression people have of your book, and so it's important to grab their attention quickly. Make sure the cover suits the genre of your book and stands out from the competition.

Back Cover Blurb

Keep the description tight. Include references to character emotion as well as story line. Use headlines to catch readers' attention. (The topic of creating effective back covers is discussed in detail in Chapter 23.)

Competitive Pricing

Determining the ideal price for your book is an extremely important aspect of marketing. Price it too low, and you run the risk of readers associating a low price with low quality. Price it too high, and you can price it right out of the market. Unfortunately, there's no magic formula for pricing. In the end, it boils down to positioning your book to be competitive, but other contributing factors include your experience as an author and the market demand for your subject matter.

It is imperative to know where competing books are priced, as they are vying for the attention of the same audience as yours. This is relatively easy to do by browsing the bookshelves on Amazon and in local bookstores. Look at books in the same genre, format (paperback, e-book, audio, and hardcover), and trim size as yours and that are of similar length. Pricing your book slightly lower than the others, especially if you are a new author, may give you a competitive edge.

When establishing the list price for paperback books, factor in how much it costs to print the book. In print-on-demand scenarios, the printing cost will be deducted from the retail price before your royalty is calculated, so you don't want to price your book so low that the printing costs cut too far into your profit. You will want to make sure you're still making enough money with each book sale to meet your revenue goals.

If you publish your paperback book on Amazon, their submission tool helps guide you through the pricing process.

Here is a pricing scenario for one of my books. The cost to print this book is $3.59, and the royalty is 60%.

> If I price this book at $10, my royalty is $2.41.
> If I price it at $9, my royalty is $1.81.
> If I price it at $8, my royalty is $1.21.

Amazon's pricing guidelines for printed books will not allow me to price this book under $5.98 or above $250.00

IngramSpark also provides a pricing tool on its website myaccount. ingramspark.com/Portal/Tools/PubCompCalculator that calculates how much you will earn from the sale of each copy of your book after entering your book's specifications (trim size, interior color and paper types, binding style, number of pages, list price).

When pricing a book, one of the questions you will probably ask yourself is whether it will be more profitable to price it low and hope to sell more copies of it, or price it higher but perhaps sell fewer copies. Here are some overly simplified scenarios that assume a $4.00 print cost and 50% royalty.

> Price it at $10. If you sell 1,000 copies, your profit will be $3,000.
> Price it at $10. If you sell 1,500 copies, your profit will be $4,500.
> Price it at $10. If you sell 2,000 copies, your profit will be $6,000.
>
> Price it at $9. If you sell 1,000 copies, your profit will be $2,500.
> Price it at $9. If you sell 1,500 copies, your profit will be $3,750.
> Price it at $9. If you sell 2,000 copies, your profit will be $5,000.
>
> Price it at $8. If you sell 1,000 copies, your profit will be $2,000.
> Price it at $8. If you sell 1,500 copies, your profit will be $3,000.
> Price it at $8. If you sell 2,000 copies, your profit will be $4,000.

Similarly, when pricing e-books it's important to factor in what competitors are doing. One method to use to get started is to take the price you set for your paperback and subtract the cost of printing. Round this number off to the nearest dollar, and then subtract one cent. (Apparently, it's been proven that prices ending in odd numbers, especially .99 are more attractive to retail buyers than prices ending in other numbers.) Compare this price to that of your competition and adjust accordingly.

If you publish your e-book on Amazon, their royalty program (which presumably has been designed to optimize sales) may help you in your pricing decision. Amazon pays authors a 35 percent royalty for e-books priced between $0.99 and $2.98; a 70 percent royalty for e-books priced between $2.99 and $9.99; and a 35 percent royalty for e-books priced $10 and above.

Determining where to price your book is a bit of a crap shoot. My best advice is to keep current with what is taking place in the industry to see what is trending, and then go from there.

Once these five requirements have been met, you're ready to start marketing your book.

SUGGESTED READING:

Beckwith, Sandra. The Book Designer (blog): *3 Fiction Marketing Success Tips for 2020.* https://www.thebookdesigner. com/2019/12/3-fiction-marketing-success-tips-for-2020/.

Bolt, Chandler. Self-Publishing School (blog): *How to Market a Book: 2020 Book Marketing Strategies to SELL.* https://self-publishing school.com/book-marketing-how-to-skyrocket-sales-of-your-book/.

Wagner-Stafford, Boni. The Book Designer (blog): *Engineer Success with a Good Marketing Strategy.* https://www.thebookdesigner. com/2019/09/engineer-success-with-a-good-marketing-strategy/.

CHAPTER 27

The Book Launch

Without promotion, something terrible hap-
pens...nothing!

—P. T. BARNUM

The day has finally come—the most exciting day in your life and career as an author—the day your book is introduced to the world. After months, maybe years of writing, you now are able to hold it in your hands, and it's time to let readers know of its existence. Or better yet, you have a few months before it is published for some prepublication promotion.

And that, of course, is the key to selling books—people won't buy them if they don't know they exist. Your marketing journey starts with a successful book launch, one that will make people aware of your book so they will buy it and perhaps even help you promote it. In addition, a successful book launch will result in early sales that give your book momentum in the marketplace.

Regardless of whether you publish traditionally or self-publish, you can do many things to launch your book so that it gets into the hands of as many readers as possible. Following are some checklists to guide you through the process. But wait—I don't recommend that you attempt to do everything on these lists—you'll drive yourself crazy if you do. Pick out a manageable number of things you feel comfortable doing and that make sense for your book.

Oh, and above all, listen to P. T. Barnum...

The Big Three

The trick to efficient and effective book promotion is to target likely buyers—easier said than done, I know. But the sooner you get your book in the hands of as many people as you can, the more momentum your book launch will have. And this is important, especially if you market your book on Amazon. If people see that your book was published a year ago, for example, and you have only a few reviews, they could interpret that as no one is interested in your book. So why should they?

The most-likely people to buy your book are going to be your fans—the people who have signed up for your e-mail list who have indicated they want to know more about you as an author and when your next book is coming out. This group should be the most important group in your promotion strategy. (See Chapter 29 for more on e-mail subscriber lists.)

The second most-likely group of people who will buy your book are the ones who learn about it from your influencers. Influencers can be other authors, bloggers, podcasters, or industry gurus—people with whom you have made contact during your writing project who have significant followings. Working with influencers is a two-way street of course—you promote their books, websites, and/or services, and they return the favor in kind.

The third most-likely group of people to buy your book are your social media followers. While some people follow others just to rack up the number of people they follow, some actually follow a person because they are interested in them and/or what they have to offer.

Long Before Your Book Is Released

- Identify your influencers (those who can get others to buy your book).
- Write and memorize your elevator speech. (Chapter 24)
- Develop an author website. (Chapter 29)
- Start a blog. (Chapter 29)
- Establish yourself in discussion groups on social media sites. (Chapter 30)
- Start building an e-mail subscriber list comprised of people who are interested in your work. (Chapter 29)
- Create your profile on Goodreads and Amazon's Author Central page. (Chapter 30)
- Make a list of book-promotion and book-listing sites. (Chapter 31)
- Order business cards and hand them out whenever appropriate. (Chapter 32)
- Draft promotional materials (postcards, bookmarks, posters, etc.). (Chapter 32)
- Determine your target market and ways to reach them. (Chapter 1)
- Check out your competitors and see what they are doing to promote their books. (Chapter 28)

One Month Before Your Book Is Released

- Compose long, medium, and short synopses for your book. (Chapter 24)
- Write a press release or hire someone to write it. (Chapter 31)
- Draft a media-kit page for your website. (Chapter 31)
- Contact your influencers. (Chapter 27)
- Put out teasers on your website, blog, e-mail list, and social media.
- Participate in guest posts and online interviews. (Chapter 31)
- Plan a launch party/event. (Chapter 27)

- Set up a blog tour. (Chapter 29)
- Start soliciting book reviews. (Chapter 25)
- Investigate paid and free advertising on social media and other venues. (Chapters 30 and 35)
- Consider creating a book trailer. (Chapter 31)
- Set up preorder options with Amazon and other distribution sites.

One Week Before the Book Is Released

- Establish a list of people to whom you will gift a copy of your book. Draft a personal request asking them to help you promote the book by spreading the word and writing a review on Amazon and Goodreads.
- Consider launching a social media contest with your book as a giveaway prize.
- Promote your book by posting the first chapter on your website.
- Repeat teasers on your website, blog, e-mail list, and social media.
- Set up a Google alert for your name and book title.

Day of the Launch

- Headline the book release on your website.
- Go live with the media kit on your website.
- Send an announcement to your e-mail subscriber list.
- Post an announcement (better yet, pin it) on your social media pages, website, and blog.
- Post an announcement on the promotional pages of your social media groups.
- Update your author pages on social media and other sites.
- Update your e-mail signature line.
- Plan a book-launch event at bookstores or other retailers that sell books; cafés, restaurants, bars; outdoor parks; libraries; or in your home.

Post Launch

- Repeat any of the above that will keep your name and book title in front of readers.

All the Time

- Have your elevator speech ready when people ask you what your book is about.
- When people tell you they liked your book, ask them if they would write a short review on Amazon and Goodreads.
- Whenever you post something about your book on social media, tell your fans, followers, and friends to feel free to re-post.

If done well, a book launch will create interest, excitement, and momentum for your book. It will also help you establish your brand and credibility as an author.

There is no best way to launch a book. Choose activities you're most comfortable with from the lists above, work hard at what you do, and hope for the best.

SUGGESTED READING:

Bogan, Francis. BookBub Partners Blog: *11 Creative Ways Authors Announced Their Book Launch.* https://insights.bookbub.com/creative-ways-authors-announced-book-launch/.

Bradshaw, Claire. "9 Handy Tips for Planning a Successful Book Launch." Writer's Edit. (No date.) https://writersedit.com/self-publishing/9-handy-tips-planning-successful-book-launch/.

Penn, Joanna. The Creative Penn (blog): *Aspects of a Book Launch.* https://www.thecreativepenn.com/aspects-of-a-book-launch/.

CHAPTER 28

Marketing Plan

The work required to become a successful author doesn't stop with the book launch—you need to do ongoing promotion. Having a marketing plan in place before you publish, even a simple one that evolves over time, is an essential part of the process regardless of whether you self-publish or go the traditional publishing route. (If your book is traditionally published, your publisher's marketing campaign will generally not be enough.)

Elements of a good marketing plan include the following.

Goals

Written goals help you to see where you are going and what changes you need to make if you are not progressing the way you had planned. Defined targets put you on a direct course of action. Set reasonable goals for the following:

> **HOURS SPENT EACH DAY ON PROMOTION.** I commit full-time to publishing novels. I wish this meant I could spend all of my time writing, but it doesn't—far from it. I can commit four to six hours per day writing. I spend the remaining hours

of the day promoting myself and my books, responding to e-mails and other correspondence, maintaining my website, and dealing with other book-related activities.

NUMBER OF BOOKS PUBLISHED. Some publishers claim you will not be considered a serious novelist until you've published at least six books. I think this is a reasonable goal.

NUMBER OF BOOKS SOLD. The truth is that most self-published authors sell fewer than 100 copies of their books, and that's because they write mediocre books and then sit back and wait for people to buy them. I didn't want to be part of that club, so when I published my first book, my goal was to sell more than 100 copies. Now, seven books later, if I haven't sold 1,000 copies in the first three months (or had 1,000 pages per day read via Kindle's lending library), I look to see where I failed. It's difficult to set forth any guidelines on this, as each author will have his or her own specific goal depending on the situation.

AMOUNT OF MONEY EARNED. Some writers begin with how much money they need to earn to break even (number of books you need to sell before realizing a financial profit). In a very simple example, let's say you price your paperback book at $12.50, your fixed costs (editing and formatting services, cover design, etc.) come to $4,000, and your variable unit costs (the cost to print the book plus shipping) are $7.50. Assuming you are able to collect 100 percent of the royalties, you will need to sell 800 books to break even. If you publish in e-format and price the e-book at $3.00, the number of books sold to break even will increase to 1,333.

AMAZON/GOODREADS REVIEWS. As mentioned earlier, online reviews are among the main things that attract customers to your books. My goal is to receive at least 100 reviews during the first year of publication with more five-star reviews than four-star reviews, more fours than threes, and so on.

WEBSITE TRAFFIC. If you decide to sell your books primarily from a website, the amount of traffic you get is extremely important. Statistics say that on average, 10 percent of your visitors will buy your book. So, if your break-even point is 800 books, you'll need 8,000 website visitors to break even if that is your only point of sale.

SOCIAL MEDIA FOLLOWERS. The number of followers you have on Twitter, Facebook, Instagram, LinkedIn, and the like can strengthen your brand by establishing connections and building relationships that may result in selling more books. Check out authors you admire and see how many followers they have for an indication of where you stand against them.

GUEST BLOGS. Exposure helps to sell books, and contributing solid content to blogs that are followed by avid readers is an excellent way to get exposure. My goal is to contribute at least one post to a blog, website, or social media page per month.

Target Groups

To reach multiple readers who might be interested in your book, consider connecting with groups or associations who can identify with your protagonist and/or story line. For example, let's say your protagonist is biracial and has a difficult time fitting in. There are probably thousands of people out there who have experienced the same thing, and many of them belong to the Association for MultiEthnic Americans (AMEA) or subscribe to *MAVIN* magazine. On AMEA's website, they list recommended books (fiction and nonfiction) for their members, and *MAVIN* magazine has an e-library available for their subscribers. This would be a good opportunity to offer some freebies or a discount for members. Since there's a group out there for just about everything, this avenue is worth pursuing.

I signed up for a Google Alert whenever the title of one of my books appears on the Internet, and that's when I discovered there are quite a few restaurants around the country and in Europe named The Coach House, which is the title of my first book. This got me to thinking about the possibility of making connections with entities or people who have something in common with my books to pursue joint ventures that could benefit both parties. Don't be afraid to try ideas that seem a little far out there. You never know when something will stick.

The Competition

Gaining a greater insight into who you are competing with and how they succeed is a key strategy for improving your own results. No matter the genre, the competition is stiff in today's book market. I pulled these figures from Amazon to show what authors are up against for a few of the common genres.

- Romance: 80,000+ books for sale on Amazon
- Historical fiction: 50,000+
- Mysteries: 70,000+
- Fantasy: 70,000+
- Coming of Age: 60,000+

It pays to know your competition and understand what they're doing, as you can learn from them what to do when it comes to your own books. If you go to the Amazon website and type "books" in the search box, what comes up across the top of the screen is a list of genre categories. Click on one of them to see on the left-hand side of the screen how many books are in your category. On the main section of this screen is a list of all the books in that particular category. You might want to look at each one's page and figure out which are most similar to yours and will tend to attract the same readers.

You can tell a lot about authors and their books from their Amazon author page (their profile, book descriptions, how they rank), website (the types of pages they've created), social media pages (what they post), and by Googling them. Join their mailing list if they have one—see what they offer their fans. See where they price their books—to be competitive, you don't want to underprice or overprice your own. Check out your competitors' social media pages too. What do they do there that catches your eye? (Warning: If you check these pages for celebrity or best-selling authors, be prepared for very little content or content that has been prepared by someone else. It is better to focus on other authors for more instructive pages.)

Where Amazon ranks a competing book will give you an idea of that book's popularity, at least in the eyes of Amazon. The Amazon Sales Rank is a number that reflects a book's popularity—the smaller the number, the better the product is selling. The algorithm Amazon uses is proprietary, and while many have speculated on what factors Amazon takes into account to determine the sales rank, no one outside of Amazon knows for sure.

You can find rankings on each book by scrolling down to the bottom of the book's page. Lower rankings mean Amazon will give a book more visibility, which will result in more sales and an even better ranking.

Learn everything you can from your competition—without becoming a copycat, of course. What strikes you as helpful as well as what turns you off can both be beneficial.

Genre Categories

Choosing the genre category for your book is important on Amazon and many other sites, as it is in these category sections that many prospective buyers browse for books. One strategy is to choose categories that are as narrowly defined as possible because they will have fewer competing books in them. Consider this example on Amazon:

Historical Fiction: 50,000+ books listed
Medieval Historical Fiction: 437

Obviously, you'd rather compete with 437 other books than with over 50,000.

The success of your book, whether you traditionally publish or self-publish, rests heavily upon you, the author. You will reach your intended audience by building a strong marketing plan and modifying it as needed.

SUGGESTED READING:

Beckwith, Sandra. The Book Designer (blog): *Three Fiction Marketing Success Tips for 2020.* https://www.thebookdesigner.com/2019/ 12/3-fiction-marketing-success-tips-for-2020/.

Friedlander, Joel. The Book Designer (blog): *Marketing Your Book.* https://www.thebookdesigner.com/marketing-your-book/.

Sansevieri, Penny. Author Marketing Experts (blog): *20 Smart Book Marketing Strategies for 2020.* https://www.amarketingexpert. com/20-book-marketing-strategies-to-be-successful-in-2020/.

Scott-Hainchek, Sayde. "How to Build a Yearlong Book Marketing Plan." The Fussy Librarian. December 1, 2019. https://www.the fussylibrarian.com/newswire/for-authors/2019/12/01/how-to-build-a-yearlong-book-marketing-plan?

Urban, Diana. "Top 10 Book Marketing Articles from BookBub in 2019." BookBub Partners. December 18, 2019. https://insights. bookbub.com/top-book-marketing-articles-bookbub-2019/?utm_ source=pemail_top-book-marketing-articles-bookbub-2019& utm_medium=email.

CHAPTER 29

Websites and Blogs

To establish yourself in the industry, to show the world who you are, and to compete on a level playing field with other authors, you will need a website and/or blog. Your website/blog is an extension of you and what you represent—it's your online promotional brochure—and the time to create one is before any books are published.

Websites

Setting up a website is important in that it will serve as an easy means for readers, fans, and others to learn about you and your work—a hub for all you do in your writing. Not only will a professional-looking website showcase your work, it will also establish you as a serious author and give you instant credibility. And a great added benefit is the opportunity to build a following by collecting the e-mail addresses of those who visit your site.

For those of you who have never developed a website and believe you don't have the skills to create one, think again. It's not that hard. I have just average computer skills and started out using Yahoo Site

Solution to create mine, then upgraded to Yahoo Site Builder. Then, when I wanted to add a blog to it and Site Builder could not accommodate one, I changed to using Wix (florenceosmund.com). But there are numerous other templates available. Just Google "website design" and you'll see tons of site-design tools, most of which offer a basic template to use for free and then one or more upgraded versions that include more sophisticated features.

If you truly can't handle designing your own website, or don't have the time, you can always hire a web designer. Be prepared to pay a minimum of $1,000 for a decent basic site.

Before creating a website, you'll need a domain name. Domain registration is cheap and easy. I used namecheap.com, but there are many others. Most web hosts offer domain registration as well.

Put thought into the name of your website. Choose one that identifies you and your books and that is easy to remember, spell, and type. You can find other tips for choosing a good domain name on thesitewizard.com/archive/domainname.shtml as well as on many other sites.

You will also need a web host in order to post your website on the Internet. I use Wix as a web host, but there are numerous others. My advice is to find one that offers 24/7 tech support. There is nothing more frustrating than being in the middle of developing a website page, running into a problem, and not having a resource to go to for help. I have found Wix offers good customer service (with a real person).

Things to include on your website are:

- A home page that welcomes people to your site and gives them an overview of what's inside
- Your bio, including interesting facts about yourself and a photo or two
- Your contact information
- A synopsis and cover image of each of your published books
- Links to where to buy your books
- Reviews and/or testimonials

- Links to other sites you think may be of interest to your audience
- Some kind of freebie (a sample of your work, writing advice, etc.)
- Relevant searchable keywords in the page titles, tags, and contents of your pages

With respect to the "Buy" links, consider adding a PayPal page to your website so people can order directly from you. This means you'll have to ship your book to the purchaser yourself, but you make up for this by enjoying 100 percent of the revenue. If you open an account with usps.com, you will be able to create a First Class mailing label that includes postage, making it easy to send books without going to a post office. But if you don't mind trips to the post office, you can send books at a very low "book rate" and save some money.

Promote your website as often as you can. Include the URL on your business cards, stationery, and social media pages. Include it in your bio and e-mail signature block. Whenever you give someone your contact information, include your website URL.

SCAM ALERT: If you decide to hire someone to help you with your website, beware of the following:

- Service providers who charge exorbitant fees for developing an easy website. I had my initial five-page website up and running with about twenty hours invested in it. If I had charged $50/hour for my time, that would have amounted to $1,000. I wouldn't pay more than that for a basic website.
- Service providers who charge a fee to manage a website you can easily manage yourself.
- High setup and monthly web-hosting fees.

Blogs

Unlike a website, which contains relatively static information, a blog is a site (often a subset of a website) that is regularly updated by someone (called a blogger) who wants to share his/her passion about certain subjects and solicit conversation about the same. Anyone can start a blog, but not everyone has the time or skills to make it successful.

It's relatively easy to create a blog—there are numerous templates from which to choose (Wix, SquareSpace, and HostGator, to name a few). Most of them require limited computer skills to use. I use Wix.

For me, there's nothing worse than a cluttered blog that forces the visitor to sift through a lot of irrelevant stuff looking for what's meaningful. Another pet peeve I have is typos in blogs. Blogs should be well thought out and proofread. Otherwise, the author lacks credibility.

To get and keep readers, it's essential to create material that is of interest to those you want as followers. Sounds like a simple concept, but it really isn't. It takes a lot of thinking and experimenting to get it right. Focus on providing your readers with free, worthwhile information, even if it means commenting on other peoples' blogs or directing them to other sites. In addition, people love tips, quizzes, checklists, top-ten lists, and "Did you know?" posts.

It's okay to have fun. Consider relaying humorous or embarrassing stories about your life as an author. I remember one mystery writer (I can't remember his name) who blogged that he feared being hauled off to jail one day if anyone of authority ever looked at the Internet search history on his computer, which included the keyword phrases such as "undetectable poison autopsy," "suffocation without marks," "death to look like a suicide," and "best crimes against mothers-in-law."

Conducting polls can generate great discussion on your blog. I've seen authors post things like:

- Choose which cover you like best.
- Tell us about your all-time favorite character in a book.

- What makes you keep turning the pages when you read?
- Join my e-mail subscriber list for a chance to win (fill in the blank).

It's one thing to create and maintain a meaningful blog, but it's quite another thing to draw people to it who then become your followers. Including the right keywords will help. Be creative. I saw on one person's blog, "Make me smile today...leave a comment or question."

Don't forget to include other links on your blog. And make it easy for readers to see what else you have to offer, including the link to buy your books.

Blog sites need to be consistently updated with new material. Too few posts and you'll appear stale. Too many may cause an overdose for your audience. Once a week to once a month appears to be an acceptable frequency range. Review your old posts and if they are out-of-date, update or archive them.

Promoting your books should be secondary on your blog. If you do a good job with the rest of it, book sales will follow.

Like websites, blogs take time to catch on. Don't get discouraged the first year.

Here are eight author blogs I follow:

> thebookdesigner.com/
> janefriedman.com/blog/
> thecreativepenn.com/blog/
> writetodone.com/
> jodyhedlund.blogspot.com/
> buildbookbuzz.com/blog/
> writersinthestormblog.com/
> livewritethrive.com/

Not everyone is a blogger. If you find it too difficult or cumbersome to maintain an interesting, current blog, don't do it. Stick with what you do well.

SCAM ALERT: Blog tours—a collection of authors who are given the opportunity to showcase their books on a predetermined number of blogs in an effort to improve name/book recognition and gain exposure and reviews—have become popular. Most tours run for two weeks. Some allow you to participate in an interview, provide a guest blog post, and offer giveaways. A tour host coordinates the process. Like everywhere else, scammers exist in this arena, and you have to fully vet them before using them. Beware of blog-tour hosts who:

- Charge large fees to participate in the tour
- Promise that the tour will result in increased sales
- Have insignificant followings
- Do not have followings that are pertinent to your book

E-mail Subscriber List

It took me a while to understand the importance of building an e-mail subscriber list, and in fact I started to build mine way too late. The time to start building one is before your first book is published.

The purpose of an e-mail subscriber list is reciprocatory—you offer people something of value in exchange for their e-mail address. The something of value can be a short story you've written, the first few chapters of one of your books, or an entire book. Don't forget that authors are readers too, so consider giving away valuable tips you've learned along the way to those who also write. This concept works in part because people who have received something of value from you appreciate the bond they have created with you and are more likely to talk about you and buy your books.

The most significant financial benefit of having a list of e-mail addresses of dedicated followers comes with your book launch. Sending a new book announcement to this group will result in early sales that will help you gain momentum in your marketing strategy.

What works best for me in finding subscribers comes via my website. On my website/blog, I include an invitation to join my e-mail subscriber list. I post this message:

> When you subscribe, you will...
>
> - Receive monthly notifications when a new post is added to my blog,
> - Learn of my future book releases (about one per year), and
> - Be added to a monthly drawing for a free copy of one of my books.

Make it easy to subscribe to your e-mail list, but more important, make it easy to unsubscribe. I use MailChimp to manage my e-mail subscriber list, and they are required by law to include an unsubscribe link. In addition, I tell subscribers they can reply to the e-mail and put UNSUBSCRIBE in the subject line.

Don't ask for too much information for people to subscribe. Be completely transparent on what they will receive by subscribing. And avoid coming across as spammy.

When you send your subscribers an e-mail, be careful with the subject line. You want to catch their attention, but you don't want to mislead or confuse them. Have you ever read a subject line and expected one thing, but when you opened the message got another? Very annoying. And if you're including some type of book promotion, make it easy for them to purchase it, but don't make it a hard sell.

When building your list, you can go for sheer numbers, but I believe a list with fewer, high-quality subscribers is more effective in the long run. It is easy to buy mailing lists, and I know authors who do it, but I personally don't believe it's worth the investment.

Promote the value of being one of your subscribers wherever you can. Put it at the end of the articles you write, in your e-mail signature block, on your website/blog, at the end of your book, in your bio, on your Facebook page, and wherever you promote your books.

Be patient. Building a quality list takes time.

Newsletters

I know what you're thinking: *Yet another thing I have to do that takes me away from my writing.* Well, you're right, and there are a ton of them. Two things to remember is that you don't have to do *all* of them. You can pick and choose. And once you've developed a method—a template, so to speak—for some of them, it becomes an easier, less time-consuming task.

Newsletters help you connect with your readers beyond your website, blog, and social media. They arrive in your readers' inboxes and therefore are more direct and personal. Newsletters can provide insight into who you are as an author and a person—something readers tend to appreciate and enjoy.

Consider these components when creating a newsletter for your readers.

1. General message—A brief message telling readers what to expect in this edition of your newsletter. Include something personal in this section.

2. Main story—This can be anything you deem interesting to your readers—an account of something that recently happened to you as an author, something that inspired you, an insight you had—anything related to the theme of your newsletter. Keep it short—I suggest no more than 300 words. Include photos. Open up to your readers. Be genuine. Make it fun, if you want.

3. If your target audience is other authors, consider a how-to section on some aspect of writing or publishing.

4. Many of your fans will be interested in what you're reading, so add a section for your recent or current reads and what you think of them. This would be a good place to promote your author-friends' works.
5. Include a section for your published books and the latest update for your current work in progress. Include a recent review or testimonial you received that was particularly complimentary or interesting for some other reason.
6. Create an events calendar—your upcoming book fairs, signings, speaking engagements, published articles. Let readers know you are 100 percent into being an author.
7. Always include a brief bio, contact information, and links to your social media, website, and blog.
8. Provide a means for readers to leave a comment or ask a question.

Always make it easy for people to subscribe and unsubscribe to your newsletter. Do not add anyone to your newsletter subscriber list unless they have signed up for it.

Keep your newsletter short—most people don't have time to read lengthy e-mails. And don't make it all about buying your books—you'll lose subscribers if you do. Use the 80/20 rule—devote 80 percent to material that will help, interest, and inspire your readers and 20 percent to promoting yourself and your books.

Frequency is something you'll have to decide for yourself depending on how much you have to say and the amount of time you are willing to devote to it. Once a month is reasonable.

Promote your newsletter everywhere—on your website/blog, in your e-mail signature block, on social media, and via word of mouth.

Several easy-to-use applications exist for formatting and distributing your newsletter—Mailchimp, Campaign Monitor, Constant Contact, and AWeber to name a few.

SUGGESTED READING:

Bradshaw, Claire. "Ultimate Guide: Establishing an Author Newsletter." Writer's Edit. (No date.) https://writersedit.com/self-publishing/ultimate-guide-establishing-author-newsletter/.

Burke, John. IngramSpark (blog): *The Complete Guide to Completing an Author Website*. https://www.ingramspark.com/blog/what-should-i-put-on-my-author-website.

Friedlander, Joel. The Book Designer (blog): *Content Creation for Bloggers: 14 Kinds of Sharable Content*. https://www.thebook designer.com/2017/05/content-creation-bloggers-14-kinds-shareable-content/

Friedman, Jane. Jane Friedman (blog): *How to Start Blogging: A Definitive Guide for Authors*. https://www.janefriedman.com/blogging-for-writers/.

Goins, Jeff. "Why Every Writer Needs an Email List." Goins, Writer. (No date.) https://goinswriter.com/email-list/.

Mudri, Jade. Website Planet (blog): *How to Create a Website—Build a Website in 4 (Easy) Steps*. https://www.websiteplanet.com/blog/how to create-a-website-build-a-website/.

Urban, Diana. BookBub Partners (blog): *45+ Author Websites with Stellar Designs* https://insights.bookbub.com/author-websites-with-stellar-designs/.

CHAPTER 30

Amazon, Goodreads, and Social Media

To sell books, you want to get exposure in places where dedicated followers go to browse and shop for them.

That's the first step. The second is to involve yourself with these venues. Amazon, the obvious retail gorilla in the room, is a must. And so is Goodreads (now owned by Amazon), the largest website network where authors have the opportunity to connect with readers. Combine these two with the many social networking sites available that are at your disposal, and you have the opportunity to reach all the readers you need to become a successful author.

Amazon

Amazon—the largest online book retailer in the world—can be your best friend when it comes to promoting and selling your books. While there are other selling platforms available, most self-published authors have found Amazon to be the most user-friendly and lucrative in the long run. Besides being a reliable selling platform, Amazon has other things to offer.

KDP

KDP (Kindle Direct Publishing) is Amazon's way for authors to sell their e-books on Amazon. Authors get 35 percent or 70 percent royalties, depending on the e-book's list price and where it's sold—one of the highest royalty percentages around. To get 70 percent, the list price of your e-book must be between $2.99 and $9.99; at least 20 percent of that of the physical version of your book; and 20 percent lower than anywhere else you have it listed for sale. The 70 percent rate applies to sales in the U.S. and most of Europe. Everything else falls under the 35 percent royalty rate.

KDP is not exclusive. Authors can upload e-books to KDP and sell the same e-book elsewhere—unless they join KDP Select, which requires ninety days of digital exclusivity. In return, KDP Select pays higher royalties for sales in otherwise lower royalty rate countries, adds the e-book to the lending library for Amazon Prime members, and offers promotional options for free and discounted books.

The majority of my income comes from the royalties I receive from Amazon Prime members borrowing my e-books from KDP's lending library. The KDP lending library royalty has been hovering around 0.5 cents per page read. My monthly goal prior to 2017 was to have 300,000 pages read for each book. That was an easy goal to achieve during a special promotion (I've had as many as 1,500,000 pages read during a month following a free promotion), but lately 300,000 has been a lofty goal to maintain for each book each month. In 2017, the market changed (for my books anyway) and reaching 150,000 pages read per month per book has become more realistic.

It's important to note that readers do not need a Kindle device to read a Kindle e-book. They read well with a free app on PCs and any tablet (like iPads) or smartphone.

Amazon Associates

Amazon Associates is a membership service that pays you for driving people to Amazon to purchase products. It uses a tracking ID in each URL to identify who directed the buyer to their site. You can use this link when promoting your own books and make an extra 4 to 8 percent on each sale. You also earn a commission from anything else that someone buys on Amazon if they initially got there through your link.

Amazon Author Central

The Amazon author page—where you can include your bio, photo, events, videos, and links to your website, blog, and Twitter page—gives the reader lots of information that in turn builds credibility. Don't be afraid to include fun information about yourself or inspiration for writing, as this helps to nurture relationships with readers.

Your Author Central page appears on every book sales page on Amazon, so it cross-links other books you've published. If someone clicks over to your author page, they can follow you and receive e-mail alerts from Amazon when you release new books.

Author Central also improves the likelihood that your book will be discovered by the search algorithm. The more active you are on your Amazon page, the greater the likelihood that the books will appear in keyword searches.

Amazon's Author Central format encourages reader feedback and author-initiated discussions, allowing authors to extend a personal touch to their readers—a connection that is good for ongoing sales.

Goodreads

With more than 20 million members, Goodreads is one of the best, if not the best, networks specifically designed for authors and readers—its primary goal being to help readers find books. Becoming a member of the Goodreads community allows readers to check out up-to-date information about you and your books, see what you look like, browse the books you've written, and read the reviews.

Here are some ways to utilize Goodreads to its fullest advantage as an author.

Author Profile

Setting up your author profile is the first step to connect with readers on Goodreads. Creating an author page not only gives you exposure, it also provides author and book statistics such as the number of fans you have, number of people who have added your book to their "To Read" list, number of ratings you have, and number of reviews. This page on the Goodreads site goodreads.com/author/program includes instructions on how to go about setting up a profile.

Your Bookshelf

Since Goodreads is all about sharing the love of books, it behooves you to talk about not only the books you've written but also books you've read. Authors are typically voracious readers, so let browsers know what you are reading. Share your picks and talk about them. Members love seeing what authors are reading and if they have any of the same book choices. Show off your understanding of the craft. Talk about characterization, pacing, setting, theme, and narrative arc. Let them know you are knowledgeable in your field.

Reviews

The more reviews you have on Goodreads the better because Goodreads features books based on the number of reviews. The more reviews your book has, the more people are likely to read it.

Ask the Author

Ask the Author is an optional feature that allows readers to submit questions directly to you. Author responses are public and displayed on the author's profile page. Questions can be about anything, and it's up to the author to answer or ignore them. Readers generally like this feature, as your responses tend to reveal more about you personally.

Reader Q&A

Similar to Ask the Author, Reader Q&A allows readers to ask questions or make comments about a specific book of yours from the book's profile page, but unlike Ask the Author, any reader can answer said questions. Answers are ranked by the number of "Likes" they receive, with the most liked getting top billing.

Discussion Groups

If you're lucky enough to have an active following, Goodreads is a great place to host a discussion about your book—a way to create interest for those who haven't read it yet. Goodreads is home to more than 20,000 book clubs and thousands more groups about nearly every topic imaginable, some of which regularly host chats with authors. Find a few groups that interest you and join them. After you've established yourself in the group, you can talk about your books and eventually contact the moderator about hosting a discussion of your book.

Advertising

Goodreads' unique advertising program allows you to target readers who are fans of other authors, for instance, those who write books similar to yours. Or you can target people who have rated your other books in hopes that if they liked one of your books, they'll like others. These pay-per-click ads cost as little as $0.15 per click. (See more about paid advertising in Chapter 35.)

Book Giveaways

According to Goodreads, on average, 750 people enter each Goodreads book giveaway, and the pre-release giveaway can be an effective way to get your book read and reviewed. Each month, more than 1,500 titles are given away on Goodreads. But not all giveaways are created equal. To get the most bang for your pre-release buck, consider running multiple giveaways, each open for three to four weeks. Your first giveaway could ideally start three months before publication. Then run a second giveaway a few weeks before publication. There is no limit to the number of giveaways you can run.

According to Goodreads, about 60 percent of giveaway winners review the books they win, so the more free books that are released, the more reviews they'll get.

Social Media

Social media is increasingly important to authors in that it allows them to have unfiltered communication with their intended audience, which in turn can lead to establishing valuable relationships. Increasing your author visibility through various social media sites allows you to meet readers, build your audience, and increase your discoverability to sell more books. Treat social media as a side job. Devote enough time to it to make it worthwhile—an hour or so a few times a week should suffice.

Finding the ideal social media channels is often an exercise in trial-and-error. For one person it might be Twitter; for someone else, it could be LinkedIn, Facebook, or Pinterest. Whatever the outlet, it's more about the quality of the connections as opposed to the quantity that will in the long run sell more books.

I personally haven't found social media sites very effective for the direct selling of books. Rather, I see them as a tool for building brand awareness, increasing website traffic, networking, and generally establishing credibility as an author. It's all about exposure—using social media wisely can increase your exposure and reap benefits in the long run.

Don't expect much to happen if all you do is post your Amazon link on a social media page over and over again. Instead, use social media to get to know other writers, talk to industry people, establish relationships with people who can make a difference, and communicate with your readers and potential fans. Ask for their opinions, make an emotional connection with them. These ties can turn into your best advocates.

Try sharing blog posts on social media, ones that your following will find interesting. Give advice. Make recommendations. Talk about other authors. And talk about you and your books…in small doses.

When in doubt, post pictures of your pets—everyone loves animals.

The ten most popular social media platforms are arguably the following.

- Facebook
- Twitter
- LinkedIn
- Pinterest
- Google Plus+

- Tumblr
- Instagram
- VK
- Flickr
- Vine

It takes time to build a following. It's okay to have only a few hundred in the beginning. It's a start. I believe it's better to have fewer followers who care about what you're saying and meaningfully interact with you than to have numerous followers who are just a number to boost your ego.

Facebook

Facebook is by far the largest and most popular social media site, and many authors love it for getting exposure for themselves and their books.

First, let me clarify the distinction between a Facebook personal profile that people use for their personal lives versus a Facebook Page they use for their business. The following is directly from the official Facebook.com site:

> *Personal profiles are for non-commercial use and represent individual people. Facebook Pages look similar to personal profiles, but they offer unique tools for businesses, brands and organizations. Facebook Pages are managed by people who have personal profiles.*

Creating a Facebook Page will keep your professional posts and other activities separate from your personal ones. Facebook Pages are viewable by anyone, even non-members, so your posts can get significant exposure with the right keywords. One of the great features of the Facebook Page is that when someone "likes" your page, it gets broadcasted to their contacts, potentially reaching many more people who may be interested in you or your books.

I like the 80/20 rule when it comes to authors posting on Facebook—80 percent of the posts are related to some aspect of the book industry and 20 percent are directly related to you and your books. The trick is to keep it interesting for your followers and potential book buyers 100 percent of the time.

For 20 percent of your posts—the ones directly related to you and your books—post milestones, book launches, impressive reviews, interviews, and book signings. People like to read something personal about you, so include interesting facts about yourself—how you got started, lessons learned along the way, what you do when you're not writing. As long as you keep it interesting, it won't be considered spammy.

For the remaining 80 percent of your posts, consider writing about fellow authors, sharing interesting facts about the book publishing industry, and offering advice.

Strike a good balance for the number of posts. Too few and people will think it's not an active and current site. Too many and people may get annoyed. Be generous with including links, not only ones directly related to you but also those that may be interesting or helpful to your audience members. Direct your visitors to places they may not otherwise have visited.

It's important to get people to "like" your Facebook Page, as search engines, such as Google, favor Facebook Pages with lots of "likes." One way to get "likes" is for you to "like" other people's pages and ask them if they will return the favor.

Facebook is all about creating relationships, whether you're using your personal profile or professional page. It is not advisable to use Facebook strictly as a selling tool. Once you make connections and earn trust, sales will come naturally as a side benefit.

Twitter

Twitter is another large social network, and its potential for promoting books is hard to deny. But beware—Twitter can be your best friend or your worst nightmare, or maybe both. Here are what I consider the positive features and precautions for this social media outlet.

POSITIVE FEATURES
- It's free.
- It's super easy to use.

- You can reach your target audience with the use of hashtags.
- Because you are limited to 280 characters, your messages are forced to be concise, therefore having a higher probability for someone reading them than if they were long and drawn out.
- Authors can support each other by retweeting posts, enlarging the audience.

PRECAUTIONS

- Like most other social media platforms, maximizing your effectiveness on Twitter can turn into a full-time job.
- How frequently you tweet and retweet is a balancing act. Too infrequent and your followers wonder if you're serious about what you're doing. Too frequent and your followers feel like they're being spammed.
- You have to consistently get more creative to get your tweets to stand out.
- Sometimes the 280-character limit gets in the way of saying everything you want to say in a single post.

You can start by making a list of the authors and experts in your genre and see who follows them, as these are likely the same people you want for your following. Use Twitter's recommendations on whom to follow. Twitter creates this list based on whom you've followed, so if you follow people in the writing industry and readers, that's mostly whom you'll see on the list.

LinkedIn

What Facebook does for social networking, LinkedIn does for business-oriented networking. With more than 50 million members worldwide, LinkedIn provides a vast pool of valuable networkers and potential buyers for your books. Just as you will want to create interesting posts for your blog and Facebook Page, you will want to do the same on LinkedIn. But, again, you don't want to make your LinkedIn site into a hard-sell endeavor. That will likely turn people off.

Use LinkedIn for offering interesting articles, making announcements, reaching out for advice, and offering advice. Increase your visibility by encouraging discussions and comments. Offer freebies. Create contests. Make it fun—even though it's business, people still like a little fun.

Pinterest

This is a site where users collect images by "pinning" them to separate boards based on themes, such as books to read. It is different from other social media sites in that the focus is more on making connections with a like-minded community and curating their boards than on "likes" and "follows." It works for authors because people use it like a search engine. For example, they might search for "literary fiction," and my book covers will pop up…okay, along with hundreds of others. But throw "Chicago" in the mix, and my book covers get pretty good exposure. And Pinterest allows you to interact with other Pinterest users and build a community that can add value to your platform.

Google Plus+

This social network—with the slogan "Real-life sharing rethought for the web"—incorporates "circles" (groups of people, such as family, friends, office colleagues, or people who share a particular interest); "hangouts" (video-chat option); "huddles" (text messaging in group chats), "instant uploads" (option to send pictures and videos); "streams" (news updates); and "sparks" (topics that you want to discuss with others).

Tumblr

Tumblr is another site where you can connect with others who share your interests and post text, photos, GIFs, and videos.

Instagram

Owned by Facebook, Instagram is a social media app that allows users to share photos and videos from a smartphone. Anyone who creates an Instagram account has a profile and a news feed. When you post a photo or video on Instagram, it is displayed on your profile. Other users who follow you will see your posts in their own feed, which makes it an interesting marketing tool for authors.

> **SCAM ALERT:** Beware of the dark side of social media—it's a place where scammers abound, and it's extremely easy for them to find you on social media and direct their message to you personally. For example, I often see ads for creating tweets or gaining followers for you that are guaranteed to reach millions. The problem is that the millions they are referring to are fake Twitter accounts. Scam artists play on your weaknesses and ignorance. Are all social media service providers bad? Of course not. But many are. Learn how to spot them. Each social media site has its share of trolls, catfish, and haters. Some sites are better than others when it comes to protecting its members against such undesirables, and each has a means of reporting abuse.

SUGGESTED READING:

Goodreads Staff. "Goodreads Authors: How to Promote Your Books on Goodreads." Goodreads. September 25, 2019. https://help. goodreads.com/s/article/Goodreads-Author-How-to-promote-your-books-on-Goodreads-1553870940588.

Lekic, Natasa (Founder). NY Book Editors (blog): *Social Media Marketing for Authors.* https://nybookeditors.com/2019/02/social-media-marketing-for-authors/.

Sansevieri, Penny. Author Marketing Experts (blog): *How to Market Your Book with Author Central—Five Quick Fixes.* https://www. amarketingexpert.com/five-quick-ways-to-ramp-up-your-amazon-author-central-page/.

CHAPTER 31

Online, Press, and Face-To-Face Exposure

t's all about exposure—the more you and your books get, the more likely you are to increase sales. Here are some ways to increase your exposure and (hopefully) sales online, with the press, and through face-to-face communication.

Book Posting Sites

One way to expose your books to potential readers is to post descriptions of the books along with purchase information on websites that match readers to books. The more sites on which you post your books, the more you will potentially enlarge your audience and platform. Launched in 2007, Goodreads is the gorilla in the room. They claim to have over 9 million members who have added more than 320 million books to their shelves.

Here are some sites other than Goodreads to consider:

askdavid.com
bookbrowse.com
bookbuzzr.com
bookgoodies.com
bookpreviewclub.com
booksie.com
booktalk.com
bookzio.com
digitalbooktoday.com
ereadergirl.com
goodkindles.net
indiebooklounge.com
indiebookoftheday.com
kboards.com
selfpublishersshowcase.com

I post my books on most of these sites, but there is no way to tell if any of them have resulted in any sales. Posting details of each book (which you have to do just once) takes only about five minutes, so I feel it's worth the effort and can't possibly hurt.

Book Trailers

A book trailer is a teaser or a promotional video that highlights the narrative arc of your book—a synopsis that doesn't give away too many details. It's pretty clear that the masses are into watching videos, and with audiences this big, one might assume book trailers are a great opportunity for authors to increase their online presence, reach a wider market, and ultimately sell more books. According to a January 2019 MerchDope article, YouTube is the second most visited website in the world with the following statistics.

- The total number of people who use YouTube: 1.3 billion.
- 300 hours of video are uploaded to YouTube every minute.
- Almost 5 billion videos are watched on YouTube every single day.
- YouTube gets over 30 million visitors per day.

In preparing to write this book, I viewed a lot of book trailers—surprisingly, 90 percent of them stank. I even found trailers for really good books that were just awful—lacking in creativity, professional image, and relevant content. Cheesy, boring, amateurish, and unimaginative videos—that's what I found. I don't know how much time and money was invested in any of them, but the majority appeared to have been shot with someone's iPhone with little forethought and questionable music playing in the background. Maybe people don't care about quality. Maybe I'm in the minority on this one.

But there are authors who claim book trailers on YouTube are an effective marketing tool, like this one youtube.com/watch?v= VSZawTU_d8Y for *The Good Girl* by Mary Kubica. Here are some suggestions for making a good book trailer.

Target Audience
Know who your potential readers are and cater your message specifically to them—what will catch their eye (and ear). Ask yourself what will inspire them to view the entire video and then (more importantly) press the "Buy" button.

Hook
A book trailer should highlight your book's hook—what makes it unique from all the others. You can do this with a headline. Keep it focused, short, and simple. A powerful hook lays the foundation for a great book trailer.

Length
Keep in mind that most people, especially those online, have short attention spans. An effective book trailer should be thirty to ninety seconds in length. Don't try to cram in a summary of the entire novel—just the

highlights. You may want to consider creating a short and longer version of the trailer for different venues.

Quality

Use high-quality photos, graphics, audio, and actors. If you can't pull this off yourself, hire a professional. Knowing how to incorporate these elements takes an eye for design and knowledge of the latest trends and software, so if you're not in the know, seek help from others. Don't plan to be in the video yourself unless you can come across as a professional actor. The same goes for voice-overs—spend time to find the right voice for your book trailer.

Content

While the primary objective is to sell more books, you may have to come in through the back door to do this effectively. You can accomplish this by talking about the idea (the theme) behind the book as much as about the book itself. In other words, don't make it a direct sell. Consider having the protagonist narrate the video and include some quotes from the book. Or minimize the dialogue and create intrigue with tantalizing music and footage. Regardless of the approach you choose, you will want viewers to walk away wanting to know more about the protagonist after hearing about his or her plight and the challenges he or she faces.

Invitation

End the trailer with an invitation for viewers to do something that will hopefully lead them to buy the book. But don't do a hard sell. Consider, for example, inviting them to visit your website or blog where you have "buy" buttons.

A book trailer doesn't have to be super expensive or complicated to be successful—it just needs to be enticing enough to cause the viewer to want to know more about you and your books. Give readers a taste of what to expect without giving too much away. Leave them wanting to know more.

Exposure through Writing

What easier way is there for writers to gain exposure than by showing off their writing skills? Consider these avenues.

Online Interviews

Many, if not most, book bloggers post author interviews on their sites. Not only does this provide an opportunity for exposure, it is also a chance for you to show off your creativity and writing style. (See "Suggested Reading" at the end of this chapter for a list of bloggers by genre.)

Articles and Blog Posts

A great way to gain exposure, increase your credibility as an author, and help your fellow authors at the same time is to write and publish articles. One platform in which to do this is EzineArticles.com, a searchable database of hundreds of thousands of original articles posted by people like you and me. After I post an article on this site, I can expect a big hike in the number of visitors to my website and many shared links. Other places to submit articles are trade publications, such as *Poets and Writers, Writer's Digest, Publishers Weekly,* and *The Writer.*

Guest posting on author-related blogs is another way to get great exposure and an indirect way to get sales. More than a few times, someone has relayed to me that they bought my book because of one of my posts they read on someone else's blog. (See Chapter 29 for a list of blogs I follow.)

Short Stories

Another way to showcase your writing skills and potentially garner new fans is by writing short stories. Here are two links to sites where you can publish short stories.

thewritelife.com/where-to-submit-short-stories/

writersdigest.com/whats-new/how-where-to-get-a-short-story-published

While I haven't done this myself, I know authors who scale their books way down, into short stories, and publish them as such. Since short stories can run anywhere from 1,500 to 30,000 words, this gives you lots of options.

Online Chat Groups

There are numerous online discussion groups you can join to get advice, give advice, and network with authors, editors, book reviewers, and publishers. The more you interact with fellow members of these groups, the more you learn and the more exposure you get for your books. Look for successful authors in these groups who have great web pages and/or blogs you can follow and learn from them.

Many groups have separate areas of the site that will allow you to post information about your book. Use these for promotions, but don't forget to provide feedback on postings from your fellow authors. Not only are you helping them gain exposure, but you will gain exposure for yourself. These groups are all about helping each other.

Following are the three most popular venues for group discussions.

Facebook

Claiming over 2 billion active users, Facebook continues to be the largest social networking site. Numerous groups of authors support each other on Facebook by chatting about marketing ideas, writing techniques, and more. Here is a link to a list of some of the Facebook groups for writers. prowritingaid.com/art/630/Our-Favorite-Facebook-Groups-for-Writers.aspx

LinkedIn

The world's largest professional network with more than 500 million members, LinkedIn is another good place to connect with other authors. Here is a link to a list of several of its groups. adazing.com/linkedin-groups-authors-should-join/

Goodreads

Launched in 2007 with over 85 million members who have added more than 2.5 billion books, Goodreads is the largest site in the world dedicated to readers where they can find, rate, and review books. Here is a link to their author-related groups. goodreads.com/group/topic/9-goodreads-authors

The Press

The news media (including TV, radio, newspapers, magazines, web pages, and blogs) can help you get exposure to assist in building your reputation as an author and lead to book sales. Through these media, you will announce the release of your book and, with any luck, get interviews and media attention. In addition, these media can help you connect with editors, producers, reporters, broadcasters, columnists, podcasters, bloggers—people who have audiences and a platform from which to promote you and your work.

What are the chances that someone with an audience will hear about you through the press and promote your work? Probably slim, but all it takes is one person with an interest in your story at that particular moment in time. It's all about timing...and a little luck. A short time after the press release for my first book *The Coach House*, I was contacted by CPRTV, a local Chicago TV program serving the Filipino/Asian/Hispanic community. Its founder, Veronica Leighton, saw the press release and thought her audience might like to learn more about the ethnic thread that runs through the book. She invited me into her studio for an interview where we talked about what influenced my decision to write this particular story, the book writing process, and the research involved.

As with your other book promotion efforts, it's all about exposure, and the more you get the better.

Press Page

Always have a press page available to send to the media when asked or to hand out at book signings, speaking engagements, conferences, and any other place where there is potential for self-promotion. Here's the link to my website press page. florenceosmund.com/press. At a minimum, include the following:

- Book summary
- Author bio and head shot
- Image of book cover
- Where to buy the book
- Author contact information

Press Releases

Press releases get the message out about your books to hundreds if not thousands of people at TV and radio stations, newspapers, magazines, bookstores, book clubs, book discussion groups, book reviewers—people who may be interested in talking about your book.

Anyone can write a press release. There are templates available on PRWeb.com, pressreleasetemplates.net, and smallbusinesspr.com for do-it-yourself ones. If you want to engage a service, try mymediainfo.com, or cision.com. A free service is Muckrack.com.

Not everyone agrees that press releases are worthwhile. My thinking is that all it takes is one person—one right person—to read it and act upon it. The right connection can potentially make a big difference. You never know.

Here are some stats on the press release I used for my novel *Regarding Anna* in March 2015. I used PRWeb.com and paid $99 for the service.

TOTAL HEADLINE IMPRESSIONS (cumulative)
Day 1: 16,179
Day 2: 18,241
Day 3: 20,120
Day 4: 21,911
Day 5: 22,007

FULL READS
Day 1: 715
Day 2: 88

Day 3: 62
Day 4: 53
Day 5: 5

MEDIA DELIVERIES: 1,561

RELEASE INTERACTIONS: 17 (1 pdf, 9 printed, 4 hovered over iFrame, 3 viewed iFrame)

OTHER SITES THAT PICKED IT UP: onenewspage.com and broadwayworld.com

Picked up by Google 9 times and Yahoo 25 times

So, what does all this mean? It appears that PRWeb did a fair job at distribution, but my release was likely just one of thousands during this time period that was read by the people who read such things. Only 4.2 percent of the people who received it actually read it, and then only seventeen people did something with it. It would be interesting to know who they were, but this data was not available. All I know is that no one contacted me and said, "I just read your press release and..."

So are press releases really worthwhile? I think they are if you have something genuinely newsworthy. Unfortunately for most of us, the publication of our latest book does not qualify. Keep in mind that press releases sit at the top of a long list of other press releases for about one nanosecond, and then they drop down the list real fast. Perhaps if you've just sold the 100,000th copy of one of your books, it would catch some attention and be newsworthy. I'll let you know if that's true when I get there.

Face-to-Face Marketing

Most people currently spend more time engaging with their cell phones, iPods, and the like than they do hearing another person's voice, let alone looking people in the eye. But while electronic communication has certainly lent itself to a substantial increase in the quantity of communication we send and receive, I don't think we should lose sight of the quality and authenticity that face-to-face communication allows.

Adding the personal touch of face-to-face communication is still important when trying to sell something to another person or group of people. It sets the foundation for trust and hopefully establishes a relationship between you and the other person—the potential buyer of your books. It allows your audience to associate a real person to your book—someone with whom they can relate or perhaps connect.

I would argue that people are more apt to buy your book if they can look you in the eye as you talk about it. Moreover, when you're face-to-face, you can read a person's body language and then adjust your message as needed. And you can engage them in the conversation, pull them into your world to further pique their interest in what you're selling. When you talk to someone in person about your books, it allows you to show them that you are excited about what you do—excited about the characters, the story line, and the process you followed in order to get published—and hopefully get them excited about it too.

Here are some face-to-face opportunities to consider.

Speaking Engagements

Public speaking is a great way to bring your message to a wider audience and letting people know you are a confident author with poise and professionalism. So if you are comfortable with it, you can use public speaking to gain credibility and exposure.

Here are some topics to consider given your qualifications.

- How to self-publish
- Promoting and marketing your book
- How to begin writing a novel
- Working with illustrators, editors, and publishers
- What inspired you to write

You may be surprised at the level of local interest in hearing from an author, even relatively new authors.

Here are some possible venues for speaking engagements.

- Public library
- Local writing groups
- Schools
- Book clubs (see below)
- Someone's workplace
- Community centers

Book Clubs & Discussion Groups

Book clubs and book discussion groups provide publicity that cannot be bought. They meet in libraries, bookstores, club houses, and peoples' homes. Most everyone you know is likely either in a book club or knows someone who is in one. Spread the word—tell your friends and family you are available to participate in book club discussions if they choose your book for their monthly read. Book-club members love to have authors present for their discussions. Bring a copy of your next book as a door prize. (I give it away to the person who has the next birthday coming up.)

I love participating in book club discussions, and my experience is that the book club members are thrilled to have me there. I have participated in many, most of them local but a couple across the country by Skype, and the feedback I have received has been invaluable. They always begin with a discussion about the story line of my book, but it inevitably ends with a discussion about the writing process. I love talking about either.

If you want to cater to book clubs, be sure to include a list of discussion questions at the end of your book or link readers to a page on your website with the questions. Craft questions to stimulate the readers' intellect, as opposed to test their memory on facts about the story line. Make it personal—try to draw them further into the story.

There are thousands of online book clubs, but since they are online and accessible to anyone, they are inundated with requests from authors, so try to be genre-specific in your queries. Here is one book-club list I found book-clubs-resource.com/online/. I am sure there are others. And you may also find clubs in your area via meetup.com.

Local Establishments

People love local authors, self-published ones included. Write letters to the editor of your local newspapers, newsletters, and trade journals. Call your local radio and TV stations and offer to do an interview. Contact your local library and bookstores and offer to do a signing or free lecture. Talk to everyone you visit about your book—your dry cleaner, dentist, doctor, and grocer. Look for bulletin boards wherever you go to post information about your website, blog, and books.

Writers Conferences and Book Fairs

Writers conferences and book fairs are great opportunities for networking, learning more about your craft and the industry, and promoting your books. You'll have the chance to meet and seek advice from fellow authors, book editors, agents, and book marketing specialists. Here is a link to a list of writers conferences for 2020. selfpublishing.com/best-writers-conference/

Family and Friends

Don't discount word-of-mouth with family and friends. If all my FB friends re-posted one of my book announcements, I would reach close to 10,000 more people. That's a lot of potential book buyers.

Thank You

I have saved the most important advice for last, and that is to say "thank you." Say it when someone has read your book, given you a review, recommended your book to others, re-posted your announcement on their Facebook page, complimented your work, and even when they offer criticism. Take it a step further by sending them a handwritten note on one of your bookmarks, business cards, or postcards. Gratitude is its own reward.

SUGGESTED READING:

(Book Marketing Tools staff). "A Step-By-Step Indie Authors Guide for Attracting Media Attention." (No date). https://bookmarketing tools.com/blog/a-step-by-step-indie-authors-guide-for-attracting-media-attention/.

Chesson, Dave. Kindlepreneur (blog): *127 of the Top Free and Paid Book Promotion Sites* https://kindlepreneur.com/list-sites-promote-free-amazon-books/.

Christie, Sally Franklin and Parsons, Jim (moderators). The Writers Chat Room http://writerschatroom.com/wp/online-writers-chat-room/.

Drake, Julia. "The Ultimate Guide to Book Trailers: How to Produce a Killer Book Promo Video." Writer's Digest. February 7, 2018. https://www.writersdigest.com/writing-articles/by-writing-goal/marketing-your-work/book-trailer-guide-how-to-produce-book-promo-video.

CHAPTER 32

Discounts, Freebies, and Promotional Items

C alling attention to your book is essential for sales, and there are many ways you can accomplish this. Three strategies are discussed in this chapter: discounting the price of your book, giving it away for a brief period of time, and creating promotional items to hand out to prospective buyers.

Discounts and Freebies

Everyone loves a sale. Discounting your book periodically will draw in people who may not have been interested when the book was at its normal price. If they like it, you've gained a fan, and fans will consider buying your other books and help spread the word on what a great author you are. I once heard from a book club member that one of my books on sale at the time caught her eye, and from that I sold twenty-five books when she chose it for her club's monthly read. You never know.

Some of you are probably asking why anyone would want to give away their books. Many authors feel that giving away their books sends a message that they put little value on their book or that they're desperate. Hear me out, there are reasons to give away books.

First, it gives you exposure you wouldn't otherwise receive, lots of exposure. During my most successful BookBub free-book promotion, I gave away over 76,000 e-books. This kind of exposure led to increased sales of the book being promoted in the days/weeks/months following the promotion, as well as in crossover sales for my other books. During the thirty days following this particular promotion, I sold substantially more than my usual monthly sales for all my books, resulting in a huge ROI.

Secondly, the more books you give away, the higher your Amazon ranking, and the higher your Amazon ranking, the better your ability to sell more books. Readers look at rankings, and so does Amazon. My books have shown up on the section of Amazon's buy page that says, "Customers who viewed this item also considered..." as well as on the opening page of some Kindle readers. This is exposure you can't buy.

Third, some of the people who download your book will write a review—reviews that will help other readers make buying decisions. During the thirty days following my biggest promotion, I received 147 Amazon reviews averaging 4.4 stars. Good reviews sell books.

And last, giving away an e-book doesn't cost anything.

KDP Select

If your book is available on Kindle, you may want to consider their KDP Select program. It costs nothing to join. Their terms and conditions are lengthy, but in a nutshell, there are two major benefits: promotional opportunities and being included in Kindle's lending library.

Two promotional opportunities are available if you join the KDP Select program. During each ninety-day enrollment period, you can make the Kindle version of your book available on Amazon for free up to five days in exchange for giving Amazon exclusivity on any digital version of the book. You can choose five one-day promotions, one five-day promotion, or any other combination you desire that adds up to five days. Or you can choose a Kindle Countdown Deal that involves limited-time discount promotions and a countdown clock showing how much time is left at the promotional price.

The second benefit of the KDP Select program is their Kindle Owners' Lending Library. If someone is an Amazon Prime member, they can borrow most Kindle books listed on Amazon (one per month) at no cost. The beauty of this is that the author earns a royalty based on pages read from the borrowed book. I earn the majority of my royalties from Prime members borrowing my books.

Why wouldn't you want to participate in the KDP Select program? If you elect to participate in KDP and you continue to sell e-books via channels other than Kindle, you will be violating the program rules, and if you breach the contract in this manner, you face forfeiting all royalties earned during the ninety days. So if you are successfully selling lots of e-books in other venues, KDP Select may not be for you.

Where to Promote Discounted and Free Books

Hundreds of sites exist where you can promote your discounted and free books—it's an evolving list, as sites frequently drop off and are added. The largest, most effective, and most expensive one is BookBub, so let me begin by discussing it.

BookBub is a service (free to readers) that helps people discover books in their favorite genre that are either deeply discounted or free during a limited promotion period. Claiming more than 10 million avid reader-members interested in thirty different genres, BookBub has noted the following demographics (from April 2017) of their members:

> 85% prefer books in e-format
> 76% of their readers are female
> 40% are employed full-time, 36% are retired
> 74% are married
> 73% are empty nesters
> 29% are 65+; 28% are age 55-64; 20% are 45-54; 14% are 35-44; 7% are 25-34; and 2% are under 25
> 30% prefer mysteries/thrillers; 13% prefer sci-fi/fantasy; 12% literary fiction; and 11% romance

BookBub used to be a self-publisher's best friend, but things changed in 2016 when (based on my observation) most of the promotions they accepted were from traditionally published books. Before this, about one in five deals submitted to them were accepted. Today, it's closer to one in ten. The cost has gone up as well—a deal (literary fiction) that cost me $220 in 2015 now costs $411. Other genres are even more expensive.

The way BookBub works is authors submit a title for consideration for a promotion spot with them. Their editorial team reviews the submission. Selection factors include the promotion price, reviews, awards, cover design, the number of retailers from which the book is available, and content (what they believe readers will enjoy).

If you are lucky enough to get your book accepted for a BookBub deal, they will promote it in one of their daily e-mails to readers who are interested in that particular genre and also put it on their website.

I haven't been able to snag a BookBub deal since 2017, when I got a deal that cost me $317 and worked out to a more than 300 percent ROI on that title alone. I also had an increase in residual crossover sales for my other books. The most successful BookBub promotion cost me $180 in 2015 with a 2,016 percent ROI (no, that is not a typo). So, if you are lucky enough to get a deal from them, and you can afford the up-front cost, BookBub is a great way to get exposure and make a financial gain.

But for the vast majority of us who can't secure a BookBub deal, there are other options for promoting our books—many are free of charge; some cost a few dollars a day; and some are more expensive. Many book-promotion sites have strict requirements (like number of four- and five-star reviews the book has) and some have no requirements. Here are the ones I've recently used that are associated with a cost to advertise.

- Authorsxp
- Bookdaily
- Bookloversheaven
- Bookpreviewclub
- Bookreadermagazine
- Bookrunes
- Booksbutterfly
- Choosybookworm
- Ereadernewstoday
- Freekindlebooksandtips
- Greatbooksgreatdeals
- Justkindlebooks
- Kindlebookreview
- Kindlenationdaily

- Newfreekindlebooks
- Readingdeals
- Thefussylibrarian

With the exception of BookBub, I have never run a promotion using just one promotion site, so it's hard to tell which ones have been the most successful for me. My strategy is to establish a budget (usually under $100), pick the site(s) that I think will give me the best exposure, and then submit to them, along with sites that don't charge anything. I typically end up with twenty or so sites for each promotion. Here are the ones I've recently used that do not charge a fee to advertise the promotion.

- Armadilloebooks
- Askdavid
- Bargainbooksy
- Bookpreviewclub
- Bookzio
- Digitalbooktoday
- Ebookshabit
- Fivestarreads
- Freebooks
- Freebooksy
- Icravefreebies
- Igniteyourbook
- Indiebookoftheday
- Itswritenow
- Readingdeals
- Thebookcircle
- Theereaderscafe

I currently have seven novels published and typically run one free or discounted promotion per month. That works well with my KDP Select enrollment. With five promotion days allowed each ninety-day enrollment period, that means each of my books gets promoted twice a year.

Promotional Materials

Promotional products can be a good marketing tool—as effective as advertising and in some ways even more, as they are longer-lasting. Give people something practical, and they will think of you whenever they use it. Furthermore, promotional items send a message to people that you are serious about what you do.

I participate in as many book fairs as I can, and that's where I get the most out of the promotional items I use. I always have an 8x10 poster of my latest book, business cards, and bookmarks on the table. I also created (on my own—no outside costs) a postcard-sized card for each of my books that includes the cover image, synopsis, and "where to buy" information. That way, visitors to my booth have something to take away with them for future reference.

Many promotional items are extremely affordable. Others will require an investment. The two must-haves are business cards and bookmarks. Other items to consider include:

- Pens/pencils
- Tote bags
- Postcards
- Posters/banners

- T-shirts
- Coffee cups
- Stickers
- Notepads

If your book calls for it, choose promotional items that reflect the theme. I know one author whose main character owned a tea store. She had tea bags made with the cover image and handed them out at book fairs. I know another author who wrote historical novels and had paper hand-fans made as a promotional item. Be creative. Have fun with it.

SUGGESTED READING:

Brandt, Jason. "Why Authors Shouldn't Give Away Free Books." Alliance of Independent Authors. February 27, 2017. https:// selfpublishingadvice.org/opinion-why-indie-authors-shouldnt-give-away-free-books/.

Collett, Glenna. Book Design Made Simple (blog): *Your Book Promotion Materials* https://www.bookdesignmadesimple.com/ book-promotion-materials/.

Klaric, Mateja. "What Can You Expect When You Offer Your Books for Free." The Writing Cooperative. March 21, 2018. https://

writingcooperative.com/why-im-offering-my-book-for-free-7831b97f4dd2.

Spatz, Steven. "Amanda Hocking Made Millions by Selling 99-Cent Books—and You Can, Too." The Writing Cooperative. October 11, 2018. https://writingcooperative.com/amanda-hocking-made-millions-by-selling-99-cent-books-and-you-can-too-ee87e470e869.

CHAPTER 33

Contests and Awards

Awards can be the catalyst your book needs to bring it out of obscurity and into the spotlight. They can create interest in your book, which may lead to more sales and other opportunities including media, agent, and publisher interest. Recognition from a prominent panel of judges can increase a book's credibility, visibility, and marketability, especially if the contest is open to both traditionally and self-published books.

The best vetted list of awards and contests that I can recommend is put out by the Alliance of Independent Authors selfpublishingadvice. org/author-awards-contests-rated-reviewed/, who rate each one after appraising them using multiple criteria, including pricing and value, quality of service, contract terms and rights, transparency, accountability, and customer satisfaction. They use three ratings:

- **RECOMMENDED**
- **MIXED**—those which are mostly positive but present some issues of minor concern.
- **CAUTION**—those with serious concerns, such as excessive entry fees, exploitative contracts, conflicts of interest, or high-pressure sales.

Are literary awards worthwhile for authors? Here are the pros and cons of writing contests.

PROS

- **MONEY:** The cash prize can range anywhere from less than a hundred dollars to many thousands.
- **PRESTIGE:** The exposure may help with sales and being noticed by the right people.
- **PUBLICATION:** Publication in a well-known magazine, website, or other venue results in recognition and potential sales.
- **LONGLIST/SHORTLIST CREDIT:** Even an honorable mention can help to get exposure for your book.
- **TIME AWAY FROM YOUR WORK:** Deadlines can work in your favor. Sometimes just having to work under a deadline helps to get projects moving and off your desk.

CONS

- **ENTRY FEES:** Many times the cash prize isn't enough to cover the cost to enter and effort you put into the project.
- **EXCLUSIVE SUBMISSIONS:** Some contests require exclusive submissions, tying up your manuscript for a period of time.
- **RISK FACTOR:** There is the risk of your winning being a long shot and your entry a waste of your time and money.

Probably the best thing that comes from winning an award is a boost to the author's ego and recognition to all others involved in the project for doing a good job. Whether winning an award will result in increased sales is questionable, but it does mean that the author's name and title of the book will get exposure, which is never a bad thing. And people do take notice that a book has won an award—authors can display medals and stickers on their books, website, e-mail signature, and anywhere else that may make a difference to a potential book purchaser.

Don't expect much of a payday if you win. There is usually very little, if any, prize money awarded, and the amount may not be much more than the entry fee.

Before you enter a writing contest, consider these words of advice:

- Double-check your eligibility before you go any further.
- Be aware of word-count restrictions, formatting preferences, and what you should and should not include with your submission.
- Take note of the deadline and give yourself plenty of time to prepare a perfect manuscript. Hire an editor or at least a proof-reader to make your submission as strong as possible.
- Review the works of the contest's previous winners to determine what the judges deem award-winning material.
- If you are a first-time entrant, start with smaller contests, then work your way up.

SCAM ALERT: Like every other aspect of publishing, there are many unethical people out there who are making a living from scamming authors with phony contests. Beware of the following:

- Contest organizers who lure you in with the promise of a publishing contract.
- Contests with high entry fees and very little payout.
- Contests hosted by an unknown sponsor with little or no track record.

SUGGESTED READING:

Friedlander, Joel. The Book Designer (blog): *Book Awards for Self-Published Authors.* https://www.thebookdesigner.com/book-awards/.

Strauss, Victoria. Victoria Strauss (blog): *Writing Contests: Facts and Fakes...and How to Tell the Difference.* https://www.victoriastrauss.com/advice/contests/.

CHAPTER 34

Brand and Platform

Y ou can differentiate yourself from other authors by developing a unique brand and building a platform to be recognized for it. Once you start doing this, people will get a sense for who you are and the types of books you write. It is a slow process, but if you take control of it early, you will avoid people drawing the wrong conclusions about your expertise, personality, and ability to sell books.

Brand

We're all familiar with the general concept of branding when it comes to our everyday lives. We immediately know what to expect when we see or hear mention of the Nike, McDonald's, or Amazon brands, for example. Branding for authors is the same concept. For authors, your brand is your name—when people hear it, you want them to immediately think of your product—your books.

Brand is how others perceive you based on the words you write, your style, the colors and theme you choose for your business cards and website, and how you present yourself in public. Your brand is reflected in your books, through your social media posts, on your website/blog, on your business cards and promotional items, and in your personal presence.

When thinking of your brand, ask yourself how you want to be perceived and then act accordingly. For example, if you want to be perceived as a serious mystery writer, don't choose a frivolous theme for your business cards and website. If you write children's books, cater to them and their parents.

A few years ago, I participated in Chicago's Printers Row Lit Fest, at which I displayed my books in a booth shared by three other authors. One author spent his time in front of the booth, practically grabbing people off the walkway in an effort to get noticed. A second author sat demurely behind the table inside the booth, often looking down at her phone. The third one spent more time chitchatting with people on the sidelines than he did paying attention to the passersby. And then there was me: I stood behind the table and tried to make eye contact with the people passing by the booth. I sold out by 2:00 p.m. and had to start taking orders. The others didn't fare that well. Okay, so it may have helped that I had a dish of Godiva chocolates readily available, but still... The point I'm trying to make is that my approach seemed to attract viable book buyers compared to what the others were doing—the manner in which I branded myself at this particular event suited my intended audience.

There are many ways to create awareness of your brand, and they are all about exposure. The more exposure you get, the more recognizable your brand will be. And the more recognizable your brand, the more sales you'll enjoy.

Expert marketers say that it takes seven to ten impressions for people to recall your brand. Here are some ways to get your brand out there.

- Write good books—this is always #1!
- Hand out business cards.
- Use a signature block on e-mails that includes links to you and your books.
- Hand out promotional items.
- Participate in interviews.
- Do speaking engagements.

- Promote your website/blog.
- Use social media pages to their fullest advantage.
- Participate in book club discussion groups.
- Participate in online discussion groups.
- Write articles.
- Guest-post on blogs.
- Exhibit in book fairs.

Caution: Like any other brand name, yours is an implied promise to the consumer that they will consistently receive a specific kind of product from you—if you deviate from it, you risk losing credibility.

Platform

Platform is an author's ability to sell books based on their background, the connections they have, and the distribution channels they use to reach an audience—it conveys an author's expertise and credibility to others in an effort to build a career. Platform gives authors visibility so that others know who they are and how to find them and their books.

If your goal is to become a successful author, you will need to build a platform, and if you begin the process before you have a book to sell, you'll be that much ahead of the game when your book is launched. NOTE: If you're a big celebrity, you can stop reading now—you have a built-in platform.

The true value in an author platform is in deepening connections with readers. It's not about book marketing and promotion...although the goals may be similar. The whole point of a platform is to market yourself as an author.

Building an author platform is a gradual process. For most of us, it involves education, experience, and hard work. It rarely happens overnight. Before I retired from a traditional office job to write novels, I worked in the corporate world. My last position was regional director of administration for a $75 billion company. It took years to attain that level position—years of gaining expertise, fostering relationships, and establishing a credible reputation—years of building an effective platform. Building an author platform is no different.

An effective platform should affirm an author's uniqueness—what sets him or her apart from competitors. To begin to establish a platform, think in terms of the following components:

- Proven abilities
- Personality
- Websites and blogs
- E-mail subscriber list
- Social media

The quality of your platform will have a direct effect on the success of your book.

Proven Abilities

Showing the world that you are a successful, credible author will naturally follow the successful, credible books you've written. But until you reach that point in your career as an author, there are things you can do to pave the way. One of the things I often preach to new authors is to proofread everything you write…yes, even text messages and social media posts. Typos, confusing/cryptic sentences, and bad grammar are not qualities of a good writer. You can demonstrate your writing skills in your blogs, website, articles, and comments to other people's blogs and articles. Let the world know that you know how to write.

Personality

Personality—derived from the Latin word *persona,* which means "mask," as used by early actors when they changed their appearance—is the combination of an individual's thoughts, characteristics, behaviors, attitudes, ideas, and habits. Personality is what makes you interesting; being interesting is how you grab people's attention and distinguish yourself from other authors. An interesting personality can help you progress in your writing career.

Your personality can shine through in many ways, not just face-to-face encounters. Your online presence will reveal your personality as well and can be helpful in attracting potential followers, fans, and book buyers.

Websites and Blogs

Having your own website is a prerequisite for launching a book—it serves as a home base for establishing relationships between you and readers. When people visit your website, it is because they want to know something more about you. What better opportunity to connect with a possible future book purchaser? Your author website is all about you—a showcase for your work, who you are, what you do, and what you want to be known for. And, unlike social media, you have total control—you don't have to fight for space or worry about some new social media posting term that limits what you can say, how much you can say, and to whom. But it can work in tandem with social media—when people are trying to find someone online, they're likely to try to find their website, and from there, they can be directed to the person's social media pages.

One of the easiest ways to establish your platform is with a blog. I've heard many stories about authors having met publishers, agents, and screenwriters through blogging. An active blog that gets hits and comments will get noticed. It may take months or even years, but eventually it will get Google's attention; then, when somebody Googles you, you'll be on the first page of the Search Engine Results Page (SERP). With consistent content and lots of patience, an author blog can take your career to the next level by connecting you with the right people.

Websites are great, but blogs offer an even better opportunity to deepen relationships with your followers in that they are interactive. Blogging is writing—it's what you do and a great way to present your skills. People are judgmental, and if visitors view your website/blog as well written and well thought out, they are more likely to consider you a serious, professional author.

Your website/blog can be an important means for readers to get to know you better and form a valuable relationship that leads to sales. Moreover, it is the perfect tool for curating your e-mail subscription list.

(See Chapter 29 for more about websites and blogs.)

E-mail Subscriber List

Imagine having at your disposal a list of people who are interested in you and your work—dedicated followers who have asked to be on the receiving end of updates about what you're working on and when a new release is about to come out. Could it get any better than that? Well, that's the beauty of an e-mail subscriber list—an easy and free way to communicate directly with real fans, a powerful way to engage with your readers.

Finding subscribers is directly related to the quality of your platform—the more exposure you get, the more relationships you develop, the more you'll discover interested readers, and the larger your subscriber list will grow. And the best way to do this is with a compelling website. (See Chapter 29 for more on website development.)

Unlike your social media pages, your e-mail list is owned by you, which gives you control over what you post to a captured audience. Be sure to offer something of value in exchange for their e-mail address. This can be done in the way of a short story you've written, a few chapters from one of your books, or an entire book. I invite people to join in exchange for a chance to win a free copy of any one of my books. For authors, I add a list of over 100 helpful links related to writing, book publishing, and promotion. This concept works in part because people who have received something of value from you appreciate the bond they've created with you and are more likely to talk about you and buy your books.

It's a long process to build a list—but if you start talking about book one with your subscribers, you will have at least a handful of people to tell about book two. Your list will grow with each new book and as readers find you.

Social Media

The key benefit of social media is engaging with people and getting exposure with posts and shares. The problem is that you can get so caught up in it, it can keep you from doing more important things. So rather than spreading yourself thin across multiple social media platforms, I suggest focusing on the two or three that are most beneficial to building your platform.

Let's start with Twitter. While this social media site has a very active author community, it does not have the same for readers. But because it is so easy to use and the least time-consuming of all social media outlets, I recommend using it for the exposure and potential one-on-one interactions with readers.

Facebook has billions (with a *b*) of monthly active users. The key to benefiting from your Facebook page is to address a niche audience—one specifically interested in your books. This means sharing only content that this audience will enjoy (so no cute cat videos unless, of course, you write about cats). Focus only on that which has the potential for establishing a connection with someone who can improve your career as a writer.

Unlike other platforms that are all about connecting, Pinterest is a place where users can share images that link to articles that interest them. Some people use it to find books to read, making it beneficial for authors. And Pinterest allows you to interact with other Pinterest users to build a community that can add value to your platform.

If your work lends itself to video, try YouTube to increase your overall Web presence. YouTube is not just a place to watch far too many interesting videos (don't even get me started on the baby animal ones). It also contains a wealth of useful advice for authors as well as opportunities to enhance and grow your platform. Possible videos you can create are:

- Book trailers
- Q&A sessions
- Live book launches
- Interviews with other authors
- How-to sessions
- Readings

"Nothing that's worthwhile is ever easy." Nicholas Sparks claims ownership of this quote, but I think he may have borrowed the premise from one of Teddy Roosevelt's famous quips. Either way, it's true. Building an author platform can be trying work, and there will be times you wonder why you're putting so much effort toward it. But it's also rewarding when you see the occasional spike in sales, new followers, or awesome review, and you can attribute it to your platform building.

A strong author platform will result in improved or increased:

- Credibility/validity
- Exposure/visibility
- Meaningful contacts
- Influence over others
- Target audience
- Fan base

You can put as little or as much time into building a platform as you deem appropriate. If your book is being traditionally published, the publisher will likely have a good deal of control over what you do to build your platform. If you are self-published, you will have full control over your destiny. You're in charge. You're the one in the driver's seat. Wait a minute. That's also the scary part.

SUGGESTED READING:

Coker, Mark. "Seven Author Branding Tips." *Publishers Weekly.* November 16, 2108. https://www.publishersweekly.com/pw/by-topic/authors/pw-select/article/78616-seven-author-branding-tips.html.

Friedman, Jane. Jane Friedman (blog): *A Definition of Author Platform.* https://www.janefriedman.com/author-platform-definition/.

McCrae, James. "How to Build a Successful Author Marketing Platform." *Forbes.* April 28, 2017. https://www.forbes.com/sites/forbescommunicationscouncil/2017/04/28/how-to-build-a-successful-author-marketing-platform/#182521e126d4.

Penn, Joanna. Joanna Penn (blog): *7 Best Ways to Build an Authentic Author Brand.* https://www.thecreativepenn.com/2017/11/10/authentic-author-brand/.

CHAPTER 35

Paid Advertising

P aid advertising can be an effective way to attract people to your site (or wherever you are doing your marketing), so you can strengthen your brand, gain fans, and increase sales. I'm a firm believer in the adage that you have to spend money to make money, but if you aren't careful, you can end up with a paid-advertising money pit into which you quickly pour dollars with no ROI.

WARNING: The reason many authors don't use paid advertising is because some aspects of it are a little difficult to understand and complicated to use. In this chapter, I try to explain the process in simple terms.

Online paid advertising comes in many different forms. The main categories include:

Pay-per-click   Display ads
Pay-per-impression   Video ads
Pay-per-download

When you choose pay-per-click advertising, you are essentially competing for advertising space with other advertisers. The way the bidding system works is that the amount you bid for a click isn't what you're actually going to pay—it's the maximum amount you'll pay to win the bid. If you're the highest bidder, most ad networks will charge you $0.01 more than the next highest bidder. The more you're willing to pay, the more likely you are to win. It's a tricky business: If you bid too low, your ad campaign may not get the exposure it deserves because the higher bidders will have won the space; and if you bid too high and others bid high too, you'll end up paying too much per click and blow your budget in a hurry. Each ad network has a different way of determining the winning bids. For example, some may favor a $0.10-per-click ad that gets clicked a thousand times over a $5-per-click ad that gets clicked only twenty times.

With pay-per-impression advertising, an author pays a certain amount each time the ad is displayed regardless of whether anyone clicks on it or not.

The pay-per-download method is for when you want to offer a free download of your book and you pay each time your book is downloaded.

Display ads have been around for centuries—you see them in newspapers and magazines and on billboards. It works the same way online—you create a static visual image of your product and are charged a one-time fee to have the ad displayed.

Video ads are similar to display ads, with a video of the product replacing the static image.

What method of paid advertising is most effective for one author may not be for another—it's all about trial and error. Keep in mind how many books you will need to sell to recoup the cost of the paid advertisement, which approach will result in a positive ROI.

There is a long list of ad networks that want you to pay for advertising, and that's because it's an easy way to make money off you. And that's not necessarily a bad thing…as long as you profit from it too.

Here is an overview of the most popular ad networks for paid advertising. For more specific details on how they work, you will need to visit their websites.

Google

Google's AdWords paid advertising pay-per-click platform (their main source of revenue, by the way) relies on the premise that people who click on the ad will be interested enough to buy the book, and even though most people will not click on it, at least many eyes will have seen the ad.

It is basically a five-step process:

1. **YOU SPECIFY A BUDGET**—the maximum amount you are willing to spend per day.
2. **THEY ASK YOU WHAT GEOGRAPHICAL AREA YOU WISH TO REACH**—U.S. only, other countries, specific cities, etc.
3. **YOU ENTER KEYWORDS RELATIVE TO YOUR AD.** This is a very important step that requires a certain amount of research to determine the most effective ones to use.
4. **YOU DETERMINE YOUR BID**—the most you're willing to pay when someone clicks on your ad.
5. **YOU CREATE YOUR AD.** Each ad is composed of a link, a headline, and two lines of text—a concise, informative call-to-action.

This link ads.google.com will take you to Google's paid advertising page.

Amazon

Amazon offers five options for paid advertising:

- **SPONSORED PRODUCT ADS**—pay-per-click, keyword-targeted display ads
- **HEADLINE SEARCH ADS**— pay-per-click, auction-based ads that let you feature up to three different products
- **PRODUCT DISPLAY ADS**—pay-per-click ads that appear on Amazon product-detail pages, customer-review pages, on top of the offer-listing page, and below search results
- **NATIVE ADS**—ads that you can place on your own website

- **VIDEO ADS**—ads that you can place on Amazon-owned sites like Amazon.com and IMDb, Amazon devices like Fire TV, and various other places

This link advertising.amazon.com will take you to Amazon's paid advertising page.

Goodreads

Goodreads also offers a pay-per-click advertising option that involves three steps.

1. Loading the book into the Goodreads system and writing a short description
2. Setting a daily budget, total budget, and bid amount (the amount charged each time someone clicks on the ad)
3. Choosing which Goodreads users will be able to see the ad, depending on age, gender, country, and genre

This link goodreads.com/advertisers will take you to Goodreads' paid advertising page.

Pinterest

Pinterest offers a variety of ad options.

- **PROMOTED PINS**—appear in the home feed and search results just like a regular Pin except that they're boosted to target a wider reach
- **ONE-TAP PINS**—user clicks are taken directly to your landing page
- **PROMOTED CAROUSELS**—multi-image ads
- **PROMOTED VIDEO PINS**—appear in the home feed, search results, and the "more like this" section
- **PROMOTED APP PINS**—allow users to download your mobile app from Pinterest

- **BUYABLE PINS**—allow users to find and buy products directly from your Pin
- **STORY PINS**—allow up to twenty pages of images, text, and links

The steps required to create a Pinterest ad are:

1. Choose a preexisting ad group or create a new one. Each ad group is independent and can have a different budget and targeting.
2. Determine the target audience.
3. Select placement for the ad.
4. Add keywords.
5. Set the start and end date for the ad campaign and a daily or lifetime budget.
6. Set the maximum bid for the ad.
7. Determine at what pace you want your ads to show throughout the day—standard or accelerated.

This link pinterest.com/business will take you to Pinterest's paid advertising page.

BookBub

BookBub offers an auction-based advertising platform their readers see at the bottom of their daily e-mails. Steps required include:

1. Create the ad.
2. Choose where you want readers to be directed when they click on your ad.
3. Set your target audience based on combinations of author interest and book categories.
4. Establish a budget and schedule.
5. Choose a bidding strategy—cost-per-click or cost-per-thousand-impressions, keeping in mind that you are bidding against other authors who are trying to reach the same readers you've targeted with your ad. The higher you bid, the more clicks or impressions you are likely to win over the competing authors.

This link bookbub.com/partners/bookbub_ads will take you to BookBub's paid advertising page.

Social Media

Social media advertising is another way to potentially drive sales to your website and grow your fanbase. The most popular social media sites are:

Facebook	Reddit
Twitter	Snapchat
YouTube	WhatsApp
Instagram	Tumblr
LinkedIn	Flickr

All offer paid advertising, each with a little something different in pricing and the way they structure their campaigns. The most common billing options are:

- **COST-PER-VIEW (CPV):** You are charged every time someone views your ad.
- **COST-PER-CLICK (CPC):** You pay for the ad each time a viewer clicks on it.
- **COST PER ACTION/CONVERSION (CPA):** You are charged when someone completes the action you specified when optimizing the ad (for example, when someone downloads an app, signs up for an e-mail newsletter, or makes a purchase).
- **COST PER LIKE (CPL):** You pay for each follower gained through the ad campaign.

Whichever paid advertising network you choose, consider tracking results on a spreadsheet so you can see trends, as daily results don't really tell you very much. Weekly and monthly trends are better indicators of whether the ad network is working for you.

If your results aren't very good in the beginning, try tweaking the various settings provided by the particular ad network. Try different keywords, cost-per-click, or target audience. If it's still not working, don't keep pouring money into it with little or no ROI and expect it to miraculously bring in a profit one day. Know when to try something else.

Paid advertising is not a quick, guaranteed way to make a profit selling your books. It requires understanding how it works, patience, and knowing when to stop.

SUGGESTED READING:

Chesson, Dave. Jane Friedman (blog): *Changes to Amazon Advertising: What Authors Need to Know.* https://www.jane friedman.com/amazon-ads-changing/.

Chesson, Dave. Kindlepreneur (blog): *How to Advertise a Book on Facebook.* https://kindlepreneur.com/how-to-advertise-book-facebook-facebook-ads-for-books/.

Robertson, Carlyn. David Gaughran (blog): *Clever Ways Authors Are Using BookBub Ads.* https://davidgaughran.com/2018/12/07/clever-book-marketing-authors-bookbub-ads/.

Shiau, Yvonne (Content Editor USA). Reedsy (blog): *Amazon Ads for Authors: Two Case Studies Showing They Do Work.* https://blog.reedsy.com/amazon-ads-for-authors-case-studies/.

Verrillo, Erica. "8 Ways to Use Goodreads to Promote Your Book." The Writing Cooperative. May 29, 2018. https://writingco operative.com/8-ways-to-use-goodreads-to-promote-your-book-461f52eec54b.

CHAPTER 36

Distribution and Sales

Once you've written a book, it's time to decide how to get it into the hands of readers. The good news is that self-published authors have the same access to online retail distribution as the major publishers, and they do not have to hire an expensive self-publishing service to get their books distributed through them.

Let me start with Amazon, the obvious gorilla in the room, which handles both print and e-book distribution.

Amazon

More than half of all book sales take place online, with Amazon the number one retailer in both print and digital formats. If you publish through Amazon's KDP subsidiary, and your book is original content that has never been published before, you most likely have what they consider worldwide rights, which means customers can purchase your print and e-book through any of the nine Amazon.com companies (United States, United Kingdom, Turkey, Spain, France, Italy, Japan, Canada, and Australia). Uploading your e-book file or print manuscript is super easy and costs nothing. Amazon makes its money by taking a percentage of your royalties.

Amazon does not require exclusivity (unless you opt in to its KDP Select service for e-books), so if you want to order print books for yourself to sell elsewhere, you can do so for the cost to print the book plus shipping.

Print Books

For print book distribution, you may want to consider print-on-demand technology, as opposed to investing in a print run (with which you produce hundreds or thousands of books at a time). Print-on-demand means that your book isn't printed until someone orders it. If books are printed only when they're ordered, you will pay more for the printing of each book, but you won't be stuck with an inventory of books if they don't sell.

The key distributor (other than Amazon) to consider for print books is IngramSpark—the largest book wholesaler/distributor in the U.S. If you go into a bookstore and order a book, they will likely order it from IngramSpark. Most libraries, schools, and other institutions also order from them.

IngramSpark does not require exclusivity and allows authors to purchase print copies of their books at cost plus shipping.

E-books

Readers can purchase e-books from a variety of online retailers (Amazon's KDP, Apple iBooks, Kobo, and Google Play, for example). To reach these different stores, authors have two options—work directly with the retailers or use an aggregator (Draft2Digital, IngramSparks, Smashwords, and Bookbaby, to name a few) that will distribute your book to a large number of stores and other venues in exchange for either a cut of your royalties or an up-front fee for each book they distribute for you.

Like so many other authors, I choose to keep things simple by working directly and exclusively with Amazon via its KDP Select program for the sale of my e-books. That's not to say it will be the best method for you. You should investigate the other methods and make the best decision based on your circumstances.

I've talked about using online retailers and aggregators to get your books in the hands of readers, but there are many other methods you can use to accomplish this, albeit on a smaller scale. Here are some to consider.

Your Website

Selling your books directly from your website is potentially the most lucrative way to sell your books, as you enjoy 100 percent of the profits. If you include a PayPal or Zelle feature on your website, you will make payment easy and avoid dealing with credit cards and personal checks. I advise including the cost of shipping in the price you set, as it keeps things simple. To encourage purchases, be sure to include on your home page the book's cover image, excerpts from good reviews of the book, and testimonials. Ship the book from your own inventory and offer to write an inscription inside the book, making it a more personal experience for the purchaser than going to a large retailer.

Book Fairs

I do very well at local book fairs. When I lived in downtown Chicago, I participated in Printers Row Lit Fest and sold out both times. Now that I live in the far north suburbs of Chicago, I attend several smaller venues and do well at those. I price my books to do little more than break even, as exposure in these instances is more important to me than income.

Community Craft Fairs

My small community of Venetian Village holds a local craft/vendor show each year. Last year was the first one I attended, and I sold twenty books—not bad for a small event. And what was even more promising was the number of people who stopped by to talk to me and left with a bookmark, business card, or some other item with my contact and book purchase information on it. Getting the word out locally where you live is a great way to get exposure.

Bookstores

While major bookstores are closing branches, the smaller independent stores appear to be hanging on. Many of them will take your books on consignment. Some have a local author section. You're probably not going to make a ton of money here, but the exposure is worth the small effort you'll make.

Book Clubs

I love when someone in a book club selects one of my books for their monthly read and invites me to join in on the discussion. The conversation always starts out about the story line of the selected book but inevitably turns to my journey as an author. Book clubs are fun. Such interactions between author and readers almost always result in invaluable feedback.

Conferences

I haven't attended very many conferences, but the ones I did attend usually resulted in meeting other authors who ended up either wanting to buy one of my books or exchange one of theirs for one of mine. Not a big money-maker, but again, you never know where such a connection can lead.

Libraries

You'll want libraries to have copies of your books. Some have a local-author section that many locals find interesting. I started out by donating a copy of each of my books to local libraries (in my case, six libraries). If they are checked out often enough, the library will purchase more so there is always one on the shelf.

Retail Shops

Small towns in particular often have boutique shops that include a book section. Approach the owner for space on their shelves. Many will be thrilled to have books written by a local author.

Book Signings

I find that book signings are more common in small towns than in large cities (at least for us relatively unknown authors), and they take place in bookstores, libraries, coffee shops, and other places locals frequent. Small businesses are usually receptive to the idea because it may attract customers, so don't miss out on this opportunity.

The above suggestions are not going to make you rich—each is just one more thing that will help you get your name and book titles out there and build your author platform and brand. And they can perhaps add some fun to your busy author life.

SUGGESTED READING:

Doppler, John. "What's the Best Way to Distribute Self-Published Books—Direct or Via an Aggregator?" Alliance of Independent Authors. January 17, 2017. https://selfpublishingadvice.org/distribute-self-published-books/.

Friedman, Jane. Jane Friedman (blog): *How to Get Your Book Distributed: What Self-Published Authors Need to Know.* https://www.janefriedman.com/get-book-distributed-self-published-authors-need-know/.

Haines, Derek. "What are the Best Ways to Sell Books Online?" Just Publishing Advice. November 17, 2019. https://justpublishingadvice.com/whats-the-best-way-to-sell-my-books-online/.

(IngramSpark Staff). IngramSpark (blog): *How to Sell Your Self-Published Books to Bookstores.* https://www.ingramspark.com/blog/how-to-sell-your-book-to-bookstores.

Williams, John Sibley. Creative Penn (blog): *How to Sell More Books at Author Events.* https://www.thecreativepenn.com/2019/06/28/book-marketing-how-to-sell-more-books-at-author-events/.

PART 5

Conclusion

The scariest moment is always just before you start.
After that, things can only get better.
—STEPHEN KING

So many people have thought about writing a book at some point in their life—starting with some glimmer of an idea that they thought would make a good story. They may have pondered it off and on for years but, for one reason or another, never acted on it. Does that sound like you? If so, I hope that after reading this book you haven't been scared off; rather, I hope you feel that now is the time to begin writing.

Anyone can write a book. It could be the worst book ever written, but it's still a book. The difference between a good book and a bad one is usually the level of effort put into it. I made many painful mistakes during the course of writing novels, but I can honestly say that I've learned from each one of them. I wrote *How to Write, Publish, and Promote a Novel* based on (in part) what I learned from my mistakes.

It bears repeating: The vast majority of first-time authors will sell fewer than 100 copies of their book (mostly to family and friends), not even recouping expenses let alone making a profit. But creating a well-written, professionally edited, marketable book that is vigorously promoted increases the odds of meeting reasonable goals. Keep this in mind as you develop your goals and objectives for writing a book.

I like this article annhandley.com/9-qualities-of-good-writing/ by Ann Handley in which she talks about nine qualities of good writing. If you're a first-time writer, it's definitely worth the read. The insight that most resonates with me is her statement that good writing:

- serves the reader, not the writer,
- has credible content,
- has likely gone through many rewrites,
- has structure and logic, and
- is simple but not simplistic.

Just as it's hard to condense an entire novel into a 500-word synopsis, it is difficult for me to summarize what I've written in *How to Write, Publish, and Promote a Novel*. But I'll try. Each bullet point represents what from my experience is an essential aspect of publishing a successful novel.

- Understand your reason and motivation for writing a book.
- Know the difference between traditional publishing and self-publishing.
- Set reasonable goals and a realistic budget.
- Know whom you are targeting to read your book.
- Understand the basic elements of writing fiction—character, plot, setting, point of view, conflict, and theme.
- Realize the importance of a professional editor and cover designer.
- Create effective advertising blurbs.
- Consider creating your own website, blog, and/or newsletter.
- Be aware of industry scams.
- Learn what makes a book highly marketable.
- Know all the avenues for promoting, distributing and selling your book.

I can't guaranty that if you follow the advice in this book that you'll be a successful author, but I can guaranty that if you do, your chances will be better than if you had done nothing. Ultimately, it all falls on you—how much time and money you are willing to invest.

Hopefully, I have given you enough fundamental information to write the book that's been inside of you just yearning to get out and haven't discouraged you with some of these eye-opening facts. I trust that after reading this book, you realize there is no secret that allows you to skip over the hard parts. (See Appendix A for a comprehensive list of things to do before, during, and after the writing of your book.)

I want to end this book with a list of self-publishing success stories—stories about people like you and me who love to write but weren't taken seriously by traditional publishers. Some of their stories seem fictional in themselves…but they're not.

E.E. Cummings
Twentieth-century poet Edward Estlin Cummings had to rely on his own finances (and, at times, his mother's) to publish his work, as traditional publishers just weren't interested in him due to his unconventional style. After self-publishing for much of his career, he eventually found the fame he deserved when he published *No Thanks*, a volume of poetry financed by his mother. On the half-title page, he listed the thirteen publishers that had rejected the book, which later became one of his classics.

Lisa Genova
In 2007, neuroscientist Lisa Genova began her writing career by self-publishing *Still Alice,* the story of a woman who slowly loses her thoughts and memories to Alzheimer's disease. To get exposure, she went as far as selling copies out of the trunk of her car for the first two years. The book was later picked up by Simon & Schuster, made the *New York Times* best-seller list, and was made into a movie starring Julianne Moore. *Still Alice* has sold millions of copies in more than twenty-five languages.

Amanda Hocking
One can't talk about self-publishing success stories without mentioning Amanda Hocking. After years of seeing her urban fantasy and paranormal romance books get rejected by agents and publishing houses, she self-published one of them in e-book format on Amazon in the hope of selling at least enough copies to finance a trip to Chicago to see her beloved Muppets on exhibit there. She managed to raise not just the $300 needed for the trip but an additional $20,000. St. Martin's Press later bought the rights to her first three novels for $2 million…and the rest is history. Hocking has published more than twenty-five novels, including the *New York Times* best-selling series the *Trylle Trilogy* and

The Kanin Chronicles, along with the *Watersong, My Blood Approves,* and *The Hollows* series.

E. L. James
While her *Fifty Shades* trilogy is controversial due to the books' sexual content and lack of literary merit, one has to give E. L. James credit for being right in her insistence that there was a large audience for this type of literature. She sold more than 100 million copies of her books, making her a poster child for self-publishing.

Michael J. Sullivan
Author Michael Sullivan started writing books to teach his dyslexic daughter to read. After spending more than ten years writing thirteen novels, he couldn't find a publisher. His wife, who believed in him and supported his work, formed her own publishing company and helped him become the successful sci-fi and fantasy writer that he is today. Sullivan has published one stand-alone novel, *Hollow World,* and three series: *The Riyria Revelations, The Riyria Chronicles,* and *Legends of the First Empire.*

Andy Weir
When Weir failed to find a publisher for his first book, *The Martian,* he began posting free chapters of it on his website. Later, he put a ninety-nine-cent version of it on Kindle. By 2013, the book had become so popular that Weir received an offer from Crown Publishing to buy the book for $100,000.

William P. Young
After having written a story with a strong Christian message, William Young wanted to present it to his children in book form for Christmas. He made fifteen copies, which he gave to his kids and a few friends. When they encouraged him to get it published for wider distribution, he polished up *The Shack* and sent it to twenty-six publishers, all of whom rejected it. So he formed his own publishing house, published it

himself, went on to sell millions of copies, and wound up on the *New York Times* best-seller list.

Follow your dreams and make them happen. Have realistic expectations, work hard, and it will pay off—that's what I believe.

I wish you every success with your book, and I hope it becomes a best seller!

Florence Osmund

I hope you found *How to Write, Publish, and Promote a Novel* helpful and will consider posting a short review on Amazon (amazon.com/author/florenceosmund) and/or Goodreads (goodreads.com/user/show/8800692-florence-osmund). Reviews and word-of-mouth referrals play an important role in helping authors promote their books, and your help in this regard is much appreciated.

Florence Osmund

Additional Resources

I n addition to the topic-specific lists of links at the end of each chapter under Suggested Reading, here are some helpful links to articles, books, and online classes that are of a more general nature.

Online Articles

Crawford, Sara. Live Write Thrive (blog): *What Does It Take to Be a Real Writer?* https://www.livewritethrive.com/2019/09/16/what-does-it-take-to-be-a-real-writer/#more-10793.

Donovan, Melissa. Writing Forward (blog): *42 Fiction Writing Tips for Novelists.* https://www.writingforward.com/storytelling/42-fiction-writing-tips-for-novelists.

Goins, Jeff. Goins Writer (blog): *The Best Books on Writing You'll Ever Read.* https://goinswriter.com/best-writing-books/.

Jenkins, Jerry. Jerry Jenkins (blog): *Writing Tips 40 Experts Wish They'd Known as Beginners.* https://jerryjenkins.com/writing-tips/.

Johnson, Fred. ProWritingAid (blog): *Advice from Kurt Vonnegut That Every Writer Needs to Read by.* https://prowritingaid.com/art/455/

Advice-from-Kurt-Vonnegut-that-Every-Writer-Needs-to-Read.
aspx.

Johnson, Steve. Publication Coach (blog): *9 Ways to Make Your Writing More Resilient.* https://www.publicationcoach.com/9-ways-to-make-your-writing-more-resilient/.

McIntyre, Ericka (Editor-in-Chief). "5 Tips to Get More Creative + Free Download with 26 Tips on Writing Fiction." Writer's Digest. (No date.) https://www.writersdigest.com/writing-fiction-5-tips-to-get-more-creative.

Mikel, Betsy. "25 Ways to Tighten Up Your Writing." Ragan. https://www.ragan.com/25-ways-to-tighten-your-writing-3/. Dec. 30, 2014.

Sansevieri, Penny. Author Marketing Experts (blog): *14 Habits of Highly Successful Authors.* https://www.amarketingexpert.com/14-habits-highly-successful-authors/.

Vos, Lesley J. Bang to Write (blog): *10 Awesome Writing Tips from Robert McKee.* http://bang2write.com/2014/07/10-awesome-writing-tips-from-robert-mckee-by-lesley-vos.html.

Writer's Relief staff. "Tips for New Fiction Authors." *Huffington Post.* https://www.huffpost.com/entry/writing-tips-advice-fiction-authors_n_1628537?guccounter=1. June 27, 2012.

Online Classes

Australian-based Open Colleges for online courses in writing, editing, and media-related training for aspiring authors, editors, and journalists.

http://www.opencolleges.edu.au/courses/writing-journalism.

List of universities offering free online courses. http://study.com/articles/10_Universities_Offering_Free_Writing_Courses_Online.html.

Writer's Digest University for online classes and webinars. https://www.writersonlineworkshops.com/.

Books

Dillard, Annie. *The Writing Life*. HarperCollins, 2013.

Hacker, Diana, and Sommers, Nancy. *Rules for Writers*. Bedford/St. Martins, 2018.

Koontz, Dean R. *How to Write Best Selling Fiction*. Writer's Digest Books, 1981.

Lamott, Anne. *Bird by Bird*. Anchor Books, 1995.

Strunk, William Jr., and White, E. B. *The Elements of Style*. Pearson (fourth edition), 2019.

The Chicago Manual of Style. University of Chicago Press (seventeenth edition), 2017.

Webster's Third New International Dictionary of the English Language. Merriam-Webster, 1993.

Things to Do Before, During, and After the Writing of Your Book

This checklist includes things you can do while you're writing the book; things you can do while your book is going through editing, formatting, and cover design; and things you can do after your book is finished.

While You're Writing the Book

- Consider developing a website/blog. (Chapter 29)
- Establish your social media pages. (Chapter 30)
- Decide whether you'll publish in paperback, e-book, Kindle, audio. (Chapter 22)
- Find an editor. (Chapter 21)
- Find a formatter. (Chapter 23)
- Find a cover illustrator/designer. (Chapter 23)
- Start developing your author platform. (Chapter 34)

While the Book Is Going Through Editing, Formatting, and Cover Design

- Hone your elevator speech and synopses. (Chapter 24)
- Locate appropriate book-posting sites. (Chapter 31)
- Find reviewers. (Chapter 25)
- Establish pricing for your book. (Chapter 26)
- Secure ISBN and LCCN numbers as appropriate. (Chapter 22)
- Establish distribution channels. (Chapter 36)
- Develop a marketing plan. (Chapter 28)

After the Book Is Finished

- Conduct the book launch. (Chapter 27)
- Establish a promotion strategy and schedule. (Part 4)

Self-Editing Checklist

Text message from a traveling husband to his wife:
"Having a wonderful time. Wish you were her."

One typo can destroy your life.

This checklist includes self-editing tips for your manuscript after you've finished writing the first draft. It's a long list, but as I've been told more than once, if writing a successful novel was easy, everyone would be doing it. The good news is that the more writing experience you have, the more of these things you will do automatically without having to rely on the checklist.

Beginning of the Book

- Does the first sentence/paragraph "hook" the reader?
- Has the stage been set—the mood, setting, time period, and tone?
- Does the reader have a good sense of the main character?
- Does action happen early on in the narrative?

Paragraphs

- Do the paragraphs transition smoothly from one to another?
- Are there any exceptionally long ones that could be shortened or split into two or more?
- Is there a paragraph break every time the subject shifts or when a new character speaks?

Scenes

- Has a setting been established for each scene?
- Does each scene have a narrative arc (beginning, middle, and ending)?
- Is every scene plausible?
- Does each scene include some level of conflict (internal or external)?
- Is there body language included for the characters when the scene requires it?
- Is each scene necessary to the story line?
- Does each scene start and end at a good point?
- Is there a natural flow and transition from one scene to another?

Chapters

- Does each chapter start with something that impels the reader to continue?
- Is there a central theme for each chapter?
- Does each chapter end with something that entices the reader to continue to the next chapter?

Characters

- Is each character unique?
- Are the characters three-dimensional? Well-developed?
- Can your readers picture the characters?

- Do the readers know the internal qualities of the main characters?
- Are the strengths and weaknesses of the main characters evident?
- Is the protagonist's goal(s) clearly defined?
- Is the protagonist sufficiently challenged throughout the book?
- Are there reasons for a reader to feel empathy for the protagonist?
- Are relationships between characters well-defined?

Dialogue

- Does the dialogue sound natural? Is there any stilted or "too perfect" dialogue that should be changed?
- Is the dialogue necessary? Does it add to the story line?
- Has dialogue been used as an information dump? If so, reconsider.
- Does the dialogue help to define the character?
- Is the dialogue consistent with the character?
- Does each character have a distinct voice?
- Have physical gestures been weaved in with the dialogue where needed?
- Has anyone's name been overused in a conversation?
- Are there any lengthy exchanges between characters that should be shortened?
- Is any dialogue preceded by text that explains what the character is about to say? If so, remove it.
- Are all of the dialogue tags necessary?

Description

- Is there enough description for the reader to visualize what you are describing?
- Has description been overdone to the point of being boring?
- Have the five senses been adequately used to describe things?
- Is there more showing than telling?

Story Line

- Is the story credible?
- Are there any plot glitches or holes?
- Is there too much backstory? If so, delete whatever isn't necessary to the story line.
- Does the story have a good climax?
- Is there enough conflict to carry the story?
- Did the protagonist change adequately given his/her challenges?
- Have details been checked for accuracy?
- Does the story line flow smoothly?
- Does the story line have a theme?

Pace

- Does the story continually move forward?
- Are there any sections of long, boring narrative? If so, omit whatever isn't important to the story line.
- Are there moments that allow the reader to breathe between high-action scenes?
- Are there any places where the action has been delayed for too long?

Writing Style

- Within each sentence, are the words in the correct order?
- Have the beginnings of sentences been switched up by varying the first word from a noun, to a pronoun, to an article, to a verb, etc.?
- Are sentence structures within a paragraph or group of paragraphs varied by mixing in short (even one-word) sentences and fragments and/or occasionally interrupting the dialogue?
- Are any of the sentences clumsy or awkward to read?
- If limited POV is the chosen narrative, have the appropriate rules been followed? No head-hopping allowed.
- Are there any clichés? If so, remove them.

- Have *ly* words been overused? If so, replace them with stronger verbs and nouns.
- Do any paragraphs include repeated words or phrases? If so, replace them with alternatives.
- Is there a good blend of narration, dialogue, and description?
- Are there weak words that could be replaced with stronger ones?

Ending of Book

- Have all the issues been resolved in the end?
- Will readers feel fulfilled when they reach the last paragraph of the book?
- Will the reader feel some type of emotion at the end?
- Will the reader be sorry to see the story end? If so, you've done a good job!

Spelling and Grammar Checking

- I'm always surprised when I see authors who have apparently not taken advantage of the spelling and grammar checkers available in Word or via downloads or online services. Just be aware that the suggestions these programs might make, especially regarding grammar, are not always correct.

FINAL TIP: Try reading the story aloud, or even better, listen to someone else read it aloud. You'll be surprised at how many problem areas are unearthed with this exercise.

About the Author

A fter a long career in the corporate world, Florence Osmund retired to write novels.

I wrote my first novel without the benefit of any training, planning, or knowledge of the publishing industry. That was in the late 1990s, when self-publishing was an unfavorable method of getting published, so when I finished writing the book, I conducted an exhaustive search for an agent. After being advised to have the manuscript professionally edited, I found someone willing to take a look at it, and she enlightened me to the fact that I had violated just about every rule on writing fiction known to man. Not to be discouraged (and because no one was going to get away with telling me my work was, well, worthless), I enrolled in classes at The University of Chicago and read every book and article I could find on how to write fiction. I rewrote my novel (it actually became two novels) and self-published them in 2012. What an eye-opening journey that was!

Today a successful author, Florence has several published novels and is a contributing writer for The Book Designer thebookdesigner.com/, a blog renown for educating and guiding authors through the publishing process. She continues to write literary fiction at her home on a small, tranquil lake in northern Illinois.

Website/Blog
florenceosmund.com

E-mail
info@florenceosmund.com

FaceBook
facebook.com/FlorenceOsmundBooks

Twitter
twitter.com/FlorenceOsmund

LinkedIn
linkedin.com/in/florenceosmund

Goodreads
goodreads.com/user/show/8800692-florence-osmund

Pinterest
pinterest.com/florenceosmund/

Amazon author page
amazon.com/author/florenceosmund

Novels by Florence Osmund

Nineteen Hundred Days

They Called Me Margaret

Living with Markus

Regarding Anna

Red Clover

Daughters

The Coach House

Index

Made in the USA
Monee, IL
22 September 2024